FOR OUR FREEDOM AND YOURS

THE JEWISH LABOUR BUND IN POLAND
1939–1949

PARKES-WIENER SERIES ON JEWISH STUDIES

Series Editors: David Cesarani and Tony Kushner

ISSN 1368-5449

The field of Jewish Studies is one of the youngest, but fastest growing and most exciting areas of scholarship in the academic world today. Named after James Parkes and Alfred Wiener, this series aims to publish new research in the field and student materials for use in the seminar room, to disseminate the latest work of established scholars and to re-issue classic studies which are currently out of print.

The selection of publications reflects the international character and diversity of Jewish Studies; it ranges over Jewish history from Abraham to modern Zionism, and Jewish culture from Moses to post-modernism. The series also reflects the inter-disciplinary approach inherent in Jewish Studies and at the cutting edge of contemporary scholarship, and provides an outlet for innovative work on the interface between Judaism and ethnicity, popular culture, gender, class, space and memory.

Other Books in the Series

Holocaust Literature: Schulz, Levi, Spiegelman and the Memory of the Offence
Gillian Banner

Remembering Cable Street: Fascism and Anti-Fascism in British Society
Edited by Tony Kushner and Nadia Valman

Sir Sidney Hamburger and Manchester Jewry: Religion, City and Community
Bill Williams

Anglo-Jewry in Changing Times: Studies in Diversity 1840–1914
Israel Finestein

Double Jeopardy: Gender and the Holocaust
Judith Tydor Baumel

Cultures of Ambivalence and Contempt: Studies in Jewish-Non-Jewish Relations
Edited by Siân Jones, Tony Kushner and Sarah Pearce

Alfred Wiener and the Making of the Wiener Library
Ben Barkow

The Berlin Haskalah and German Religious Thought: Orphans of Knowledge
David Sorkin

Myths in Israeli Culture: Captives of a Dream
Nurith Gertz

The Jewish Immigrant in England 1870–1914, Third Edition
Lloyd P. Gartner

State and Society in Roman Galilee, A.D. 132–212, Second Edition
Martin Goodman

Disraeli's Jewishness
Edited by Todd M. Endelman and Tony Kushner

Claude Montefiore: His Life and Thought
Daniel R. Langton

FOR OUR FREEDOM AND YOURS

The Jewish Labour Bund
in Poland 1939–1949

DANIEL BLATMAN

Translator
NAFTALI GREENWOOD

VALLENTINE MITCHELL
LONDON • PORTLAND, OR

First published in 2003 in Great Britain by
VALLENTINE MITCHELL
Crown House, 47 Chase Side, Southgate
London N14 5BP

and in the United States of America by
VALLENTINE MITCHELL
c/o International Specialized Book Services, Inc.
920 NE 58th Avenue, Suite 300
Portland, OR 97213-3786

Website: www.vmbooks.com

British Library Cataloguing in Publication Data

Blatman, Daniel
    For our freedom and yours: the Jewish Labour Bund in
Poland (1939–1949). – (Parkes–Wiener series on Jewish
studies)
    1. Allgemeyner Idisher arbeyterbund in Lita, Poylen un
Rusland 2. Jews – Politics and government 3. Socialism and
Judaism 4. Poland – Politics and government – 1918–1945
5. Poland – Politics and government – 1945–1989
I. Title
943.8′004924

ISBN 0-85303-449-4 (cloth)
ISBN 0-85303-458-3 (paper)
ISSN 1368-5449

Library of Congress Cataloging-in-Publication Data

Blatman, Daniel, 1953–
    [Lema'an herutenu ve-herutkhem. English]
    For our freedom and yours: the Jewish Labour Bund in Poland, 1939–1949/ Daniel Blatman.
    p. cm. – (Parkes–Wiener series on Jewish studies)
    ISBN 0-85303-449-4 (cloth) – ISBN 0-85303-458-3 (pbk.)
    1. Jews–Poland–Politics and government. 2. Ogâlny çydowski Zwiñzek Robotniczy
"Bund" w Polsce. 3. World War, 1939–1945–Jewish resistance–Poland. 4. Holocaust,
Jewish (1939–1945)–Poland. 5. Poland–Ethnic relations. I. Title. II. Series.

DS135.P6 B53413 2003
940.53′1832′09438–dc21

2002038945

Typeset in Janson 11/13pt by Cambridge Photosetting Services, Cambridge
Printed in Great Britain by MPG Books Ltd, Bodmin, Cornwall

In memory of my father
Sholem Blatman
A Jewish worker from Warsaw

Contents

Acknowledgements

The publication of this book was supported by grants of The Koret Jewish Studies Publication Programme and The Lucius N. Littauer Foundation.

Abbreviations and Glossary

AAN	Archiwum Akt Nowych, Warsaw.
Agudath Israel	ultra-orthodox Jewish party.
AJDC	Archives of the American Jewish Joint Distribution Committee, New York.
AK	Armia Krajowa: Home Army, the underground armed forces on Polish soil, under the authority of the Polish government-in-exile.
Akiva	non-socialist youth pioneer Zionist organization.
Aktiv	active members of the youth movements and political organizations in Poland.
AKWD	*Armia Krajowa w Dokumentach* (see Bibliography).
AL	Armia Ludowa: People's army, Polish communist underground.
Arbeter Ring	Workers' Circle, Jewish local workers' organizations in the United States.
AŻIH	Archiwum Żydowskiego Instytuto Historycznego, Warsaw.
BA	Bund Archives, Yivo, New York.
Berichah	(lit. 'flight'). Mass migratory movement of Jews after the war from Poland to Israel, organized by Zionist activists.
Betar	Zionist revisionist youth organization.
Central Committee	main policy-making committee of the Bund.
CKŻP	Centralny Komitet Żydów w Polsce: Central Committee of the Jews in Poland (after the war).
Delegatura	underground representative of the Polish government-in-exile on Polish soil.
DPSR	*Documents on Polish–Soviet Relations* (see Bibliography)
Dror (Dror hettaluts)	youth pioneer socialist Zionist movement.
FPO	Faraynikte Partizaner Organizatsye: United Parti-

	sans' Organization: underground Jewish organization in the Wilno ghetto.
HaShomer haTsa'ir	youth zionist pro-Soviet movement.
HHA	HaShomer haTsa'ir Archives, Giv'at Haviva.
HIAS	Hebrew Sheltering and Immigrant Aid Society.
HICEM	Roof Organization of HIAS–ICA–Emigdirect, the Jewish Emigration Society.
Itonut	*Itonut haMahteret haYehudit beVarsha:* Jewish underground press in Warsaw (see Bibliography).
JDC	American-Jewish Joint Distribution Committee.
JLC	Jewish Labour Committee.
Judenrat/ Judenräte	Councils of Jewish elders in the occupied areas of Poland.
KC–PZPR	Komitet Centralny, Polska Zjednoczona Partia Robotnicza: Central Committee of the Polish United Workers' Party (the Communist Party).
KRN	*Krajowa Rada Narodowa:* Homeland National Council (pro-communist).
Left Po'aley Tsiyon	Socialist, pro-Soviet, Zionist organization.
MA	Moreshet Archives, Giv'at Haviva.
NKVD	Soviet People's Commissariat for Internal Affairs.
ODC	Oral Documentation Centre, Institute of Contemporary Jewry, Jerusalem.
ORT	Organization for Rehabilitation and Training.
PKP	Polityczny Komitet Porozumiewawczy: Political consultative committee of the Polish resistance.
PKWN	Polski Komitet Wyzwolenia Narodowego: Polish national committee of liberation (pro-communist).
PPR	Polska Partia Robotnicza: Polish Workers' Party (pro-communist).
PPS	Polska Partia Socjalistyczna: Polish Socialist Party.
PRO	public record office, London.
PSL	Polskie Stronnictwo Ludowe: Polish Peasant Party.
PS	Polish Socialists.
PZPR	Polska Zjednoczona Partia Robotnicza: Polish United Workers' Party (the Communist Party).
The Representation	American representation of the Bund in Poland.
Right Po'aley Tsiyon	Zionist socialist party.

SD	Sicherheitspolizei: German Security Police.
Sejm	Polish parliament.
SKIF	Sotsyalistishe Kinder Farband: Union of Socialist Children (affiliated to the Bund).
Toporol	Towarzystwo Popierania Rolnictwa: Jewish association for aiding agriculture (pre-war period).
TOZ	Towarzystwo Ochrony Zdrowia: Society for the preservation of health.
Tsisho	Tsentrale Yidishe Shul Organizatsye: Central Yiddish Schools Organization (socialist).
Tsukunft	youth organization of the Bund.
WRN	Wolność-Równosc-Niepodległość: Freedom, Equality, Independence (socialist underground in Poland).
Yikor	Yidishe Kultur Organizatsye: Society for Yiddish Culture.
YIVO	Yidisher Vaysnshaftlekher Institut, New York.
YVA	Yad Vashem Archives, Jerusalem.
Żegota	Council for Aid to Jews in Poland (1942).
ŻKA	Żydowski Komitet Antyhitlerlowski: Jewish Anti-Hitler Committee (became the Jewish Antifascist Committee).
ŻKN	Żydowski Komitet Narodowy: Jewish National Committee (political committee of the underground in the Warsaw ghetto).
ŻOB	Żydowska Organizacja Bojowa: Jewish Fighting Organization.
ZPP	Związek Patriotów Polskich: Union of Polish patriots (Moscow, pro-communist).
ŻSS	Żydowska Samopomoc Społeczna: Jewish public self-help.
ZWZ	Związek Walki Zbrojnej: Union of Armed Struggle (became the AK).

List of Illustrations

1. Jews being transferred into the Warsaw ghetto.
2. Jews selling armbands with the Star of David in the Warsaw ghetto.
3. Beggars in the streets of the Warsaw ghetto.
4. A sweetshop in the Warsaw ghetto.
5. A coffee shop in the Warsaw ghetto.
6. Selling potatoes in the Warsaw ghetto.
7. A ration card, issued by the *Judenrat* in the Warsaw ghetto.
8. One of the street markets in the Warsaw ghetto.
9. Smugglers bringing goods into the Warsaw ghetto.
10. The Jewish police in the Warsaw ghetto.
11. Jews about to be deported, Umschlagplatz.
12. Henryk Erlich.
13. Wiktor Alter.
14. Abrasha Blum and his wife, Luba.

Introduction

This study is the result of the residual feeling in the heart of a student who completed his studies with the conviction that he had not mastered his entire discipline properly. For anyone who was born into the peculiar realities of Israel in the 1950s, the Holocaust and, especially, the ghetto uprisings were central episodes in the fashioning of consciousness and national identity. However, when I completed high school and, years later, studies in history at the Hebrew University of Jerusalem, I still had the perplexing feeling that I had not obtained a clear view of the full picture. My generation, that of the 'sabras' in fledgling Israel, had hardly been informed about a lengthy chapter in Eastern European Jewish history – that of the Jewish labour movement, the Bund. This 'black hole' sensation remained with me when I chose my field of specialization and academic discipline, the history of Eastern European Jewry during the Holocaust. Therefore, research and writing about the Bund during the Holocaust also constitute a personal attempt to understand a chapter in Jewish history that still awaits exhaustive examination and historiography.

The origins of my irksome personal feeling should, perhaps, be sought somewhere in the middle of March 1942, when seven underground activists affiliated with the main political movements met in the soup kitchen on Orla Street in the Warsaw ghetto. Two of them, Maurycy Orzech and Abrasha Blum, were the leaders of the Jewish labour Bund, in the ghetto. The agenda of the seven men included debating the appropriate response to many reports that had been reaching the ghetto about the annihilation of the Jews.

They were days of continual hardship and dread. The underground press in the ghetto was publishing comprehensive articles, and diarists were recording lengthy entries, about horrific murders among Jews throughout Lithuania, Belarus and Ukraine. Entire Jewish communities were being obliterated; the extermination operation was spreading like a bushfire. Amidst the grim reportage, one can sense the writers' sense of helplessness. One of the underground newspapers expressed this feeling: 'We are facing a vastly powerful enemy with neither assistance nor counsel, unarmed and defenceless. Maybe a miracle, so common a phenomenon in the history of our people, will save us.'[1]

That meeting in March 1942 marked the first attempt to establish a united Jewish fighting organization in the Warsaw ghetto, one that would assume responsibility for defending the ghetto when the Germans decided to evacuate it. The Bund leaders, for various reasons, refused to participate in such an organization, preferring to reinforce their underground cells separately. They were confident that their sympathizers and friends in Polish underground circles, especially among the Polish socialists, would help and support them. The rest of the story, as we know, was totally different.

Obviously, this clandestine meeting was of no critical importance in the ability or inability of the Jewish underground in the Warsaw ghetto to counteract the deportation of Jews for extermination. Nevertheless for many years, it casted a shadow over the history of the Bund during the Holocaust. This is due to the way the historiography of Jewish resistance during the Holocaust placed special emphasis on the Warsaw ghetto uprising and took the Bund to task for its role in the Jewish rising and resistance. The historical account of the Warsaw ghetto uprising, based heavily on the memoirs and writings of those warriors who survived, established the Bund's guilt categorically. Its leaders' resistance impeded, at an early phase, the establishment of the Jewish Fighting Organization (ŻOB) in the ghetto and, perforce, nipped in the bud the possibility of earlier and more effective organizational action by young underground members against the Germans and their schemes.

The history of the Bund in its last decade in Poland was written by various historians, but mainly at only one level – that of the Jewish resistance. Israeli historiography of the Holocaust expresses this clearly. The events of March 1942 are described at length in the writings of almost all uprising leaders who belonged to Zionist youth movements and parties – Yitzhak Zuckerman, Haika Grosman and Abba Kovner, who survived, and Hersh Berlinski and Mordechai Tenenbaum-Tamaroff, who perished. However, the few Bund activists who survived hardly mention them. Marek Edelman does not refer to this event as a meaningful landmark in Bund history during the Holocaust. Neither does Bernard Goldstein or Ya'akov Tselemenski. Their attitude toward the occurrences of that time assigns them a totally different meaning. The struggle against Nazism was not the mission of Jews only, and the establishment of a separate Jewish fighting organization was not necessarily the best way to carry out this mission in the spring of 1942.

Unlike the uprising leaders in the Zionist youth movements, who after the war castigated the Bund for this episode, Marek Edelman, the Bund delegate to the ŻOB leadership, distanced himself from this dispute for years. After he wrote his important, perspicacious report on the deportation and the uprising several months after the war ended, he elected to steer clear of this post mortem. Many years later, when he again began to make reference to what happened in the ghetto, his writings were full of bitterness and pain. He criticized what he called the exaggerated, somewhat obsessive, preoccupation with the warrior-heroes, and insisted that the nameless people, families and individuals whom he saw walking toward the railroad cars be lauded for their valour.

In a nutshell, we have the gist of two narratives. One gives primacy to the particularistic Jewish fate and the need for Jewish national solidarity; the other emphasizes the solidarity of all suffering peoples and all victims of Nazi persecution. The two narratives rest on two political traditions that came into being in the late nineteenth century – almost in the same year – and two political ideological frameworks that coalesced in the 40 years preceding the Second World War. They included educational and cultural enterprises, trade and party organizations, youth movements, sports organizations, women's organizations, writers' clubs – everything that an early twentieth-century political movement and culture could offer. They were vastly dissimilar, but they shared the wish to find a modern and comprehensive solution to the problem of Jewish existence. One of them was Zionism, which treated the destructive and menacing presence of anti-Semitism as the central issue and offered only one solution: to separate the Jews from their surroundings and place them within an autonomous territorial setting. The second was Bundism, which urged the Jews to integrate into surrounding society in Eastern Europe and to participate in an all-out struggle for a just, tolerant society – a socialistic, democratic and pluralistic one.

The General Alliance of Jewish Workers in Lithuania, Poland and Russia – the Bund (Algemayner Idisher Arbeter-Bund in Lite, Poyln un Rusland) – came into being and coalesced against the backdrop of the Jewish reality in Eastern Europe in the 1880s and 1890s. These were dramatic watershed years in Eastern European Jewish history. Old ways and settings of life and traditional leadership groups were steadily losing the influence they had exerted for years and were being supplanted by new political organizations and parties that advocated revolutionary, total solutions to the basic problems of the Jewish people.

The vision of social revolution, on the one hand, and the ambition to effect a national rebirth in the historical homeland, on the other, presented the young generation of Eastern European Jews with a sweeping, almost messianic challenge: '[The] search for total solutions to problems that could be resolved only in part', as the historian Jonathan Frankel put it,[2] drove tens of thousands of young Jews, dreamers and believers, to the shores of the Promised Land and into the ranks of the revolutionary movements and labour organizations. The Bund was a product of this social and political reality.

These watershed years also led to the creation of a new Jewish social class – a large Jewish proletariat in the *shtetlakh* of the Pale of Settlement that differed in its sociological and economic characteristics from the Russian, Lithuanian or Polish worker. Jewish workers were the most deprived, repressed group among the national groups that populated their surroundings. They were virtually unrepresented in advanced and developing industries but were dominant in unskilled, labour-intensive workshops. They were restricted to primitive workplaces, the lowliest terms of labour and remuneration, and limited employment opportunities. They hardly ever found work in plants owned by non-Jews and did not always manage to retain their jobs even in Jewish-owned establishments. Jewish plant owners often preferred non-Jews over fellow Jews; the former were usually less educated, willing to work on the Sabbath and less inclined to unionize.

From its very outset, the Bund moulded itself in the tradition of illegal activity and members' self-sacrifice. The centrepiece of its political heritage was the ethos of struggle against a hostile and oppressive regime, that of the tsars and their lackeys. Many Bundists forfeited their lives or their freedom for this heritage of struggle, which was of general revolutionary nature. Alongside it, the Bund fostered what it considered the special cultural heritage of the Jewish people – a heritage shaped by Yiddish, the special national language of Eastern European Jewry. The more involved the Bund became in Jewish life, especially in the 1930s in Poland, the more it distanced itself from the traditional ideological imperatives that had guided it during its formative years. The Bundist ideology, attentive from its inception to the reality and living needs of the Jewish grassroots, became flexible and pragmatic in interwar Poland. The more intensively active the Bund became in Jewish education, organizing of workers, Jewish cultural activity and struggle against anti-Semitism, the more it underscored its Jewish national identity. In its own way, the Bund gave the complicated, bumpy course of Jewish existence during the interwar years a direction and filled it with content. Realities, however, overwhelmed the Bund's ability to offer a substantive solution. Like all other Jewish political movements and organizations it could offer only a partial solution.

Within a few months, starting in early September 1939, the settings of Jewish life in Poland disintegrated in succession. Amidst this labyrinthine and tragic reality, the Bund activists, like the others, attempted to find their way and sustain some kind of public activity in the underground. The history of the Bund during those years should be examined from an inclusive, comparative perspective that takes into account, among other things, the special Bundist narrative. An outside perspective, stemming from the world of other political movements that were active in the underground – Zionist or communist – should be avoided. It has been the tendency to examine the movement's successes and failures from one perspective only: the similar fate that faced all Jews under Nazi occupation. This, however, cannot shed light on the history of the Bund during the Holocaust. A political movement with an extensive set of historical images does not change its stripes overnight, even if reality does so. Reality is a concept that denotes the here-and-now, something that exists as a setting within which events take shape. A set of images, in contrast, is a heritage transmitted over generations in the way a movement understands its historical role and missions. These shape its members' attitude toward daily affairs and guide them in solving current problems on the agenda. In this sense, the Bund was no different from any other political movement, Jewish or non-Jewish, during World War II and the Holocaust.

This study examines the last decade in the history of the Bund in Eastern Europe. The story begins in 1939, when the strength and influence of the party in Jewish public life in Poland reached its peak, and ends in 1949, when the Communist regime in Poland liquidated the Bund as an autonomous political player. Thus, the study probes the behaviour of a party with a singular worldview amidst a reality that changed several times within one decade but headed in one direction only – the end of Bund history in Eastern Europe, as part of the liquidation of Eastern European Jewish life generally. 'The Bund lost to history – that's all', Marek Edelman once said. The results of this loss would be perceptible in the Jewish collective memory for many years.

This study is the outgrowth of a PhD dissertation written for the Hebrew University of Jerusalem. It was published in Hebrew in 1996 and, in advance of the English edition, several chapters were rewritten and others were thoroughly revised. Additional documentary material and new studies and points of view shed different light on various episodes in the history of the years of the Bund's activity. Various institutions aided and supported me during the many years that I devoted to this endeavour. Foremost among them is my academic and research home, the Institute of Contemporary Jewry at the Hebrew University of Jerusalem, and Yad Vashem, also in Jerusalem. I thank all the institutions that allowed me to participate in their research activities and provided stipends and funds that allowed me to devote time to the task of writing: the Center for Advanced Holocaust Studies at the United States Holocaust Memorial Museum in Washington DC; the Centre d'études des religions du livre (CERL) of the CNRS in Paris; the Jewish Historical Institute in Warsaw; the YIVO Institute in New York; and the Guteiner Institute for Study of the Jewish Labour Movement at the University of Haifa.

The colleagues who assisted and supported me in the various phases and metamorphoses of this work are too numerous to list. I am deeply indebted to them all. I thank Yehuda Bauer, Ezra Mendelsohn, Jonathan Frankel, David Bankier and Dalia Ofer of the Institute for Contemporary Jewry, and Matityahu Mintz of Tel Aviv University; Antony Polonsky of Brandeis University, Michael Marrus of the University of Toronto, David Engel of NYU, Jack Jacobs of CUNY and Feliks Tych of the University of Warsaw and the Jewish Historical Institute; the staff of the many archives and libraries, especially Marek Web and Leo Greenbaum of YIVO and Ya'akov Lozowick and Robert Rozett of Yad Vashem. My most profound gratitude is extended to Israel Gutman, my teacher and mentor, whose special personality, even more than his vast knowledge and sagacity, contributed to the shaping of my research worldview and my approach to the Holocaust.

I owe particular gratitude to my daughters, Na'ama and Nitzan, who had to spend much of their adolescence in the company of the Bund in Poland during the Holocaust. Finally, this book is devoted, with abundant love, to Renée.

NOTES

1. *Słowo Młodych*, February–March 1942, in J. Kermish, Y. Bialostocki and I. Shaham (eds), *Itonut haMahteret haYehudit beVarsha* (hereafter *Itonut*) 6 vols (Jerusalem: Yad Vashem, 1979–97), Vol. 5, p. 274.
2. J. Frankel, *Socialism, Nationalism, and the Russian Jews 1862–1917* (New York: Cambridge University Press, 1981), p. 560.

1

Occupation

THOSE WHO FLED, THOSE WHO STAYED

On the night of 1 September 1939 German soldiers crossed the Polish border near the town of Gleiwitz. The massive German offensive, spanning a front 1,250 miles long on the ground, in the air, and at sea, deployed 58 divisions, some armoured, with 2,800 tanks. The German air force fielded approximately 2,000 craft, including 900 bombers that dropped thousands of tons of bombs on Polish industrial centres and cities. The Poles countered this mammoth military force with 32 infantry divisions, 11 cavalry brigades, one armoured brigade, and 433 aircraft, many of which were not combat-worthy. The German naval fleet also had a clear advantage over the small Polish fleet that attempted to secure the country's shores on the Baltic Sea. The Wehrmacht advanced swiftly; within three days it was clear that the Polish army had almost totally collapsed and that the country would soon, very soon, be under German occupation.[1]

On the second day of the war, the Germans began to subject Warsaw to pitiless aerial bombardment that inflicted mass devastation and casualties as the Polish air force looked on helplessly. The Sejm (Polish parliament) held its last meeting on 2 September 1939. The country's leaders offered different assessments about the state of the war, and some, even during those days, evidently floated proposals about the need to withdraw the Polish army to the east and to attempt to set up a new defence line.[2] A turning point occurred on the night of 7 September, when Polish radio announced that the government had decided to evacuate the capital, and urged all men capable of bearing arms to head to the east. Despair and helplessness mounted. The government's retreat to the east left Warsaw without any central ruling agency that could organize the town and its inhabitants to confront the encroaching German siege.

Many Jews, including most political leaders, public figures, party functionaries and various social and cultural activists, also began streaming eastward that day. They fled from the Germans in desperation, leaving behind their families, homes and property.

Two days earlier, on 5 September 1939, the Bund leadership knew that the Polish government intended to abandon the capital. The government called a press conference that day, with the participation of newspaper editors in Warsaw and high-ranking journalists, several of whom were Jewish: Ben-Zion Chilinowicz and Heschel Gottleib of *Moment*; Nathan Schwalb of *Nasz Przegląd*, Mendel Mozes of the Jewish Telegraphic Agency, Moshe Indelman of *Haynt* and Pinchas Schwartz of the Bund newspaper *Folkstsaytung*. After the press conference, the participants were apprised in detail of the government's intent to evacuate the capital in the near future. Schwartz immediately contacted Bund leader Henryk Erlich and asked him to rush the party Central Committee into session so he could report his information to the members.[3] Late that evening, evidently, the Central Committee convened along with members of the *Folkstsaytung* editorial board. The rumour spread swiftly among party activists in Warsaw, and dozens of members congregated in the yard of the editorial board building at 7 Nowolipie Street, where the meeting was being held, to wait for the movement leadership's decision at that grim hour.[4]

The party leaders vacillated about whether to urge all ranking members and party-affiliated journalists to leave Warsaw at once or to postpone the decision to some later time when the situation would become clear. Schwarz reported at the meeting that the government had decided to reserve several places on a train out of Warsaw for Jewish journalists and three Bund leaders: Henryk Erlich, Wiktor Alter and Schwarz himself. Most of the participants believed the movement leadership should leave Warsaw and attempt to reorganize the party's work and the publication of its newspaper in the east. However, several party leaders, especially Vladimir Kossovski and Maurycy Orzech, opposed the majority opinion, arguing that rank-and-file members and their own Polish counterparts in the Polska Partia Socjalistyczna (PPS) and the Polish trade unions would take a dim view of an outflux of the Bund leadership from the capital at this time. Orzech inveighed against the climate of defeatism that had spread among the members. Warsaw could not possibly fall to the Germans without a battle, he said; the Bund should urge the Jewish proletariat to stay and prepare to defend the capital shoulder-to-shoulder with the Polish proletariat.[5]

The Central Committee adjourned without taking a definite decision. The movement leaders evidently decided to wait one more day, in order to elicit the opinion of the PPS leadership concerning the evacuation. After the meeting, Orzech met with one of these leaders, Zygmunt Zaremba, a founding member of the Warsaw Labour

Committee for Social Assistance (Warszawski robotniczny komitet pomocy społecznej), which aimed to assist the thousands of refugees who were streaming into the town.[6] Zaremba disapproved of the decision of the Bund leadership and the *Folkstsaytung* journalists to leave Warsaw, considering it an expression of defeatism and escapism. Zaremba told Orzech, according to the latter, that he would spare no effort to keep the journalists and employees of the PPS newspapers, *Robotnik* and *Dziennik Ludowy*, in town.[7]

The events of 5–6 September highlighted the confusion and bewilderment that had gripped the Bund leadership as the Germans verged on the gates of Warsaw. On 6 September, Erlich and Alter informed Schwarz that they would not board the outgoing train; instead, they would wait for the town council meeting that was scheduled for 7 September, as requested by the mayor, Stefan Starzyński.[8] Two writers for the *Folkstsaytung*, Wiktor Schulman and Baruch Schefner, chose to leave in their stead. Ultimately, only Schwartz and Schefner left, Schulman having missed the train. In his memoirs, Schwartz reports Erlich's parting remarks:

> I ask you officially ... It is not a matter of personal considerations but of party mission; you, Schefner, and Schulman have to leave at once so the *Folkstsaytung* can be issued somewhere else in this world, and Alter and I must stay. I tell you this categorically, not personally but in the name of the party![9]

Erlich's attitude was influenced by his meeting with Zaremba on 5 September, after the Central Committee meeting. The PPS activist advised the Bund leader that it was too early to panic; even though the army was collapsing, the capital should not be abandoned without a struggle. Orzech aptly expressed the Bund's dilemma in the matter of leaving by telling Shloime Mendelsohn, a member of the Central Committee and a leading figure in Tshiso, that 'the party is committing suicide' by leaving Warsaw.[10]

From the standpoint of the Bund, which felt dutybound to remain loyal to the Polish – and especially the Polish proletariat – struggle against the fascist invader, the evacuation of members and leaders from Warsaw was tantamount to a retreat from an important principle.

The indecision continued the next day, 6 September. Erlich and Alter again met with members of the PPS secretariat to discuss the possibilities of labour action in German-occupied Warsaw. The secretary-general of the PPS, Kazimierz Pużak, invested little hope in the government's intention to set up a defence line along the Volga and San Rivers, because he assumed that the Ukrainians and the Byelorussians would not assist the Poles there. As for Bund leaders' departure from Warsaw, Pużak's attitude was clear: they should leave, because they were in immeasurably greater danger than the leaders of the PPS, who could leave the occupied city at some later time.[11]

On 6 September, in its last meeting, the Central Committee decided once and for all that the leadership should leave Warsaw that night. On the night of 6–7 September, Colonel Roman Umiastowski announced over the Polish radio that men able to bear arms should leave the capital. In the aftermath of the government's frantic departure – at approximately 2 a.m. on 7 September – the Bund's leaders and activists were more firmly committed to the decision they had made the previous day. The Central Committee decision envisaged a two-phase evacuation. The following would leave on the morning of 7 September: Yekutiel Portnoi, Leivik Hodes, Vladimir Kossovski, Sarah Shweber, Emanuel Szerer and Alexander Erlich (Henryk Erlich's son). The others would wait until after the town council meeting the next day. Several hours after the Central Committee meeting ended, however, the party leaders and the Bund delegates to the town council, Erlich and Alter, were informed by Starzyński that the council would not convene and that the Germans might enter Warsaw at any moment. In response, all members of the Central Committee decided to leave town.[12]

The leaders' indecision in the 48 hours preceding the exodus from Warsaw had no impact on the calculus of the rank and file. As tens of thousands made their escape amidst general pandemonium, ordinary party members could not stay in touch with the leadership; their decision to leave Warsaw or stay behind was hardly affected by the decisions of the Central Committee. A small group of second-rank activists – mainly members of Tsukunft (the youth organization of the Bund), section heads in the trade unions and employees of the Tshiso education system (about 200 people in all) – gathered on the night of 6 September (including several with their families) in Praga, in eastern Warsaw, and waited there for the Central Committee to make up its mind concerning departure.[13] It seems, however, that they were never apprised of the Bund leadership's decision, so they left on their own counsel. In the estimation of members from Warsaw who accompanied Orzech to Kovno in late September 1939, some 500–600 party members and activists left Warsaw at that time.[14] The senior members departed because their membership in a Jewish-socialist party placed them in special jeopardy at the hands of the Nazi occupier. On 5 September, for example, Jerzy Gliksman, brother of Wiktor Alter, left along with his family. In his memoirs, Gliksman wrote that his parents, concerned for his fate because he was a recognized political figure, persuaded him to go although he wished to wait until joined by his brother.[15]

Activists in political parties and movements streamed eastward from Warsaw in groups.[16] Members of the Bund Central Committee left Warsaw in two groups toward two different destinations. One included most of the older members, chiefly those who were too old to help the Polish government carry out its plans to defend the Lublin area. The members of this group left for Mińsk Mazowiecki, Kałuszyn and Siedlce, in an attempt to reach Brześć nad Bugiem, where the Central Committee intended to convene and decide what to do next under the new circumstances. The second group, the most prominent members of which were Wiktor Alter and Bernard Goldstein, headed for Lublin via Międzyrzec. On 9 September 1939, they reached Międzyrzec, where they consulted among each other about where to go from there. Transport problems, the masses of refugees on the roads, and the German bombardments made Lublin a difficult destination; several young members of Tsukunft decided to return to Warsaw. Alter and Goldstein continued toward Lublin and reached that town on 11 September.[17]

The act of splitting into groups and the composition of each group show that the party's leading members, at the time they left Warsaw, had decided that several of their number should leave Poland and attempt to reach Lithuania and that others should remain in Poland to participate in the government's self-defence efforts and attempt to sustain movement work. This was not a systematic decision: each individual joined the group of his or her choice. Bund activist Yehoshua Ofman, in a letter in late September 1939 to colleagues in New York, wrote that he had encountered Henryk Erlich, Shloime Mendelsohn, Emanuel Szerer and other members of the Central Committee in Siedlce and tried to persuade them to head for Wilno* at once. It is clear that the encounter preceded the Red Army's occupation of eastern Poland (on 17 September), because the Central Committee members said that they wished to wait several days longer before deciding where to go. Maurycy Orzech, who had reached Brześć nad Bugiem on 16 or 17 September, did choose to leave for Wilno immediately – as did

---

*Note that place names are given as they were during the war years. Hence Wilno (now Vilnius).

Ofman and several additional members – without waiting for a decision by other Central Committee members who were staying in Brześć nad Bugiem.[18]

After the Soviet army entered eastern Poland, the leadership members totally revised their plans concerning the destinations and goals of their departure. The Central Committee members learned of the Soviet invasion of eastern Poland on 18 September, after they had reached Pińsk. The members of the group that was staying in Pińsk at this time immediately fell into disagreement about the direction they should head in view of the new political situation. They finally decided that Portnoi, Chaim-Meir Wasser and Hodes would try to cross into Lithuania and reach Wilno, and that Erlich, Mendelsohn and Shweber would return to Brześć nad Bugiem and thence attempt to reach Lublin via Kowel. Mendelsohn and Erlich resolved to stay with the throng of refugees, including some Bund members, that had reached the Lublin area, and Shweber decided to attempt to return from Lublin to Warsaw.[19] The group that had reached Lublin with Wiktor Alter on 11 September also revised its plans after discovering that the Red Army had invaded eastern Poland and would advance to Lublin. Alter headed for Kowel in an attempt to reach the Lithuanian border, but was captured by the Soviets and imprisoned. Goldstein managed to return to Warsaw on 3 October 1939.[20]

In contrast to the cluster of major party activists, Central Committee members and important functionaries, who even then were guided by political considerations, the ordinary party member wished only to find a safe haven from the perils of the Nazi occupation as quickly as possible. Herman Kruk, for example – an important cultural activist in Warsaw and director of the Groser Library – reached Sarny on 17 September with several movement members. Discovering there that the Russians had entered eastern Poland, they went on to Luck, where they established a local committee that raised money and provided relief for a group of Bund members who had reached this town. On 8 October 1939 these members decided to cross into Lithuania and move on to Wilno.[21]

From the second week of the war, the Germans stepped up their aerial bombardments of and artillery barrages against besieged Warsaw to shatter the resistance of the inhabitants and the remnants of the Polish army that, after the government had fled, heroically continued to defend the Polish capital. In his diary of 12 September 1939, the Hebrew teacher Chaim-Aharon Kaplan aptly captured the atmosphere of devastation that had overtaken Warsaw:

It is beyond my pen to describe the destruction and ruin that the enemy's planes have wrought on our lovely capital. Entire blocks have been turned into ashes and magnificent palaces into rubble. … Dante's description of the Inferno is mild compared to the inferno raging in the streets of Warsaw.[22]

The new activist core of the Bund, the cadre that would lead the party during the occupation, began to coalesce during the siege. Two people spearheaded this reorganization: Szmuel Zygielbojm ('Artur'), who had come to Warsaw from Łódź on 8 September, and the engineer Abraham (Abrasha) Blum, a member of the Tsukunft Central Committee and the Warsaw committee of the Bund. Party activity during the German siege of Warsaw focused on three endeavours: continued publication of the party newspaper *Folkstsaytung*, assistance to the PPS in efforts to establish a labour brigade that would help defend the city under Mayor Stefan Starzyński and General Walerjan Czuma, and relief for Bund-member refugees who had reached Warsaw.

The Bund found it difficult to integrate into the labour brigade that the PPS had established. On 10 September the PPS leaders and the heads of the Polish trade unions issued advertisements urging workers to volunteer for the Warsaw Defence Labour Brigades (Robotniczy batalionów obrony Warszawy), commanded by Captain Marjan Kenig. Polish workers aged 17–55 were summoned to fight shoulder to shoulder with the Polish army in defence of the capital, 'in the tradition of proletarian struggle for freedom and independence'.[23] The establishment of these volunteer units was the initiative of two PPS leaders, Zygmunt Zaremba and Mieczysław Niedziałkowski. Zygielbojm, who had been in contact with them from the day he returned to Warsaw, pressured them to allow the formation of Jewish proletarian units. In his memoirs, Zaremba described his meeting with Zygielbojm:

> One of those who came in from Łódź was an acquaintance of mine, Shlomo [*sic*] Zygielbojm-Artur, the labour leader. He turned to me in poor health, his face ashen and webbed with creases. He could hardly stand, but his spirit sizzled with an inner fire. Zygielbojm found a group of Bundists in Warsaw and asked how he could contribute to the defence and collaborate with us. I suggested that he refer all persons fit and suitable for combat to the labour brigades. He accepted my proposal enthusiastically, and within a few days several groups of Jewish workers, organized by Zygielbojm, were added to our units.[24]

The annexation of Jewish workers to the PPS battalion seems not to have been as simple as Zaremba describes it. The PPS leaders categorically rejected Zygielbojm's request for the formation of separate units for Jewish workers. Posters urging Polish workers to mobilize made no mention of Jewish workers. Only the Bundist newspaper *Folkstsaytung* urged Jewish workers, in an advertisement, to take part in the PPS-organized formations. Zygielbojm admitted that he had not managed to allay the PPS leaders' anger about what they called the Bund's 'escape'. However, even though separate volunteer units were not established for Jewish workers, thousands of them heeded the call and joined the brigade, which attained a total strength of some 12,000.[25]

Back on 7 September, after the party leadership had left, the members who remained in Warsaw decided to continue issuing the *Folkstsaytung* there. That day, several employees of the newspaper met at the editorial offices with party activists Blum, Lozer Klog, Sonya Nowogrodzki (the wife of Emanuel Nowogrodzki, secretary of the Bund Central Committee, who was in New York at that time on party business), David Klayn and Szmuel Kaplan, Bund activists in Kalisz who had fled from that city to Warsaw. Abrasha Blum organized the work of the editorial board, and the newspaper continued to appear on most days of the Germans siege of Warsaw. Most other Jewish newspapers, by contrast, were discontinued in the first week of the war. *Haynt* stopped appearing on 6 September and *Moment* on 11 September; by the second half of September only the *Folkstsaytung* and *Nasz Przegląd* were still in circulation. The *Folkstsaytung* was the last Jewish newspaper published in Warsaw, its final issue appearing the day before Yom Kippur, 22 September 1939. Despite the harsh conditions of the siege, the staff managed to print several thousand copies each day.[26]

Two soup kitchens were established at this time – on Długa Street and on Zamenhofa Street – for the party member refugees who were thronging Warsaw. Sonya Nowogrodzki made it her responsibility to organize the relief work. After Warsaw fell, on 1 October 1939, the members added several additional distribution stations for food staples and tea on Nalewki, Nowolipie, Śliska and Muranowska Streets. In mid-October, Shlomo Abramsohn, Mania Zygielbojm (Szmuel Zygielbojm's wife), and Luba Gilinski (wife of Shlomo Gilinski, director of the Medem Sanatorium, who had left Warsaw) reopened the sanatorium after the JDC activist Leib Neustadt promised to assist them in so doing.[27] The members evidently had enough money for this initial welfare activity, the Central Committee members having left Abrasha Blum with the party cash-box containing several thousand złoty before they left Warsaw. Departing party members also left $2,000 with Zygielbojm, after he promised to arrange reimbursement through Bund supporters in New York.[28]

The occupation of Warsaw on 1 October and the introduction of German military rule forced the party in one stroke to go underground and adopt a new setting of activity. The new core of the underground Central Committee – Zygielbojm, Goldstein, Blum and Sonya Nowogrodzki – went into action during the month-long siege and in the weeks following the fall of Warsaw. In early October, as the members debated whether to stay in Warsaw or to move eastward, Zygielbojm insisted that Sonya Nowogrodzki and Goldstein leave town – Nowogrodzki because of the state of her health and Goldstein because he was a well-known political figure in Warsaw.[29] Several months later, only Zygielbojm left Warsaw because his opposition in the Warsaw *Judenrat* to the attempt to ghettoize the Jews in November 1939 had aroused concerns for his life.

The Bund was the first Jewish political agency that organized for underground work in Warsaw. The other Jewish parties were left with hardly any activists in the capital, but several major Bund activists remained there and replaced the veteran leadership. Unlike the other parties and movements, the Bund survived the crisis without serious disruption. Abrasha Blum, 34 years old, had carried out most of his pre-war activity among the young members of Tsukunft and was now authorized by the movement leaders to carry on. Zygielbojm had the tenure and experience to make important contacts with members of the PPS – contacts that a young and less-known member such as Blum could not make. They were subsequently joined by several women with experience in education and welfare, such as Sonya Nowogrodzki and Mania Zygielbojm. They and several staff members of the *Folkstsaytung* enabled the work of the movement, which had become so important at this time of general collapse, to continue. The Bund's relationship with a large Polish party, the PPS, facilitated its organizational work at this time, even though the exodus of Bund leaders from the besieged capital prompted some PPS members to question the Bund's loyalty to the Polish cause. Although these doubts, which predated the occupation, now became more acute, the parties managed to collaborate in Warsaw's brave fight against the Germans. These factors fortified the confidence of the Bund in its ability to continue functioning under the conditions of German occupation.

Among the players that would eventually make up the Jewish political Underground in Warsaw, all but the Bund were paralysed. The youth movement leadership left Warsaw to the east, leaving behind only the youngest members, who were unable to organize activity of any kind. On 7 September 1939, for example, the HaShomer haTsa'ir (youth socialist–Zionist organization) cell ceremoniously dissolved itself and destroyed all movement documents lest they fall into German hands. The collapse of the movement upon the occupation came as a severe shock to the young members, most of whom stayed with their parents after the adult leaders left.[30] In contrast, the leadership of Tsukunft did not leave *en bloc*. The movement's major activists – Yosef Lifschitz, Lucjan Blit and Leon Oller – left in the manner of the central committee members, but several adult activists stayed behind and undertook to keep the work going. Blum, 31-year-old Israel Grilak, and 30-year-old Hennoch Rus became figures of authority in the eyes of the young members of Tsukunft and SKIF. Before the siege ended, these young people were taking part in distributing the *Folkstsaytung*, forwarding notices and maintaining liaison among members. Thus another basis for future underground activity was created.

Thus, from the very first months, the Bund successfully built an infrastructure for underground activity, even though the purpose of the activity was not yet defined and the members of the local leadership in Warsaw considered it their mission to organize activity there, not to form a new leadership that would replace the departed one. Only over the next few months was a new framework created, in which this young group would play a central role in party history during the Holocaust.

Łódź fell to the Germans on 8 September 1939, by which time thousands of Jews, including Bund members, had fled toward Warsaw. The first meeting of the local Bund Central Committee was scheduled for 5 September. Szmuel Milman, its chairman, sought to convene it in order to appoint a group of activists that would take over the committee's functions after the leadership left town. However, the meeting was thwarted by the chaos that overtook Łódź shortly before the Germans entered and by the departure of several committee members in the direction of Warsaw.[31] On 2 or 3 September 1939 members of Tsukunft convened to volunteer for the Polish army.[32] This, too, did not come to pass because the Germans advanced swiftly and occupied the city. Szmuel Zygielbojm left the city, as we recall, and reached Warsaw on 8 September 1939.[33]

The response of the major Bund activists in Łódź to the German occupation is puzzling. As prominent activists such as Zygielbojm, Milman, Ephraim Zalmanowits and Benjamin Wirovski (a member of the town council who wrote for the newspaper *Der Lodźer Weker*) hurriedly left town and moved to Warsaw, other members preferred to wait or did not leave at all. Alexander Margulis, a doctor and a Bund delegate to the Łódź town council, stayed because he was committed to his duties as director of the hospital in Radogoszcz.[34] Chaim-Leib Poznanski, another Bund delegate to the Łódź town council, made the same decision.[35] Yosef Morgenthaler, a major activist in the Jewish textile workers' union, left for Warsaw but returned to Łódź in late September.[36] The lives of Jewish political activists in Łódź were endangered by anti-Jewish violence perpetrated by the SS Einsatzcommando 2, under the command of Fritz-Wilhelm Liphart, which entered Łódź on 11 September 1939, in the wake of Wehrmacht forces. The Einsatzcommando was joined by a unit of the Selbstschutz (self-defence), established by *Volksdeutsche* (ethnic German) civilians who resided in Łódź, nearly all of whom sympathized with the Nazi regime. These units wrought violence against Poles and Jews, foremost political activists in left-wing units and members of the Polish intelligentsia, but above all they assailed Jews in the streets and plundered and looted Jewish property.[37]

Ya'akov Nirenberg, a Bund activist in the Łódź ghetto, stated in his memoirs that the members had decided to leave several party journalists and Tsukunft members in Łódź to destroy party documents before the occupation.[38] In fact, however, journalists and Tsukunft members joined the exodus with their families, while well-known members of the Bund leadership stayed behind. Unlike the Central Committee members in Warsaw, all of whom left town, the members in Łódź considered themselves local activists and not national leaders of a Jewish party. In Łódź, as stated, the question of departure was not debated; those who left did so frantically and hastily, each prompted by his or her political, personal and family considerations.

Almost all the Bund leaders who remained in Łódź fell victim to the spate of arrests and murders that the Germans perpetrated among the Jewish and Polish political leadership in Łódź during the first few months of the occupation. The Germans, equipped with a list bearing the names of the local Bund leaders, arrested seven leading figures in September, including Chaim-Leib Poznanski and Yosef Morgenthaler. They also interned Leib Hollanderski, a leader of Left Po'aley Tsiyon (the socialist, pro-Soviet, Zionist party), and two PPS leaders in the town. In November 1939 Alexander Margulis was arrested in a round-up of most members of the first Łódź *Judenrat*. The Bund members and the other inmates were interned in a camp established in Radogoszcz, a suburb of Łódź. Margulis and other inmates were murdered in the middle of November; Poznanski, Morgenthaler, Hersh Meir Zilberberg (secretary of the *Folkstsaytung* in Łódź), and additional members were deported in March 1940 to camps in the *Generalgouvernement*, never to return.[39]

In Kraków, Bund members held a meeting on the evening of 1 September 1939, when the German invasion of Poland became known. The question of leaving the city was not debated at this meeting; the members' main concern was how to cooperate with the PPS to offer material assistance to the families of members of the two parties who had been drafted. Two days later, PPS members advised their Bund counterparts that it would be best for them to leave. Here again, however, not all of the leading group left. The first to go were the heads of the local branch and the main activists: Leon Feiner, Henryk Schrayber, the brothers Ignacy and Max Aleksandrowitz, Salo Fiszgrund and Michał Szuldenfrei. They left for Lwów, as did most Jewish refugees who fled from that area. Less famous members in this town, in contrast, did not rush to leave, and those who departed waited until 7 September to do so, after the government urged young people to head for the east.[40] Most members of the leading cadre returned to their cities several months after the Polish army surrendered to the Red Army in Lwów on 22 September 1939. Ya'akov Tselemenski, one of the prominent members in the group of young Bund members in Kraków, wrote in his memoirs that various activists returned to Kraków to avoid the danger that the communist authorities held in store for Bund members. Furthermore, their employment opportunities in Lwów were severely limited, since the strong communist trade unions there presented them with the risk of denunciation.[41] In late 1939 and in January 1940, most young Bund activists who had risen in the ranks in the latter half of the 1930s returned to Kraków: Tselemenski, however, did not return. Feiner remained in Lwów, was arrested by the Soviets on 19 July 1940, as he set out for Wilno, and was sentenced to 15 years in prison for anti-communist activity. Schrayber was arrested in the summer of 1940 and sent to a labour camp in the Urals, where he perished.[42] In no other city in Poland, as in Kraków, did so many Bund activists return to their homes in the German-occupied area. The main reason for this evidently has to do with the special complexion that the Bund had acquired in this city before the war. The Bund was weaker in Kraków, as in all of Galicia, than in Congress Poland, but in Kraków a group of activists consolidated whose strong personal and organizational abilities elevated them to leading positions in the Bund and earned them much appreciation among players in Kraków's Polish Left. These Bundists formed a very strong relationship with the PPS and collaborated with Polish workers not only in demonstrations, rallies and protest activities against the regime and the fascist opposition, but also in social assistance and cultural activity.[43]

In the spring of 1940 the governor-general, Hans Frank, decided to banish most of the Jews of Kraków from this city, which had been designated the capital of the *Generalgouvernement*. The city was to be *Judenfrei* – cleansed of Jews – by 1 November 1940, since, in Frank's view, it was preposterous to force Wehrmacht officers and German bureaucrats who lived in Kraków to live in the proximity of Jews.[44] The resulting deportation swept up some 40,000 indigenous Jews and almost all the Bund activists who had returned to Kraków. These Bundists relocated to Warsaw and helped reorganize the Bund in the underground.

In Częstochowa, the main visible impact of the Bund before the war focused on the activity of the health-care organization TOZ (*Towarzystwo Ochrony Zdrowia*), in which the two Bund leaders in this town, Liber Brener and Mordechai Kusznir, were active. Since the city fell to the German army at the early occasion of 3 September, Bund activists in Częstochowa neither met nor consulted with each other, and did not manage to prepare for departure. Most members who left Częstochowa returned to their homes by 18 September. Apart from two important activists – Avraham Rosenblatt, who moved to Lwów, and Yitzchak Stopnitzer, who moved to Będzin, Bundists either remained in Częstochowa or returned to this town by the end of September.[45]

The Germans occupied Piotrków-Trybunalski on 5 September 1939, but hardly any Bund activists there left town. In Piotrków-Trybunalski, which had a Jewish population of 10,500, the local Bund leaders (Zalman Tenenberg and Ya'akov-Reuven Berliner) had headed the *kehilla* before the war began, and did not even consider the possibility of leaving because the Germans reached the area in the first few days of September.[46] In the years preceding the war, the Bund held almost total control of the *kehilla* institutions in Piotrków-Trybunalski and accounted for nearly all Jewish delegates to the town council. In no other Polish city did the party have such influence in Jewish life. Piotrków-Trybunalski was an important PPS stronghold, and its city hall, led by the Polish Left, made efforts in the 1930s to integrate the Jews into municipal life. The Bund–PPS cooperation in local politics played an important role in the party activists' initial decision to leave or stay. Another probable contributing factor in their decision to stay was the peripheral location of Piotrków, meaning that the town's Bund activists, although well known locally, did not fear for their lives as did move-ment activists in Warsaw. The activists may also have been influenced in their decision by their pivotal role in community leadership and sense of responsibility as the German occupation condemned the town to so grave an ordeal.

Lublin was one of the last cities to fall to the Germans (on 18 September 1939), and party members there apparently held no discus-sion about staying or leaving before the arrival of Bund activists who had left Warsaw. The first to arrive from Warsaw were Pinchas Schwartz and Baruch Schefner, the journalists who left on the government train, followed by Wiktor Alter and Bernard Goldstein. Schwarz and Schefner tried to persuade activists in Lublin, headed by Bella Szapiro, to leave town before the Germans moved in. The response of the Lublin members was affected by vagueness about the future of Lublin in the first few weeks of the war, especially until the Soviet invasion on 17 September. Goldstein wrote that Lublin was being flooded by commu-nist propaganda, asserting that the Red Army had entered Poland to help the Poles in their war against the Germans. When the city fell to the Germans with no intervention on the part of the Red Army, the Bundists decided to attempt to head north towards Wilno. This decision, too, was taken in conjunction with PPS activists and trade unionists who, shortly before the town surrendered to the Germans, had estab-lished a coordinating council of sorts between the Jewish and the Polish proletariat.[47] The most important Bund activists – Aharon Nissenboym, Bella Szapiro and Shlomo Hirszenhorn – left Lublin on 18 September 1939. Ya'akov Nissenbaum, Bella Szapiro's husband and the pre-war editor of the newspaper *Lubliner Togblat*, also left. On 19 September Szapiro, Nissenboym and Hirshhorn reached Luck, where a group of functionaries and activists from Warsaw had gathered. In early October the members of this group decided to head for Wilno. The only exceptions were Bella Szapiro and her husband, who chose to return to Lublin[48] lest the Soviet security authorities captured and imprisoned them for their activity in the Bund.[49]

Bund leaders and activists did not respond identically to the German occupation in September 1939. Members decided to stay or head east mainly depending on their function in the party. Important activists, especially in Warsaw, felt in greater danger than did rank-and-file members. Many activists fled from Warsaw, and the departure of the leadership had an effect on ordinary members in this city. Chaim Babitz a member of the *Folkstsaytung* staff, recalls that the leaders' decision to evacuate had an adverse effect on members and heightened their sense of danger upon the Germans' arrival.[50] In contrast, young members of Tsukunft and petty movement activists in peripheral towns preferred to stay put because of the responsibility and duty that they sensed toward the other remaining members and young people. The great departure panic that occurred in Warsaw was not observed in peripheral towns, where members felt themselves in no greater danger from the Germans than other Jews. Many members elected to remain with their families even though they were active in the Bund or the trade unions. Relations with colleagues and friends in the PPS or the Polish trade unions also figured in Bund members' decisions to leave and, especially, to return to their homes. In localities where PPS members and Bundists interacted closely and amiably, it seems that few of the latter fled in September and many returned in late 1939 and early 1940. The importance of these relations is illustrated in the vacillations of the leaders in Warsaw shortly before they left the city after several PPS activists ruled out frantic retreat. Of course, various members' decisions to flee or stay were also influenced by objective factors. The most important of these factors was the pace at which the Wehrmacht advanced, for the German forces blocked departure from localities that they occupied during the first few days of the war. The arrival of Soviet forces in eastern Poland in September also caused grave concern among Bund members because of the hostility of the Communist regime toward their movement. Thus, many members decided to stay at home, preferring the safety of their families and communities to a migration into an unknown that involved many dangers. In this sense, Bund members were no different from Jews generally.

It is hard to determine exactly how many Bund activists left their homes in September and remained in the Soviet occupation zone. In the summer of 1940 many Jewish refugees from Poland were exiled to the Soviet interior and sent to quarantine camps and labour camps in the northern and eastern sections of the USSR, after the Communist regime failed to 'passportize' and Sovietize the refugee population in early 1940.[51] After the Polish government-in-exile in London and the Soviet government concluded their agreement on 31 July 1941, hundreds of thousands of Polish citizens were released from labour camps in the Soviet interior. A group of ten liberated Bund activists gathered in Kuibyshev, where Poland had its embassy at that time. In their estimation, some 2,000 Bund and Tsukunft members, along with their families, were in the Soviet Union in the summer of 1941.[52] After the war (in June 1946), Salo Fiszgrund and Michał Szuldenfrei, the leaders of the

Bund in Poland at that time, estimated that about a thousand veteran Bundists returned to Poland upon the repatriation from the Soviet Union.[53] In other words, most Bund members and sympathizers did not leave their homes when the war broke out, and most of those who fled to the east returned to their homes in the *Generalgouvernement* before this became impossible. Most of the latter were senior or petty officials: members of trade unions, party journalists who left the peripheral towns and secretaries of branches of the youth organizations. Few members of the activist cadre, let alone party sympathizers, left their homes at the onset of the German occupation.

THE RED TERROR

On 17 September 1939 the Red Army crossed the eastern frontier of Poland and began to claim the USSR's entitlements under the Soviet–German pact of late August that year. This agreement did not sketch the exact border between the German and Soviet occupation zones, although it stated that the border would follow the Narew, Vistula and San Rivers. Among the Baltic countries, Lithuania would be assigned to the German sphere of influence and Latvia and Estonia to the Soviet sphere. The rapid collapse of the Polish army and the Wehrmacht's advance to the negotiated border (the Vistula), after only a week of fighting, stunned Stalin and his generals. They were unprepared for so swift a German victory and had not completed their own ground-work for the invasion of Poland. The Germans' pursuit of the defeated Polish army brought them to Białystok, Łomża and Brześć nad Bugiem in the north, Przemyśl in the south and the outskirts of Lwów – areas that the German–Soviet accord assigned to Russian control. On 18 September, the German ambassador to Moscow, Friedrich von Schulenburg, advised Stalin that the Wehrmacht would withdraw from the eastern provinces of Poland and turn them over to the Red Army. On 28 September 1939 the German and Soviet foreign ministers, Joachim von Ribbentrop and Vyacheslav Molotov, signed the final agreement concerning the partition frontiers in Poland. The new border was marked along the Rivers Narew, Bug and San. Stalin ceded the area between the Vistula and the Bug, the Lublin district and parts of the Warsaw district; in return, all of Lithuania, including Wilno, went over to the Soviet sphere of influence.

The abrupt changeover from German to Soviet rule in the eastern areas sowed confusion and chaos among the local Jewish population and the many refugees who had streamed into these regions. The six weeks between the middle of September 1939 and the end of October were especially critical for members of the Bund, many of whose fate was sealed at that time.

The Soviet army occupied Wilno on 19 September 1939, and remained there until 28 October, when it turned over the city to the government of Lithuania. Several Jewish refugees arrived from Poland during this time, but the large wave of refugees reached Wilno only after the Soviets left. During their six weeks of control in Wilno, the Russians obliterated the infrastructure of Bund activity there and interned almost all of the movement leaders. The first arrested were Anna Rozental, a Bund leader in Wilno about 70 years of age and Ya'akov Zhloźnikov, a trade unionist. Rozental apparently furnished her interrogators with a list of important Bund and trade union activists in Wilno. Shortly after these two were seized, Yosef Taytel and Yosef Aronovitz, the latter elected to the deputy chair of the *kehilla* as a Bund candidate, were also detained.[54] Zhloźnikov and Taytel were banished to a camp in the vicinity of Minsk, and on 28 April 1940 were sent from this location to camps in the Soviet interior, never to return. In November 1940 Aronovitz was prosecuted for anti-revolutionary activity and sentenced to eight years in prison. Shortly after his trial, he died in prison. Anna Rozental perished in prison in late 1941.[55]

The wave of arrests included activists in other eastern Polish towns. Shaul Goldman, a member of the Bund Central Committee and head of the Białystok branch, was arrested on 2 October 1939; after a lengthy stay in prison he was deported to Siberia on 20 May 1941, along with his family. Binyamin Floymenboym, a teacher who headed the Yiddishist teachers' union in Białystok and represented the Bund on the town council, was arrested by the Soviets and subsequently vanished.[56] On 5 October 1939 Leib Shiffers, a Bund delegate to the town council and chairman of the local party branch, and Berl Abramovitz, a cultural activist in Grodno and an editor of the Bundist journal *Grodner Shtime*, were arrested in Grodno.[57] In Pińsk, some ten Bund members and trade unionists, headed by Aharon-Yudel Shlikman (the local leader of the movement), were arrested in late December 1939. Most of the arrestees worked at the match factory in Pińsk, where the labour force was famously and staunchly pro-Bund.[58] The Soviets also arrested Bund members Mordechai Posisorski in Łomża and Ida Sabaticki in Slonim. In Brześć nad Bugiem, Yisrael-Meir Tenenbaum, a *kehilla* activist and a Bund delegate to the town council, and David Shneider, a teacher and an activist in the cultural associations, were arrested.[59] Additional party members arrested included Shaya Bernstein in Włodzimierz Wołyński and Yitzchak-Ezra Glazer, Shaya Forer, and Shlomo Rogovitz in Prużana.[60] In Baranowicze, Równe and smaller localities such as Stolyn and Krynki the Soviets hunted down Bund members in order to imprison them.[61] Within two months or so, the Soviets had incarcerated the movement's leadership and terminated its activity throughout the occupied territories from Lwów to Wilno. They persecuted no other Jewish movement or party with such intensity.

In contrast to the mass imprisonment of Bund members in the annexed areas to the east, movement leaders who moved from Warsaw and other German-held cities to refugee centres in eastern Poland were hardly harmed. Most members of the party Central Committee were not arrested, except for Erlich (imprisoned on 4 October in Brześć nad Bugiem) and Alter (incarcerated on 26 September in Kowel). This is because the refugees from Warsaw – with the obvious exceptions of the senior leaders of the Bund, who were famous public figures – were less known in eastern Poland. The spate of arrests of Bund activists and the imprisonment of Erlich and Alter served as a serious warning for Bund members who reached the Soviet territories.

Before Erlich and Alter were arrested, most members of the Bund misjudged the danger they faced from the Soviet regime. The contingent of party members from Białystok, who stayed in Wilno, decided to return to their home town when the Germans left it and the Soviets came in. The Bund members in greatest danger were those who lived in Wilno, but they did not sense the menace that the Soviets' advent created for them.[62]

Maurycy Orzech, a member of the Warsaw group that had set out from Wilno to Kovno on 19 September, was one of the few who perceived the danger. In late September, he wrote the following to Nowogrodzki in New York: 'I do not want to remain in Kovno; I want to reach Paris. The situation in Lithuania is not safe at all, especially after the agreement between Hitler and Stalin … We should all leave this place and go to Sweden or Denmark; I am very concerned about the future that awaits the Jews in the Bolshevik occupied territories …'[63]

In early October, after Alter and Erlich had been arrested and the extent of the Soviet manhunt for local activists had become known, the mood among Bund refugees in the eastern areas changed. The activists who had been with Erlich in Brześć nad Bugiem were in a state of severe panic. A few members decided to move to Białystok and, once there, held a series of consultations with other members on whether to return to their homes, to continue to Warsaw, or to head for Wilno which too was under Soviet occupation.[64] In October 1939 dozens of Bund members asked themselves this question. Here, as with the question of leaving at the onset of the occupation, each member made his or her own decision in view of the position in the movement and the extent of danger presented by the NKVD. Lesser-known members decided to cross the border to Wilno even before the Soviets left the city in late October.[65] Many decided to return to their homes: Szapiro to Lublin, Tselemenski and Fiszgrund to Kraków, and Goldstein to Warsaw. Even Shloime Mendelsohn, the Tsisho leader, wished to return to Warsaw but yielded to his comrades' entreaties that he remain in Białystok.[66]

In contrast to Bund members, who feared capture and imprisonment by the Soviets if they crossed into Wilno, activists of the Zionist organizations make a swift exodus to Wilno before the Soviets could leave and the borders be closed. The Soviet authorities, wishing to earn the sympathies of members of Zionist youth movements that were to some extent pro-Soviet, treated them gently at the beginning of the occupation. In contrast, they regarded the Bund as a reactionary and anti-Bolshevist force. The Bund's strong influence among members of the Jewish working class immediately before the war, and its vigorous objections to the nature of Stalin's regime in the Soviet Union, made it a dangerous rival that had to be eliminated. Bund members in the eastern territories were in serious danger of their lives at that time. Wilno was not an option for them; unlike Zionist activists they did not regard it as a way-station *en route* to Palestine and could not continue to operate there under Soviet rule. Thus, their only alternative was to attempt to return to their homes, since in no German-occupied city – with the exception of Łódź, where Jewish and Polish activists on the Left had been imprisoned as equals – had the German occupier waged an all-out war against Jewish political activists. The only reason that few prominent Bundists eventually returned, it seems, is that in late October 1939 Wilno was transferred to the government of Lithuania and became a safe haven for them.

DISSENT AND INDECISION

Bund members and associates in Britain and the United States believed that prominent Bundists – members of the Central Committee and well-known activists – should strive to leave Lithuania as quickly as possible. Indeed, they took several measures to make this possible even before they obtained the consent of the committee members in Wilno to leave for the West. In December 1939 Berl Rosner, head of the Friends of the Bund association in London, advised Emanuel Nowogrodzki in New York that 24 Bund leaders in Wilno could be furnished with British visas for $10,000. Nowogrodzki and Jacob Pat, a Bund official who had reached the United States before the war and who served from the board secretariat of the Jewish Labour Committee (JLC) in New York at that time, obtained $6,000 for this purpose from the Board secretariat; they planned to raise the rest of the money by canvassing Bund sympathizers in the United States.[67] Nowogrodzki assured the secretariat of the British Labour Party, which had helped obtain these visas, that the Bund would provide the secretariat with £2,000 sterling to guarantee the members' travel expenses to the United States. To prevent them from becoming wards of the state or the British labour organizations, Nowogrodzki undertook to send them monthly support from New York. For several months at this time he also attempted to obtain, with the assistance of Yosef Horn, a Bund member in Argentina, entrance visas to Argentina for 20 party members in Wilno.[68] The Bundists targeted for rescue, however, headed neither for Britain nor for Argentina in early 1940 – not only because difficulties came up in obtaining the visas but also because several important members were concerned about being the first public figures and leaders of the party to leave the danger zone, and in fact to emigrate from Poland. The Central Committee elected to remain in Wilno, and slowly made this city the headquarters of Polish Bund activity. In the aftermath of the calm that ensued in early 1940 and the consolidation of the Lithuanian rule in Wilno, it was also hoped that the members there could ride out the war safely by staying put.[69]

On the assumption that Wilno would become the movement's organizational hub – the conduit of relief activity and contact with underground Bund activists who remained in Warsaw – the party leadership attempted to make contact with the activist cadre in the Polish capital. In December 1939 Mordechai Tsanin, a journalist closely associated with the Bund, travelled to Warsaw in the party's service, delivering money and announcements to the Bund activists in Warsaw. According to Tsanin's memoirs, Shloime Mendelsohn and Chaim-Meir Wasser, members of the Central Committee, also wanted to go to Warsaw, but the other members thwarted this – Mendelsohn because of his shaky health and Wasser because his activity in the Soviet Union after the October Revolution had betrayed him to the NKVD. Tsanin writes that four Bund couriers headed from Wilno toward Warsaw at this time, and two of them were captured.[70]

In the first few months of 1940, before they began to leave Wilno, the members of the Bund leadership thought mostly about raising funds from American comrades and friends to assist colleagues who had remained in Warsaw and to help the Bundist refugees who had gathered in Wilno. In February 1940 members of the Central Committee in Wilno believed they would need $15,000 to provide members of the movement in Poland with relief and organization.[71]

It was not easy to raise such a sum at that time, since the Jewish Labour Committee (JLC), the main organization that supported the Bund and its members, was financially strapped. Jacob Pat explained to his comrades in Wilno that despite its good intentions, the JLC could help only a small group of movement leaders and their families, to the exclusion of the masses of workers that remained in Poland and Wilno. The latter collectivity, said Pat, should avail itself of the relief operations of the American-Jewish Joint Distribution Committee (JDC).[72] Nowogrodzki, on his part, toiled prodigiously to raise funds from American and European friends and activists for his comrades in Wilno. Between December 1939 and December 1940, he marshalled more than $6,000 from Bund members and his own friends in New York, Zurich and Copenhagen, and forwarded the money to Wilno. He also assembled a shipment of several hundred food parcels for Warsaw and other cities in Poland.[73] It is difficult to state with certainty whether all of the money sent from Wilno to Warsaw actually reached the underground Bund leadership in Warsaw. Shloime Mendelsohn, who reached Sweden from Wilno in November 1940, received confirmation from Sonya Nowogrodzki that she had received $2,300 from Wilno.[74] The receipt of funds from Wilno at that time is corroborated by a report from the Bund underground committee in Warsaw to New York in March 1942, including a review of the movement's clandestine activity between 1940 and early 1942.[75] These actions by the Bund leadership in Wilno played an important role in the coalescence of the Bund underground in Warsaw during the first few months of the occupation.

Some 16,000 Jewish refugees gathered in Lithuania in early 1940. By June of that year, when Lithuania lost its independence and was annexed by the Soviet Union, two centres of Jewish refugees had evolved there – one in Wilno (approx. 14,000 refugees) and one in Kovno (1,800). According to data collected by the JDC, the refugee population included 2,440 yeshiva students, 171 rabbis, 2,065 members of Zionist pioneering youth movements – and some 400 members of the Bund.[76] In December 1939 a general committee for Jewish refugees was established in Wilno under Dr Ya'akov Robinson. Moses Beckelman of the JDC reached Wilno at this time and coordinated relief operations for the refugees. Between September 1939 and June 1940, when the Soviet Union annexed Wilno, the JDC provided more than $717,000 in refugee aid, fed 7,000 people in public soup kitchens, distributed clothing to some 8,000 refugees and gave them a regular weekly allowance of 13 litt (about $6) – just enough for basic needs and rent.[77]

When actions to organize refugee relief first began, a severe disagreement erupted between the Bund leaders and the JDC activists in Wilno. The Bund wished to represent itself *vis-à-vis* the JDC instead of obtaining assistance for its members through the general refugee committee. In early November 1939 Shloime Mendelsohn and Moses Beckelman held a meeting that was evidently attended by Isaac Giterman, a leading JDC official in Warsaw who had conducted a fierce dispute with the Bund before the war, who objected to separate relations between the JDC and the Bund, and even argued that relations with a socialist oppositionist party such as the Bund actually militated against the JDC's interests in Poland.[78] Mendelsohn presented Beckelman with a series of Bund demands: that 'the Joint' provide with Bund activists in Wilno sums of money for members who remained in Warsaw; that the Bund be given a separate budget for the development of labourer-refugee workshops; that the Polish złoty that Bund members had brought from Poland be replaced with Lithuanian litts; and that Bund members be allowed to buy their own clothing instead of obtaining it through JDC relief channels, as did the other refugees in Wilno. Beckelman replied that there was no obstacle to honouring the work-shop request, such an enterprise being consistent with the JDC approach. Neither did he object to forwarding money to members in Poland, although he stated that the decision was not his to make since the JDC had not yet elaborated its policy toward the occupied territories. However, he flatly rejected two demands: replacing złotys with litts and allowing the Bund to buy its own clothing for member refugees. The JDC cannot enter into currency trading, he told Mendelsohn, and the clothing demand would set a precedent for other political groups to follow. In Beckelman's opinion, Mendelsohn was seeking the JDC's principled consent to segregating Bund members from other refugees and had not given much thought to the magnitude of assistance that party members needed.[79] The Bund members in Kovno also opposed assistance through the Joint Refugee Committee. Beckelman visited Kovno in the middle of October 1939, and managed to reach terms with the small group of Bundists there. They found housing and jobs on a farm a short distance from Kovno and established a collective that obtained assistance from the JDC. Although the Lithuanian authorities limited their freedom of movement and barred them from the city itself, they avoided economic hardship.[80]

The Bund leaders in Wilno found it hard to accept the JDC officials' refusal to honour their demands for autonomy in their relations with this organization. They impugned the JDC's motives and traced its opposition to rejection of the Bund's ideational and ideological doctrines. Mendelsohn expressed these feelings in one of his letters to New York:

> We are stirring up lots of trouble and embarrassment because of Giterman. Our refugees are not being helped because they are our refugees; unfortunately, they are 'political'. It's an infuriating tactic to use in apportioning coats, blankets, shoes, etc. I spoke about it with Beckelman, but to no avail. Couldn't the JDC tell its representatives to set aside a special reserve of several thousand dollars and spare us this hassle and unpleasantness?[81]

Among the refugees who reached Wilno were about 150 teachers and faculty members of Yiddish schools in Poland, including well-known educators such as Shlomo Gilinski and Chaim-Shlomo Kazdan. These Tsisho activists wished to re-establish the Yiddish schools in this city with authorization from the Lithuanian government. They also wanted to help comrades in Warsaw who were sustaining educational activity of some kind after the war in Poland had ended. Mendelsohn, Beckelman and Giterman discussed this matter, too, in a talk they held in November 1939. However, just as they had not managed to work out an understanding on refugee relief, so they could not agree on a budget for Tsisho activities in Wilno. Mendelsohn alleged that the JDC was forwarding large sums of money to yeshivas and other institutions of religious education, and discriminating against Yiddish-language schools associated with the labour movement.[82]

JDC officials were afraid that a separate relationship with the Bund would embroil them in trouble with the Lithuanian government. Information from Lithuania that reached members of the Jewish Labour Committee evoked concern that the Lithuanian government took a dim view of the Bund's activity in Wilno. The JLC officials forwarded this information to their JDC counterparts in New York.[83] The government's attitude toward the Bund may have originated not in the socialist complexion of the latter, as Beckelman believed,[84] but in its unwillingness to tolerate a permanent beehive of illegal activities (border

running and underground contacts) between Wilno and occupied
Poland. The government preferred to see the refugees from Poland
remove themselves promptly from Lithuanian soil. The JDC, in turn –
echoing its policy in Poland before the war – preferred to deny the
government any pretext to halt the relief work.

The problems that arose between the Bund and the JDC representatives in Wilno were explored in January 1940 when Beckelman met
in Paris with Morris Troper, head of the JDC office in Europe. The
JDC secretariat in New York instructed Troper to attempt to reach
terms with the Bund. At the recommendation of a sympathetic JDC
official – Joseph J. Schwartz, secretary of the JDC at the time – Troper
accepted the logic of the Bund members, who argued that their
movement could not join the general refugee committee because one-
third of the committee members represented non-proletarian if not
anti-proletarian political entities such as the Orthodox.[85] In their
summarizing memorandum, Troper and Beckelman stated that several
of the Bund's demands should be met even if they deviated from the
JDC's policy principles for its activity in Wilno, i.e., to apportion relief
on the basis of party key.[86] The JDC and the Bund leadership concluded
an agreement of this nature in March–April 1940. Instead of coming
aboard the Joint Refugee Committee, the Bund established a committee
of its own that coordinated the receipt of assistance for party members
with members of the Joint Refugee Committee.

What was the crux of the dispute concerning the Bund joining the
Joint Refugee Committee and obtaining assistance for the Tshiso
schools? Evidently, it was a struggle among interest groups, mainly in
view of several petty demands that Mendelsohn and his comrades
bruited with Beckelman in November 1939. In the matter of assistance
for schools, for example, the Bund's arguments were groundless. In
December 1939 the JDC forwarded money to the Jewish education
systems in Wilno. Tsisho received 5,750 litt, Tarbut 1,540, Tahkemoni
3,550 and Shulkult 1,000. These last three were identified with Zionism.
Additionally, the Jewish Labour Committee provided Tshiso in Wilno
with $3,000 between January and March 1940.[87] In March 1940 the
JDC Cultural Committee decided to allocate $7,000 for educational
and cultural activity in Wilno. Of this sum, $3,000 was set aside for
the needs of the numerous yeshiva students who had reached Wilno;
the rest was apportioned among the Jewish education systems.[88]

However, the root of the discord that erupted in Wilno between
Bund activists and JDC officials concerned the Bund's relationship
with other political entities for cooperative purposes. Until September

1939, the party leaders had categorically ruled out any political relationship; now, for the first time since the war broke out, they had to rethink the matter. At first glance, there was no ideological reason for the Bund to object to joining the Joint Refugee Committee. After all, the committee engaged not in political work but in the distribution of assistance and relief. Before the war, the Bund had not flinched from social and cultural cooperation with Jewish parties such as Left Po'aley Tsiyon and Yiddishist circles in Tshiso, which shared much of its worldview, and in its capacity in the community administrations it had cooperated with public agencies that were far from its worldview. Thus, the root of the dissension in Wilno concerned how to define the Joint Refugee Committee's work: was it political, or simply humanitarian?

Representation on the Joint Refugee Committee was apportioned by a sectorial party key that gave the Orthodox camp and the Zionist organizations a majority. The Bund members suspected that the committee was in fact a political framework and that the Bund's humble representation would not suffice to protect its rights. The suspicion and hostility that typified the party's attitude toward most political Jewish organizations in Poland before the war resurfaced in Wilno. Furthermore, the Bundists – leaders and rank and file alike – regarded themselves, in contrast to other refugees, as political refugees who had nothing in common with the collectivity of Jewish fugitives. They had come to Wilno because they were members of a socialist and Jewish party that was being persecuted by the Nazis and the Soviet regime. The Bundists intended to re-establish the party centre in Wilno, whence they would maintain contact with their comrades in the occupied territories. Since they perceived their work as political – transcending mere social assistance – they saw no place for collaboration with other political parties or entities. In the very first months of the war, the Bund leaders were already perturbed about the Jews' position in the anti-Nazi struggle. In a letter to Adolph Held, president of the Jewish Labour Committee, Mendelsohn said:

> We accept the relationship between the fate of the Jewish masses and that of the working masses in various countries. It is in our interest to cooperate with the non-Jewish working class. How does this principle correspond to the general Jewish goals of the war? What are the Jewish goals of the war? This matter makes the Jewish problem an international problem that ties in with Palestinism and Zionism. How can the world Jewish working class interrelate thus with the international proletariat?[89]

From the standpoint of the Bund leadership in Wilno, joining the Joint Refugee Committee at this time was tantamount to admitting that the Jews had collective and particularistic interests in this war. The Bund ruled out partnership with various Jewish political entities not only in early 1940 but even in the grim times that followed. The compromise ultimately attained in the matter of the refugee committee in Wilno was the first of similar settlements that the Bund worked out with other Jewish political entities during the war. The party maintained its separate framework of activity, but participated in a coordinating agency that mediated between it and a pan-Jewish organization.

RESCUE

The Red Army entered Lithuania in June 1940. A Communist government was established there, and in August of that year Lithuania applied to join the Soviet Union as a Soviet republic. In July the government ordered the de-activation of Jewish institutions of national nature. Thus the Palestine Agency was shut down, followed several months later by the office of the Hebrew Sheltering and Immigrant Aid Society (HIAS). As this occurred, the Wehrmacht in the West completed its occupation of the Low Countries and defeated France. The hopes of Bundist refugees – especially in Wilno, where the Central Committee members were staying, that Wilno would become the party's centre during the war, were dashed. They knew how dangerous the Soviet regime was for them, and the need to leave Lithuania became palpable and urgent.

The advent of the Red Army, and the reincarnation of Lithuania as a Soviet republic spread fear and panic among the Bund members in Wilno. The Soviet secret police inspired such terror that even rank-and-file Bundists, not known to be active party members, fled to out-of-town hideouts and waited to see how the new regime would behave.[90] But the Soviets refrained from harassing Jewish political activists and even allowed many of them to leave. When the issue of visas for Dutch Curaçao via Japan began,[91] an effort was made to include important activists among their recipients. Among the Bund activists and political figures of whom the Soviet security police were aware, Yekutiel Portnoy and Vladimir Kossovski, for example, received such visas in August 1940.[92] Other members left several months later after obtaining Soviet transit visas in October or November of 1940.[93] To procure transit visas to cross the Soviet Union to Japan, it was necessary to provide the NKVD with lists of visa applicants.[94]

For understandable reasons, Bund members were in no hurry to disclose their comrades' names to the committee that dealt in obtaining transit visas. They hoped to procure American entry visas directly from the US Consulate in Kovno before all the consulates there were shut down at the end of August 1940. During the Soviets' first week in the city, Hersh Gotgeshtalt, a member of the Tsukunft Central Committee before the war, sent the Jewish Labour Committee a list with the names of members who needed US entry visas.[95] When it became clear that it was impossible to leave except by crossing the Soviet Union, Chaim Fizshitz, who before the war headed an office that the Bund had established in Warsaw to assist Jews who wished to emigrate from Poland, prepared a list of Bundist refugees in Wilno and presented it to the Soviets. The Soviet security police responded somewhat oddly. They imprisoned Fizshitz, who met his death in a labour camp in Siberia. However, they did not harm the other Bundists who appeared on the list, and in 1941 they safely reached Kobe, Japan.[96]

Emanuel Nowogrodzki made prodigious efforts to extricate party members from Wilno and bring them to the United States. With the assistance of William Green, the highly influential president of the American Federation of Labour, the JLC furnished the American immigration authorities with three lists of Jewish labour activists from Poland who needed visas. The names were ranked by the extent of danger that each person faced. List A was composed of 50 names of the highest priority, including all party leaders, well-known journalists in the Yiddish press and cultural activists closely associated with the Bund, such as Zelik Kalmanowitz, the famous YIVO scholar at Wilno. Lists B and C also included members of Left Po'aley Tsiyon and activists' relatives. In all, the three lists contained 94 names, all of refugees from Wilno. About 70 of these refugees reached the United States by April 1941.[97]

In August 1940 Shloime Mendelsohn and Emanuel Szerer managed to reach Stockholm, following a sophisticated escape operation. (They had sneaked aboard a German train from Berlin to Memel and thence crossed the sea to Sweden by procuring a boat.) Once in Stockholm and provisioned with appropriate papers,[98] they established a centre that coordinated rescue efforts for Bund members in Wilno. The Bund and the PPS collaborated in efforts to rescue anti-Soviet socialists from Lithuania. In the United States these efforts were coordinated by Emanuel Nowogrodzki and Professor Oskar Lange, a former lecturer

in economics at the Jagiellonian University in Kraków who taught at
the University of Chicago. Lange was a leading player in the New
York-based Polish Socialist Alliance, which was active in 1940 in
rescuing Polish socialists who had reached Wilno and were at risk of
Soviet deportation and imprisonment. Lange put Nowogrodzki in
touch with two Swedish senators, Gunnar Myrdal and Britt G. Ohlin,
who were friends of the PPS in Sweden.[99] Nowogrodzki sent Myrdal
two lists of Bund members in Wilno and asked him to furnish these
members with transit visas across Sweden *en route* to the United States.
He stressed that the expenses of the travel and the stay in Sweden
would be covered by the Bund mission in New York.[100] In August and
September 1940, Myrdal and Władysław Malinowski, a PPS activist
who reached Stockholm, attempted to obtain transit visas for 12 Bund
leaders in Wilno. They failed because the Swedish government was
willing to issue transit visas only to persons who already held entry
visas to the United States.[101]

Few Bund members in Wilno were able to obtain such a visa during those months. Malinowski informed Nowogrodzki that one could
obtain transit visas via Berlin, but this of course was too dangerous for
leftist Jewish activists from Poland. In the end, only Szerer, Mendelsohn and Malinowski procured visas to cross Sweden on their way to
the United States.[102] The other Bund members who managed to leave
for the United States did so, like most other refugees, via the Soviet
Union and Japan.

Nowogrodzki and the Jewish Labour Committee officials entered
into an acrid dispute concerning the distribution of funds meant to pay
for the transport of refugees from Wilno to the United States. The
Jewish Labour Committee collected about $100,000 by September
1940. According to Nowogrodzki's reckoning, travel from Wilno to the
United States via Vladivostok and Yokohama would cost $518 person,
meaning that the JLC money would suffice for only 200 refugees.[103]
The high cost of the trip and the limited resources available touched
off struggles among members of the Jewish Labour Committee.
Nowogrodzki made efforts to include as many Bund members among
the departees as possible – first the party leaders, then members of the
activist cadre, and only afterwards (if possible) their families. He explained
these priorities to Shloime Mendelsohn and Emanuel Szerer:

> What's the use of bringing over several hundred women and
> children? Yes, they are the families of people who are leaving, but
> not all of those are important activists in the movement. The

Jewish Labour Committee rejects this advice in the matter of the departees' wives and children. The list they presented to Washington included 11 members of Po'aley Tsiyon. When they began to deal with the second list, the one that contains the Bundists, it turned out that there wasn't enough money. We're being discriminated against in this matter.[104]

Jacob Pat and Nachum Khanin, secretary of the *Arbeter Ring* (Workers' Circle) in New York, categorically rejected Nowogrodzki's computations. They considered the refugees' departure from Wilno a rescue action that transcended any political or partisan calculus, and dismissed Nowogrodzki's view that political personalities should be rescued first and their families afterwards (if possible). Pat took the unusual step of informing Mendelsohn and Szerer that he was dissociating himself from the Bund mission in New York and its decisions. Khanin notified both of them that the disagreements between the JLC and the Bund Committee in New York were so profound that he eagerly awaited the party leaders' arrival in New York so he could smooth the ruffled feathers.[105]

The operation that removed refugees via the Soviet Union ended in January 1941. According to Warhaftig, 2,800 refugees from Lithuania reached Japan and 200 went directly to Shanghai.[106] As stated, about 400 Bund-member refugees had gathered in Wilno in late 1939. By November 1941, in Nowogrodzki's estimation, 200 had left Wilno and reached the United States or Canada. Another 46 members had joined the group of Jewish refugees in Shanghai.[107] Thus, the US Bund activists and the JLC officials managed to remove the majority of members from Wilno and deliver them to safe havens. Those rescued included almost all members of the Central Committee, the cultural functionaries and the journalists, whose arrival in New York in 1941 transformed the work of the Bund mission in the United States.

Another cluster of Bund members that had gathered in Marseilles made its way from France to Lisbon in the summer of 1940, with the assistance of the Jewish Labour Committee. Fifteen Bund members fled from Belgium and northern France upon the German invasion in May 1940, including Szmuel Zygielbojm, who left Warsaw in late 1939 and reached France, and Frantz Kurski, the journalist and veteran party archivist. They sailed to New York with the help of $5,000 that Jacob Pat, by means of HICEM (the Jewish emigration society), sent to Lisbon to cover the expenses of their voyage.[108] When Zygielbojm and Kurski sailed (they reached the United States in advance of their colleagues from Wilno), the rescue of the Bund leadership and veteran activists from occupied Europe was completed.

NOTES

1. *The Historical Encyclopedia of World War II* (New York: Facts on File, 1980), p. 390; G. L. Weinberg, *A World at War: A Global History of World War II* (New York: Cambridge University Press, 1994), pp. 48ff.
2. A. Albert, *Najnowsza historia Polski 1918–1980* (London: Puls, 1991), pp. 297–8.
3. P. Schwartz, *Dos is Geven der Anhayb* (New York: Arbeter Ring, 1943), p. 24.
4. Orzech to Nowogrodzki, 28 September 1939, Bund Archives (BA), ME-17/11; interview by the author with Chaim Babitz, a member of the *Folkstsaytung* editorial board, 20 March 1989.
5. Orzech to Nowogrodzki, ibid.
6. W. Bartoszewski, *1859 Dni Warszawy* (Kraków: Znak, 1984), p. 31.
7. Orzech to Nowogrodzki (see note 4); see also K. Pużak, 'Wspomnienia 1939-1945', *Zeszyty Historyczne*, 41 (1977), pp. 7–12.
8. Erlich's wife, Sofia Dubnow-Erlich, told Schwartz that the two party leaders had decided to stay in Warsaw for the time being at the request of Mayor Starzyński, and to take part in an emergency meeting of the town council. Schwartz, *Dos is geven der anhayb*, p. 45.
9. Ibid., pp. 46–7.
10. Orzech to Nowogrodzki (see note 4).
11. Ibid. In this matter see also Lucjan Blit, 'Henryk Erlich and Victor Alter in Soviet Russia', in S. A. Portnoy (ed.), *Henryk Erlich and Victor Alter: Two Heroes and Martyrs for Jewish Socialism* (New York: Ktav, 1990), p. 90.
12. See Bartoszewski, *1859 Dni Warszawy*, pp. 31–2; and Albert, *Najnowsza historia Polski*, pp. 299–300. On the decision of the Bund leadership to leave Warsaw, see Orzech to Nowogrodzki (see note 4).
13. Orzech to Nowogrodzki, ibid.
14. Bund members in Kovno to Nowogrodzki, 24 September 1939, BA, M-7/12.
15. J. Gliksman, *Tell the West* (New York: Greshman Press, 1948), p. 24. See also Y. Rotenberg, *Fun Varshe biz Shankhay* (Mexico City: Shlomo Mendelsohn-fund, 1948), pp. 12–15. According to Rotenberg, he had decided to leave town mainly because of pressure from his brother, who persuaded him that as a member of the Bund he would be risking his life by staying there. See also Ofman to Nowogrodzki, 24 September 1939, BA, M-7/12.
16. Z. Warhaftig, *Palit veSarid Bimey haShoa* (Jerusalem: Yad Vashem, 1984), p. 17; I. Gutman, *Mered haNetsurim* (Tel Aviv: Sifriat Poalim, 1963), pp. 73–4.
17. Members in Kovno to Nowogrodzki (see note 4); B. Goldstein, *Finf Yor in Varshever Geto* (New York: Unser Tsayt, 1947), pp. 77–8; Portnoy, *Henryk Erlich*, pp. 91–2; Mayus, 'Historishe Tog in Lublin', *Unser Tsayt*, 8 (1941), pp. 25–6.
18. Ofman to Nowogrodzki (see note 15); Orzech to Nowogrodzki (see note 4).
19. Rotenberg, *Fun Varshe*, pp. 107, 111, 121.
20. Goldstein, *Finf Yor*, pp. 81–4.
21. H. Kruk, 'Der Vanderveg fun a Krigs-Palis', YIVO, Sutzkever-Kaczerkinski, RG-223.
22. C.A. Kaplan, *Scroll of Agony: The Warsaw Diary of Chaim A. Kaplan* (London: Hamish Hamilton, 1966), p. 11.
23. See W. Suleja, *Polska Partia Socjalistyczna 1892–1948, Zarys dziejów* (Warsaw:

Wydawnictwo Szkolne i Pedagogiczne, 1988), pp. 220–21; and Bartoszewski, *1859 Dni Warszawy*, pp. 39–40.

24. Z. Zaremba, *Wojna i konspiracja* (Kraków: Wydawnictwo Literackie, 1991), pp. 82–3.
25. Zygielbojm to Nowogrodzki, 10 February 1940, BA, MG-2/5.
26. Zygielbojm to Nowogrodzki, ibid.; H. Kupersztayn, 'Di Bundishe *Folkstsaytung* bes der Nazi-Daytshe Balagerung fun Varshe', *Unser Tsayt*, 10 (1984), pp. 10–11; D. Klayn, *Mitn Malakh Hamaves untern Orem: Mayne Iberlebungen in Poyln bes der Nazi Okupatsie*, (Tel Aviv: Peretz Farlag, 1968), pp. 27–9; and Goldstein, *Finf yor*, p. 114.
27. Memoirs of Shlomo Abramsohn, an employee of the Medem Sanatorium, about the work done there during the Nazi occupation, BA, M-12/6a.
28. Zygielbojm to Nowogrodzki (see note 25).
29. Ibid.
30. Gutman, *Mered haNetsurim*, p. 57; I. Gutman and D. Blatman, 'Youth and Resistance Movements in Historical Perspective', *Yad Vashem Studies*, 23 (1993), pp. 9–10.
31. A. Wolf-Yasni, *Di Geshikhte fun Yidn in Łódź in di Yorn fun der Daytsher Yidn-Oysratung*, Vol. 1 (Tel Aviv: Peretz Farlag, 1960), p. 86.
32. Interview by the author with Bono Winer, a leading figure in Tsukunft in Łódź, 29–30 June 1988.
33. Zygielbojm to Nowogrodzki (see note 25).
34. Y. S. Hertz (ed.), *Doyres Bundistn*, Vol. 2 (New York: Unser Tsayt, 1956), p. 167.
35. Ibid., Vol. 1, p. 438.
36. Ibid., Vol. 2, p. 179.
37. Z. Piechota, 'Eksterminacja inteligencji oraz grup przywódczych w Łódź i okręgu Łódźkim w latach 1939-1940', *Biuletyn Okręgowej Komisji Badania Zbrodni Hitlerowskich w Łódźi*, I (1989), pp. 13–14; M. Cygański, *Z dziejów okupacji hitlerowskiej w Łódźi 1939–1945* (Łódź: Wydawnictwo Łódźkie, 1965), pp. 35–6; Wolf-Yasni, *Di geshikhte*, pp. 89–90; D. Dambrowska and A. Wein (eds), *Pinkas haKehillot—Polin*, Vol. 1 (Jerusalem: Yad Vashem, 1976), pp. 22–3.
38. Y. Nirenberg, 'Di Geshikhte fun Lodzer geto', in Y. S. Hertz (ed.), *In die Yorn fun Yidishn Khurbn* (New York: Unser Tsayt, 1948), p. 220. Concerning the departure of Tsukunft members, see Winer interview (note 32).
39. Y. S. Hertz, *Di Geshikhte fun Bund in Lodz* (New York: Unser Tsayt, 1958), pp. 439–40.
40. Y. Tselemenski, *Mitn Farshnitenem Folk* (New York: Unser Tsayt, 1963), pp. 11–12.
41. Ibid., pp. 16–17.
42. Hertz (ed.), *Doyres Bundistn*, Vol. 2, pp. 82, 193.
43. Examples are the Bund-PPS joint committee, established in 1939 and headed by Leon Feiner and Mieczysław Bobrowski of the PPS; the workers' committee for assistance to escapees from Germany (*Robotniczy komitet pomocy uchodzcom z Niemiec*), which aided 450 persons anti-Nazi political refugees who had fled from Czechoslovakia and Jewish refugees deported from Germany. See memorandum from the committee to David Dubinski of the Jewish Labour Committee in New York, dated 7 June 1939, BA, MG-9/215.
44. I. Arad, I. Gutman and A. Margaliot (eds), *Documents on the Holocaust* (Jerusalem: Yad Vashem, 1981), pp. 197–8; concerning the deportation and its circumstances, see R. Hilberg, *The Destruction of the European Jews*, Vol. 1 (New York: Holmes & Meier, 1985), pp. 208–9.
45. Hertz (ed.), *Doyres Bundistn*, Vol. 2, pp. 316–17; M. Kushnir, 'Di Tetikayt fun Bund in der Tsayt fun der Hitleristisher Okupatsya in Tsenstochow', in Hertz, *In di Yorn*, pp. 306–7, and Kushnir to the Bund Historical Commission in Poland, 18 September 1946, Archiwum Akt Nowych (AAN), Warsaw, KC PZPR, 30/IV-18.

46. Concerning the status of the Bund in Piotrkow before the war see Y. Meltz and N. Levi-Landau (eds), *Piotrków-Tribunalski vehaSeviva* (Tel Aviv: Piotrkow Tryb. Landsmanschaften, n.d.), pp. 159–61; interview by the author with Ya'akov Leber, a Bund activist in the city, 27 January 1988.
47. Schwartz, *Dos is Geven*, pp. 100–1; Goldstein, *Finf Yor*, pp. 82–3.
48. Kruk, 'Der Vanderveg fun a Krigs-Palis'.
49. M. Zaltzman, *Bella Szapiro – di Populere Froyn-Geshtalt* (Paris, 1983), pp. 39–40.
50. Babitz (see note 4).
51. Y. Litvak, *Pelitim Yehudim miPolin biVerit-haMo'atsot, 1939–1946* (Tel Aviv: HaKibuts HaMe'uhad, 1988), pp. 112–18; B. Z. Pinczuk, *Yehudei Berit-haMo'atsot mul Penei haShoa, Mehkar beVe'ayot haHaglaya veHapinuy* (Tel Aviv: HaAguda leHeker Toledot haYehudim, 1979), pp. 20–21, 54–5.
52. M. Bernstein, 'Bundistn in Ratnfarband bes der Tsveyter Velt-Milkhome', *Unser Tsayt*, 11/12 (1957), p. 90.
53. Fiszgrund and Szuldenfrei to Bund activists in Paris, 4 June 1946, AAN, KC PZPR, 30/IV-3, file 11.
54. Hertz (ed.), *Doyres Bundistn*, Vol. 1, pp. 191–2.
55. Y.A., 'Mit 35 Yor Tsorik …', *Unser Tsayt*, 2 (1975), pp. 28–9; M.K., 'Yosef Aronovitz in Sovietishe Tefisa', *Unser Tsayt*, 7/8 (1951), pp. 39–40.
56. *Forverts*, 11 November 1939; Hertz (ed.) *Doyres Bundistn*, Vol. 2, pp. 145–6, 492–3.
57. 'Di Iberlebungen fun Bundistn unter der Sovietisher Hershaft bet der Milkhome', *Unser Shtime* (Paris), 20, 21, 22 (in June 1951); *Enziklopedia Shel Galuyot – Grodno* (Jerusalem: Enziklopedia Shel Galuyot, 1973), p. 402; Hertz (ed.) *Doyres Bundistn*, Vol. 2, pp. 278–9; Vol. 3 (1968), p. 52.
58. *Pinsk, Sefer zikaron leKehilat Pinsk-Karlyn*, A (Tel Aviv: Irgun Yotsei Pinsk biMedinat Israel, 1966), p. 527; Hertz (ed.), *Doyres Bundistn*, Vol. 2, pp. 264–5.
59. Bernstein 'Bundistn in Ratnfarband', p. 89; M.K., 'Yosef Aronovich', p. 40; Hertz (ed.) *Doyres Bundistn*, Vol. 2, pp. 312, 320.
60. M.K., 'Yosef Aronovich', p. 40.
61. Bernstein, 'Bundistn in Ratnfarband', p. 89.
62. Orzech to Nowogrodzki (see note 4); Ofman to Nowogrodzki (see note 15).
63. Orzech to Nowogrodzki, ibid.
64. Rotenberg, *Fun Varshe*, pp. 147, 151–2.
65. For example, the group that was with Kruk and that reached Vilna on 10 October 1939. See Kruk, 'Der Vanderveg fun a Krigs-Palis'.
66. Rotenberg, *Fun Varshe*, p. 147.
67. Minutes of the relief committee for the Bund in Poland, which had been set up in New York, 16 December 1939, BA, ME-18/31; Rosner to Nowogrodzki, 2 February 1940, BA, MG-1/6.
68. Nowogrodzki to the Labour Party Secretariat, 17 January 1940, BA, MG-1/6; Nowogrodzki to Horn, 1 December 1939, BA, MG-1/6, 20 January 1940, BA, MG-1/50.
69. Warhaftig, *Palit veSarid*, pp. 41–2. Warhaftig adds that other political players, both in Zionist circles and in Agudath Israel, shared this hope.
70. M. Tsanin, *Grenetsn biz zum Himl* (Tel Aviv: HaMenora, 1970), pp. 17–18, and Tsanin's testimony on 9 October 1978, Oral Documentation Centre (ODC), The Institute of Contemporary Jewry, Jerusalem, 8 (20).
71. Portnoy, Wasser and Mendelsohn to the secretariat of the JLC, 5 February 1940, BA, MG-1/36.
72. Pat to Nyomark, 6 February 1940, BA, MG-2/47.
73. Nowogrodzki to Friedman, 23 March 1940, BA, MG-1/5; to Nyomark, 6 February 1940, BA, MG-2/47; to Fedelstein, 16 December 1940, BA, MG-1/6; to Abramsohn, 5 September 1940, BA, MG-1/63; to the HIAS office in New York, BA, MG-1/5;

to Kurski, 27 January 1941, BA, ME-18/6; Pat to Zygielbojm, 19 November 1940, BA, M-16/151-D; 11 December 1940, BA, MG-1/55.

74. Nowogrodzki reported these details in a letter to Zygielbojm, 13 November 1940, BA, MG-2/32.

75. Hertz (ed.), *In di Yorn*, p. 15.

76. D. Levin, *The Lesser of Two Evils: Eastern European Jewry Under Soviet Rule, 1939–1941* (Philadelphia, PA: Jewish Publication Society, 1995) , pp. 200–1; I. Arad, 'Concentration of Refugees in Vilno on the Eve of the Holocaust', *Yad Vashem Studies*, 9 (1973), pp. 201–14; Y. Bauer, 'Rescue Operations through Vilno', *Yad Vashem Studies*, 9 (1973), pp. 215–23.

77. Y. Bauer, *American Jewry and the Holocaust* (Detroit: Wayne University Press, 1981), p. 113; Warhaftig, *Palit veSarid*, p. 62.

78. Isaac Giterman and Leib Neustadt, directors of the JDC office in Warsaw, were summoned on 17 July 1939, for a talk with a police inspector in Warsaw. This encounter inspired concern among JDC activists and other public figures that the government might restrict the organization's relief activities in Poland. In Giterman's estimation, the Polish police suspected the JDC's relationship with Jewish political agencies in Poland, especially the Bund. Giterman to JDC, 17 July 1939, American Jewish Joint Distribution Committee Archives (AJDC), New York, 795.

79. Memorandum from Beckelman to Troper, 28 December 1939, AJDC/818.

80. Summary of memorandum from Morris Troper, prepared by Henrieta Bukhman, secretary of the JDC committee for Poland and Eastern Europe, 12 January 1940, AJDC/818; Orzech to Pat, 11 October, 1939, BA, ME-17/11.

81. Mendelsohn to Nowogrodzki, 21 November 1939, quoted from a letter from Nowogrodzki to Morris Waldman, a leading American Jewish Committee official, 9 December 1939, BA, MG-1/147.

82. Pat to Bukhman, 4 April 1940, AJDC/828; Mendelsohn to Nowogrodzki, 16 November 1939, in his letter to Waldman, 9 December 1939, BA, MG/1-47.

83. Hyman to Harry Schneidermann, 22 April 1940, AJDC/818.

84. Beckelman to Troper, 28 December 1939, AJDC/818.

85. Schwartz wrote to Troper that Alexander Kahan, representing the JDC, and Jacob Pat and Benjamin Minkoff, members of the JLC, had met in New York to reach terms that would end the disputes between the Bund and the JDC in Vilna. Schwartz to Troper, 2 February 1940, AJDC/818.

86. Troper to JDC Secretariat in New York, 12 January 1940, AJDC/818.

87. Pat to Mendelsohn, 24 January 1940, BA, MG-2/47.

88. Pat to Bukhman, 4 April 1940, AJDC/828.

89. Mendelsohn to Held, 3 March 1940, BA, MG-1/36.

90. Rotenberg, *Fun Varshe*, pp. 227–8.

91. Warhaftig, *Palit veSarid*, pp. 100–11. In his estimation, the Dutch consul Jan Zwartendik and the Japanese consul Sempo Sugihara distributed 1,200–1,400 entry visas for Dutch Curacao via Japan in July–August 1940.

92. Hertz (ed.), *Doyres Bundistn*, Vol. 1, pp. 58, 141.

93. Rotenberg, *Fun Varshe*, p .292.

94. Warhaftig, *Palit veSarid*, p. 121.

95. Tsanin, *Grenetsn*, p. 146; P. Schwartz, 'Biographia fun Herman Kruk', in H. Kruk, *Togbukh fun Vilner Geto* (New York: YIVO, 1961), p. xxxiii.

96. Rotenberg, *Fun Varshe*, p. 308.

97. List of names prepared by Nowogrodzki, BA, MG-1/59; Pat and Tabtsinski to Mendelsohn, 7 September 1940, BA, MG-1/36; Nowogrodzki to Erlich and Alter, 8 November 1941, BA, M-7/20.

98. They evidently obtained their transit permits with the assistance of the German

consul in Memel and made use of his connections with an affluent Jewish merchant, a friend of the Bund, who paid for the visas personally. Tsanin, ODC 8(20).

99. Nowogrodzki to Myrdal, 8 May 1940, BA, MG-1/5; Jerzy Trzaska, secretary of the Polish Socialist Alliance in New York, to secretary of the Bund mission in New York, 19 October 1940, BA, MG-1/54.

100. Nowogrodzki to Myrdal, 8 May 1940, BA, MG-1/5.

101. Malinowski to Bund mission in New York, 4 August 1940, BA, MG-1/6; Lange to Nowogrodzki, 16 August 1940, BA, MG-1/5.

102. Malinowski to Bund mission in New York, 4 August 1940, BA, MG-1/6.

103. Pat to Mendelsohn and Szerer, 13 September 1940, BA, MG-1/36; Nowogrodzki to Mendelsohn and Szerer, 30 August 1940, BA, MG-1/36. Pat did his own reckoning and found that the $100,000 would suffice to rescue 500 refugees, not only 200, as Nowogrodzki claimed.

104. Nowogrodzki to Mendelsohn and Szerer, 30 August 1940, BA, MG-1/36.

105. Pat to Mendelsohn and Szerer, 14 September 1940, BA, MG-1/36; Khanin to Mendelsohn and Szerer, 1 October 1940, BA, MG-1/36.

106. Warhaftig, *Palit veSarid*, p. 182.

107. Nowogrodzki to Erlich and Alter, 8 November 1941, BA, M-7/20.

108. Pat to Zygielbojm, 6 August 1940, BA, M-16/151.

2

Underground and Society: Poland 1940–42

BUNDISTS AND THE GHETTO LEADERSHIP

The order concerning the formation of councils of Jewish elders – *Judenräte* – in the occupied areas in Poland appeared in Reinhard Heydrich's *Schnellbrief*, on 21 September 1939. The practical guideline for implementation of this instruction was issued by the General-gouverneur, Hans Frank, on 28 November of that year.[1]

Isaiah Trunk, in his study of the *Judenrat*, divided the members of the councils included in his enquiry by their pre-war political affiliations. According to his reckoning, 6.7 per cent of Jewish council members were Bundists as against (about) 77 per cent affiliated with Zionist factions, 11.3 per cent with Agudath Israel (the ultra-Orthodox Jewish Party), 2.7 per cent with the communists, and 2.2 per cent with the Volkist Party.[2] These figures indicate that Bund members were not strongly represented on the Jewish councils. First, the Bund did not have a tradition of work in the Jewish communities' administrations, and when the *kehilla* disintegrated in the first days of the occupation, the Bundists did not marshal the wisdom to persevere in vital public work. They may also have been afraid of exposure to the German authorities as activists in a socialist party. Perhaps, too, the negative attitude of the party leadership in Warsaw towards membership in the *Judenrat* affected them.

The establishment of the *Judenrat* presented the Bund activists with a public challenge that posed a serious ideological problem. On the one hand, they wished to assume responsibility and be active within the imposed but indispensable community structure; on the other hand, they feared that such activity would make them unwilling collaborators with the German authorities and tarnish the party's image as the leading player in the anti-Nazi resistance. As stated, the Bund lacked the years of experience in public community activity that the Zionist parties such as Agudath Israel and other groups had amassed. Only in 1936 did it resume its activity in the *kehilla* after its leaders had for years boycotted the *kehilla* and treated it as an anachronistic clerical setting that clashed with the activity and interests of the proletariat. In the last pre-war years, as the Bund expanded its popular base and transformed itself from a small, homogeneous workers' movement into a Jewish party with a rising membership in grass-roots and traditional social groups, the party leadership revised its attitude toward the *kehilla*.[3] Although the *Judenrat* was imposed on the Jews, it was a successor to the *kehilla* in a sense, and the Bund activists neither disregard nor spurned it *ab initio*. In Warsaw, a committee to deal with the needs of the Jewish population was established in September 1939, during the German siege. This Jewish civic committee was formed at the behest of the mayor of Warsaw, Stefan Starzyński, as part of the citizens' committee that had coalesced during the siege. It was headed by Moshe Kerner, a former senator in the Polish Sejm, who administered it along with Avraham Gepner, the engineer Stanisław Szarszewski, Adam Czerniaków and the engineer Marek Lichtenbaum. The committee membership included figures who remained in Warsaw, such as Apolinary Hartglas, one of the leaders of the Zionist movement in Poland, and Professor Avraham Weiss, a Mizrahi activist.[4] Bund activists did not participate in the committee, which was established in the second week of September 1939. The party leaders left Warsaw in the first week of the war, and the only member of the Central Committee who stayed was Szmuel Zygielbojm, who had reached Warsaw from Łódź on 8 September, together with young members of Tsukunft and rank-and-file activists. Czerniaków, whom Starzyński appointed on 3 September to head the Jewish citizens' committee, was unacquainted with these Bundists. The product of a middle-class, assimilationist Jewish upbringing, he naturally preferred to staff the committee with close associates among the few public activists who remained in Warsaw. Only when the Jewish citizens' committee became the first *Judenrat* – after the city was occupied in early October 1939 – was Szmuel Zygielbojm annexed to the committee as the Bund's representative.

After Warsaw fell in early October, the Germans had selected 12 hostages among the town leaders, including two Jews: Avraham Gepner, one of the most prominent Jewish businessmen in Warsaw before the war and chairman of the Warsaw Jewish Chamber of Commerce, and Zygielbojm.[5] The abduction of Gepner, an important personality in Warsaw economic life, is understandable, for the Germans sought hostages who belonged to the city's public leadership stratum, but their choice of Zygielbojm is puzzling. For example, Czerniaków wrote in his diary of 29–30 September 1939, that he had offered himself as one of the two Jewish hostages, but the Germans had turned him down.[6] It was evidently Starzyński who decided to include a Bund activist among the hostages, in the belief that the Bund – even though most of its activists had left town – represented much of the town's Jewish population, as indicated in the results of the December 1938 municipal elections. According to another conjecture, Esther Iweneska, a Bund delegate to the municipal council, was targeted as one of the two Jewish hostages, but Zygielbojm, as the only member of the Central Committee who remained in town, volunteered to take her place.[7] When Czerniaków established the *Judenrat* in early October 1939, it was only natural for him to add Zygielbojm's name to the 24-member list, since he intended to give the council the complexion of a public agency whose members represented most political entities in the pre-war Jewish scene.

Zygielbojm's term of service in the *Judenrat* lasted only about one month. In early November 1939, Standarteführer-SS Rudolf Batz, ostensibly acting on behalf of the military commander of Warsaw, General von Neumann-Neurode, issued an order stipulating the establishment of a separate quarter in Warsaw for the town's 150,000 Jews. This sent the members of the *Judenrat* into a panic, especially since the Germans allotted only three days for implementation. Zygielbojm, like other members of the council, opposed cooperation with the Germans in implementing the order. In an article he published after he left Poland, he retold the crux of his remarks at the *Judenrat* meeting on 4 November 1939,[8] immediately after Batz handed down his order:

A historical decision has been made … I feel I lack the moral strength to take part in such a measure. My heart tells me that I will have forfeited the right to live if a ghetto is established and my head remains intact; therefore, I return my mandate. I know it is the chairman's duty to inform the Gestapo of my resignation at once. I am willing to bear the consequences of this measure. I cannot act in any other way.[9]

The ghetto in Warsaw was not established by the stipulated deadline. A *Judenrat* delegation including Czerniaków, Hartglas and Weiss returned to Neumann-Neurode on 5 November 1939, and in the aftermath of this the order concerning formation of the ghetto was rescinded. Zygielbojm resigned from the council and left Warsaw, as did functionaries of other parties who sat on this first *Judenrat*. In January 1940 Zygielbojm began a journey that took him first to France, where he stayed until the defeat of that country in the summer of 1940, and then to New York.

Zygielbojm's resignation and departure from Poland left the Bund without representation on the Warsaw *Judenrat*. After he left Warsaw in early 1940, the Central Committee of the Bund met to consider the possibility of filling his place in the Jewish council with another member. Instead, it was decided to send no Bund representative to the *Judenrat*; the committee resolved to explain its negative attitude toward membership in the *Judenrat* to Bund activists in other cities.[10] The negative attitude of the Bund Central Committee toward the Warsaw *Judenrat* originated mainly in the way in which that body attempted to cope with the multitude of economic and social problems facing the ghettoized Jews. In May 1940 the *Judenrat* decided to cover its cash deficit of 30,000 złoty by imposing a poll tax on the entire Jewish population – one złoty per month, collected at the time ration cards were distributed.[11] The Bund took a dim view of this policy, which imposed an equal burden on the rich and the poor alike.[12] Public criticism of the *Judenrat* in Warsaw mounted in 1941 as the hardships of ghetto life worsened. The Bund accused the *Judenrat* of abandoning the Jewish population to starvation and distress, of collaborating with the Germans in abductions to labour camps, of negligence in caring for children and teenagers, and of implementing a policy that allowed the rich to get richer and pauperized the poor and the downtrodden.[13] Writers in the movement's underground press did not hesitate to threaten the *Judenrat* members with a reckoning after the war.[14]

In Piotrków Trybunalski the *Judenrat* was established on 5 September 1939 – as soon as the Germans entered the city – and the Bund played a central role in it, in contrast to its categorical rejection of the *Judenrat* in Warsaw. Moshe-Chaim Lau, rabbi of the *kehilla*, became acting chairman of the council, but refused to take the job officially. About a month later, on 13 October 1939, the Germans appointed Zalman Tenenberg to chair the council. Tenenberg had been one of the town's outstanding Jewish public activists before the war – chairman of the *kehilla* council, a principal in the Organization for Rehabilitation and Training (ORT) school, secretary of the Jewish trade unions in Piotrków and a Bund delegate to the municipal council.[15]

Tenenberg's appointment as chairman of the *Judenrat*, and the type of council that he established, expressed continuity between the pre-war *kehilla* in Piotrków-Trybunalski and the *Judenrat* in the same town under Nazi rule. The Bund had been a major political actor in Jewish life in Piotrków before the war, receiving six of the 16 mandates in the elections to the local *kehilla* council in September 1937. Ya'akov-Reuven Berliner was chosen to head the *kehilla* committee, and Tenenberg was appointed chair of the *kehilla* council. In elections for the Piotrków municipal council before the war, the Bund received seven of the nine mandates that the Jewish lists earned.[16] Piotrków was known for its proletarian nature, and leftist parties carried much influence among Jews and Poles alike. After undertaking to head the *Judenrat*, Tenenberg installed several party comrades in key functions on the council. Ignacy Samsonowicz was the secretary and Zalman Staszewski (formerly a municipal councillor representing the Bund) was the treasurer. Leon Kimelman, Tanhum Fraynd, Szmuel Zeitan, Morris Mayerowicz and Moshe Shternfeld also served on the *Judenrat* board along with representatives of Left Po'aley Tsiyon, the General Zionists, Agudath Israel and public figures affiliated with the merchants' and artisans' associations.[17] Conspicuous in his avoidance of the Jewish council was Bund member Ya'akov-Reuven Berliner, who evidently refused to serve on a body established by the Germans.[18]

The ghetto in Piotrków Trybunalski was established in November 1939. It was an open ghetto and the Germans applied no particular stringency in inspecting its exit permits. By applying connections that he had cultivated with the German authorities, Tenenberg managed to ease the Jews' hardships in this city:

> They usually treated the rules of movement leniently here ... Jews walked around freely and fearlessly, and at regular times they were allowed to leave the ghetto, and the Jews would circulate at a certain hour in the crisp air in the town environs. They were also allowed to ride a small train to the nearby summer homes and enjoy the forest air ... Many artisans – tailors, shoemakers, carpenters, painters – practiced their craft and made a good living ... The president of the *kehilla*, Tenenberg, was an expert in these matters. He redeemed for money various objects that one would expect to be confiscated, and whenever anyone was sentenced to prison or death, he would smooth things out by means of subventions.[19]

The Piotrków *Judenrat*, which the Jews in this city respected for its efforts to improve living conditions in the ghetto, faced a severe problem: thousands of refugees had arrived in the first months of the occupation from the western part of the country which the Reich had annexed. Thus Piotrków, where one could make a living and live satisfactorily in the early phases of the occupation,[20] was settled by Jews who had been banished from their homes or had fled them because of intolerable living conditions.

In early 1940 Bund members came from Piotrków-Trybunalski and Lublin (where Bundists also participated in the *Judenrat*) for a meeting with members of their party's Underground Central Committee in Warsaw. They explained that they had become active in the *Judenrat* in their places of residence in the wish to share responsibility for dealing with the Jews' day-to-day problems there. The Bund leaders in Warsaw accepted this argument and did not attempt to force their colleagues from Lublin and Piotrków to act against their will.[21] The Central Committee debated the matter again in early 1941, and despite derogatory remarks about the *Judenrat*, did not resolve to urge party members to avoid the councils.[22] However, the Bund leadership in Warsaw definitely took a dim view of the activity of party members in the *Judenrat* of Piotrków Trybunalski. Ya'akov Tselemenski, an emissary of the Central Committee, expressed the prevalent opinion among Bund members in Warsaw – that a Bundist could not be a member of a *Judenrat* – to Tenenberg and his comrades in one of his visits to the town. Tenenberg advised Tselemenski that he and his comrades found no satisfaction in their work for the *Judenrat*.[23]

Bund members had to cope with the question of joining or avoiding the *Judenrat* in almost every town where they had participated in the *kehilla* leadership before the occupation. Bundists in Lublin debated the issue; the opponents, headed by Bella Szapiro, vetoed such participation outright. Nevertheless, several *kehilla* activists who were members or associates of the movement – Aharon Bach, Alexander Lewi and Ya'akov Kellner – joined the *Judenrat*, led by Mark Alten.[24] In Międzyrzec, Bund member Khezekel Stein joined the *Judenrat* that had been established in November 1939, in defiance of his comrades in the city. Stein, who had been a member of the *kehilla* administration before the war, resigned from the *Judenrat* in late 1940. In March 1942 the chairman of the *Judenrat*, Shimon Klurberg, asked him to return. The matter was debated among the members, who decided to allow him to re-enlist in the *Judenrat* in order to engage in education and welfare. Stein joined the *Judenrat* on 17 March 1942, and remained active until July of that year.[25] In Kalisz, whence almost all Jews had been banished to the *General-gouvernement* by the end of 1939, Bund activists Moshe Szlumfer (a former member of the town council), and Lazar Mintz, joined the *Judenrat* that was established on 15 October 1939.[26] However, in Tarnów – where the Bund had built up much power and influence in Jewish public life before the war – Bundists did not join the *Judenrat*. In an activists' assembly it was decided that the Bund in Tarnów would have nothing to do with the *Judenrat*. Asher Blayvays, the major activist in Tarnów after the war, wrote that Moshe Fayerayzen, one of the party activists, was placed under pressure to join the *Judenrat* and that the Bund was threatened, in the event that it refused to post a delegate to the council, with the withholding of meals for members at the council's public soup kitchen.[27] In Będzin, the most important Bundists in town, Yitzhak Stopnitser and Yitzhak-Mordechai Pesachzon, chaired a meeting in early 1940 in which they resolved not to join the *Judenrat* that Moshe Merin had established. In Sosnowiec, in contrast, Yitzhak Tswaybel, a Bundist and the Bund representative in the *kehilla*, belonged to the first *Judenrat*, in which most members were erstwhile members of the *kehilla*.[28]

Relations between the Bund and the *Judenrat* in the Łódź ghetto were affected by the special existential conditions and problems of this ghetto, and by the personality and *modus operandi* of Mordechai Chaim Rumkowski, chairman of the *Judenrat*. In Łódź, almost no economic setting or semblance of social assistance could operate unless the *Judenrat* was somehow involved. However, political groups that opposed the *Judenrat*, foremost among the labour parties, sought to maintain organizational independence, continue to function within a framework of ideational and political activity, and assure their members basic living conditions. Thus, the Bundists and Rumkowski worked out a relationship in which consent and understanding alternated with struggles and collisions.

Thirty Jewish public figures in Łódź from before the war, including activists in the former parties, took part in the first *Judenrat*, which Rumkowski established in October 1939. This lasted until 11 November 1939, and one of its members was a Bundist.[29] Party members also served in the ghetto police. Bono Winer, a Tsukunft activist in the ghetto, related that the party Central Committee had decided to post two Bund members to the police to ensure channels of information and liaison with the ghetto leadership.[30]

Bund activists who remained in Łódź after the occupation did not dare hold meetings and underground gatherings lest they be captured by the Germans. Only after the ghetto was sealed did movement activity resume. The organization of a Bund underground committee in Łódź evidently began at an encounter of members of Tsukunft in the ghetto on 21 June 1940. Their main concern was to find jobs for movement members or to arrange medical assistance for the many members who had fallen ill. Their activity in these regards were overshadowed by the harsh conditions in the ghetto and accompanied by despair and anguish over the deaths of members, on a daily basis, from the diseases that swept through the ghetto in its initial period.[31]

In response to the hardships that the ghetto experienced during these months, the Bund repeatedly portrayed itself to the Jewish public as a movement that would struggle for workers' living conditions. On 29 June 1940 the Bund activists held a conference in the ghetto and advocated struggle against the ghetto authorities to improve workers' living conditions.[32] In July–September 1940, labour groupings in the ghetto waged such a struggle in advertisements urging workers in the various *ressortes* (workshops) to fight for elementary living entitlements.[33]

Was it the Bund that stirred ferment in the ghetto and organized the demonstrations? Ya'akov Nirenberg, an important activist in the Bund underground in Łódź, wrote in his memoirs that Bund members indeed organized the first demonstrations, which activists in other labour parties joined later. According to another view, the demonstrations were spontaneous and attracted elements of the ghetto underworld who wished to create turmoil.[34] It is clear, however, that the Bundists who participated in this struggle against the ghetto authorities, like their counterparts in Po'aley Tsiyon and the Communist Party, did not take this action for political considerations. Only one consideration informed workers in the ghetto: the economic struggle for basic needs, so that they and their families might survive. As the demonstrations and strikes continued (evidently in late August or early September 1940), Rumkowski summoned a joint delegation of labour parties to discuss their demands. The Bund sent four delegates: Moshe Lederman, Golda Yakobowicz-Zilberberg, Ya'akov Nirenberg and Esther Weinberg. Before they met with Rumkowski, the Bund activists conferred with their counterparts in Po'aley Tsiyon and the Communist Party. The Bundists decided to meet with Rumkowski as representatives not of their party but of the workers collectively. At this preliminary encounter they elaborated their demands to Rumkowski with respect to improvements in workers' living conditions. After the assignation with Rumkowski, the *ressortes* doubled the food rations and the assistance given to workers' children. Even after the labour representatives and the chairman of the *Judenrat* worked out these understandings, however, the anti-Rumkowski opposition remained active until early 1941. On 20 October 1940, workers at the carpentry held protest rallies that spread to other workplaces. At the end of that month, several dozen Bund members held a quiet demonstration that did not result in interference by the ghetto police (*Jüdischer Ordnungsdienst*), and in December 1940, at a large workers' assembly organized by the Bund – in which party member Moshe Lederman delivered a speech – the outcry for large demonstrations against the *Judenrat* resumed.[35]

Workers took to the street again in 1941. On 23 January, some 350 workers at the carpenters' workshop on Drukarska Street went on strike for larger bread rations, better pay and lunch without ration cards. When the strike erupted, some 70 members of the ghetto police went to the workshop and evicted the workers forcibly.[36] In the aftermath of this labour action, three Bund members who worked at the carpentry were arrested.[37] On 6 March 1941 some 700 persons demonstrated for improved food rations and larger support allowances. As the demonstration was being dispersed, several participants were arrested, including Bund members Yerachmiel Weinberg, Yosef Weinberg, Hersh Hoffman, Yosef Feldman and Mendel Feldman. A month later, they were released after promising to desist from organizing further demonstrations in the ghetto. In the winter of 1941, in an attempt to impose control over the new wave of demonstrations, Rumkowski allowed the labour parties to take over management of the ghetto's 12 soup kitchens, two of which were given to Bund members.[38]

The Bund was only one of several political players that took part in the overall organizational effort against Rumkowski. However, it was clear that the movement's ability to be a leading player in this action rested on the broad support that it commanded in the ghetto, in continuation of its strong standing in Łódź before the war. The lengthy struggle against the ghetto authorities and the spirited activity of Bund members in this struggle apparently earned the movement additional sympathy. In late September 1940 some 50 Bund activists met at the kitchen on Lutomierska Street for a conference of the party's ghetto leadership. The speakers at this conference, the leading Bundists in the ghetto, reported details that they had received about Bund activity in the Warsaw ghetto, the imprisonment of members in Wilno by the Soviets and the requests and demands that had been presented to Rumkowski in the matter of improving the living conditions of the groups of workers. The participants in the gathering decided to expand the Bund's cooperation with Left Po'aley Tsiyon and to establish a small committee (an *Aktiv*) to continue directing party activity in the underground.[39] However, the efflorescence of political activity in the ghetto was shortlived. As Rumkowski tightened his grip in the ghetto and packed the *Judenrat* with his loyalists, the Bund, like other parties, steadily lost its ability to influence the course of ghetto life.

UNDERGROUND WORK: FOR WHAT PURPOSE?

The underground Bund in Warsaw completed its clandestine restruc-
turing even before ghettoization. The underground movement was
composed of a small core group of activists who bore the brunt of the
clandestine work, backed by a circle of party members and sympathizers
who stayed in partial contact with the core activists and participated in
social and cultural activities that the Bund organized in the ghetto.
According to Bernard Goldstein, who describes this structure in his
memoirs, a national party council, a Bund Central Committee, committees of Tsukunft and SKIF, and party committees for health, finance
and archives were established.[40] Although the underground Central
Committee of the Bund had 14 members, seven or eight major activists
did most of the work. Although the framework that Goldstein describes
seemed robust, it hardly functioned under deep underground conditions
and lacked all operational significance. In contrast to the 14 members
of the Central Committee, the Underground Committee of Tsukunft
and SKIF had only six or seven members, but they created an infrastructure for extensive educational and cultural activity. They included
Abrasha Blum (who also sat on the Bund Central Committee), Shlomo
Pav, Hennoch Rus, Velvel Ruzowski, Berek Schnaydmil and Moshe
Koyfman. Six of the party Central Committee played a main role in
the underground work: Maurycy Orzech, Bernard Goldstein, Sonya
Nowogrodzki, Leon Feiner (who had returned from the Soviet Union
to Warsaw after being liberated from Soviet prison in the summer of
1941), Ya'akov Tselemenski and Lozer Klog.[41]

Occupation and ghettoization forced Jewish parties of all political
complexions to revise their *modus operandi* in one stroke. They had lost
their old power bases, and the group of activists who had remained
behind after the veteran leadership left devoted most of its thinking to
arranging support for surviving activists and members. In this respect,
the Bund leadership was no different from the leadership of the other
parties. Orzech and Nowogrodzki participated in the operations of the
Jewish Self-Help (Żydowska Samopomoc Społeczna: ŻSS),[42] funded
largely by the Joint Distribution Committee, in which public figures
such as Ringelblum and JDC officials Yitzhak Giterman and David
Guzik took part. However, even in this public system, which earned the
ghetto inhabitants' total sympathy for its honesty and the loyalties of
its activists, was not free of 'pull' and pressure that party activists applied
to reserve a larger share of the scanty relief funds for their members
and activists.[43] The Bund operated ten public kitchens that distributed

scanty daily rations – a bowl of soup and a small portion of bread. These kitchens served the Bund, as similar institutions did for other parties, as forums for political debates, lectures and cultural activities.[44] In 1940–42, the Bund remained the largest Jewish party in the Warsaw ghetto, although for obvious reasons the number of its supporters and sympathizers is difficult to estimate. Marek Edelman, later to represent the Bund in the Jewish Fighting Organization (ŻOB), wrote that about 2,000 participants took part in conferences marking the Bund's 44th anniversary, which was observed in assemblies in the ghetto in October–November 1941.[45]

The internal debate in the Bund on the nature of underground work took place between the young people of Tsukunft and the members of the veteran leadership. The latter were embroiled in a struggle for existence. They set up and ran the soup kitchens, organized conferences to mark special occasions such as May Day and the party anniversary, and disseminated the party ideology in the underground press. The young people wrestled with the question of how to give Jewish youth, idle in the absence of schools and facing terrible hardship, a setting that would support them and somehow make their lives meaningful.

The first edition of *Yugent Shtime* (Voice of Youth), the main underground organ of Tsukunft in the ghetto, appeared in October 1940. Its salient feature was a short article, rendered in the style of political propaganda, that had a clear purpose – to attempt to give party youth a sense of belonging, hope and strength to endure. This article-cum-broadsheet presented youngsters with a vision of the new future that would emerge from the suffering that humankind was currently experiencing – the victory that would come and portend equality, fraternity of peoples and liberation from the yoke of tyranny. These slogans and cliches resembled those that frequently appeared in the broadsheets of all movements and parties. This particular article, however, also mentioned several heroes whom every young Bundist knew well: Hersh Lekert, Koloman Walisz (a leader of the Austrian *Schutzbund* who was executed in 1934) and Stefan Okszje, a Polish socialist who was executed in 1905 after having placed a bomb in a police station in the Praga quarter of Warsaw. The writer asserts: 'We, the Jewish youth, educated … [in their spirit] do not know the meaning of retreat.'[46] One may, of course, regard all of this as an anecdote or merely the propaganda of a political movement that was attempting to lure to its underground ranks those who had remained loyal to the movement after the disintegration occasioned by the Nazi occupation. However, the publications also carried a covert educational and political

message, and made an attempt to persuade teenagers loyal to the movement that, even under the harsh situations currently prevailing, one
must not lose hope.

The ramparts that separated the Jews from the population at large
were painfully wounding to Bund members generally and to young
Bundists in particular. The matter transcended the horrific hardship that
spread through the ghetto and assailed the entire Jewish collectivity.
For Bundists, the walls represented a terrible insult in that they were
separated from their Polish counterparts. They spared no effort to
convince themselves that the walls really did not exist. This belief,
which reflected more naïvety than sober analysis of the reality that the
Nazis had imposed on occupied Poland, was reflected in the pages of the
young Bundists' newspaper, *Yugent Shtime*. Of the Jewish underground
publications in the Warsaw ghetto, only *Yugent Shtime* was capable of
printing the following in December 1940:

> We are surrounded by mighty walls. There is no way out. Every
> wall seems to mock you as you approach it: You'll go no farther,
> and everything on my other side is hidden from you now and
> forevermore. You have no contact whatsoever with the outside
> world.
>
> But those walls and the people who built them and stand behind
> them are mistaken. Things are no longer the way they were many
> years ago, when Jews were imprisoned in ghettos. Those Jews
> submissively thanked God for letting them to live their tranquil
> lives and thanked His great name for having doomed them to grey,
> gloomy lives of black bile, without so much as a ray of light from
> the outside, from the great and illuminating world.
>
> Things are different today. Today we know that even when they
> wish to isolate us, thousands of fibres connect us with all the
> workers, all the proletarians on the other side. Our thoughts are
> with them, and we are fully confident that they are with us whole-
> heartedly.[47]

One of the issues that perturbed the ghetto leadership of Tsukunft
was how to reach the largest possible number of teenagers and children
in the ghetto. In the absence of a regular education system, workplaces
and a supportive family setting, young Jews in the ghetto were following a downward path toward spiritual degeneration, not to mention

the spread of other negative phenomena: cheap places of entertainment, coffee-houses, games of fortune and various kinds of underworld activity. Tsukunft was an educational movement above all. As such, it attempted, despite its limited resources, to respond to the unstructured nature of the youngsters' lives and the atmosphere of nihilism that was spreading among them. One of the articles that addressed this issue asserted that Nazism's war against the Jewish people was not merely physical: it aimed also to lead the Jews to spiritual extinction. *Yugent Shtime* urged young people to regard reading a book, studying and overcoming the tendency to live without moral reckonings as weapons no less important than rifles in the struggle to stamp out fascism.[48]

The youth movements struggled prodigiously to maintain educational settings in the ghetto for children and teenagers. Hundreds of underground classes (each known as a *komplet*) operated in building courtyards and food kitchens. Thousands of children and young people attended these classes, along with additional educational settings such as primary and high schools, if only on a part-time basis. It was a Sisyphean effort that had to be repeated each day, and success was measured in terms of an increase in the number of children who attended these educational and cultural activities. On 15 January 1941 Tsukunft members organized a Mendele Mokher Seforim memorial study evening. The 600 teenagers who came to listen to a recital of his letters and lectures on his works gave the organizers much happiness; for them, it was 'an authentic celebration of youth'.[49] In 1941 Tsukunft arranged dozens of events in the ghetto – lectures and evening recitals on Yiddish culture, performances by creative artists in this language, courses and lectures on the history of the Jewish and the general labour movement, Jewish and Polish history, music and poetry encounters, activities in kindergartens and wall newspapers written by children, to name only a few. On 30 March 1942, by which time the movement leadership was perturbed and preoccupied by the most terrible matter of all – reports that reached the ghetto about the extermination of Jews in the Soviet areas – the movement surreptitiously held a special evening for its activists on the 'March revolutions': the upheavals in 1848, the Paris Commune (1871) and the 1917 Russian revolution. The author of the *Togbukh Tsukunft* summarized the event as 'a successful evening [that] took place in a festive atmosphere around well-appointed tables'.[50]

The conspicuous feature of the Tsukunft newspapers was the continual search for a way to win the hearts of teenagers and to concern themselves with issues that mattered to them. In this regard, a discussion held in late March 1941 offers an insight into the disagreements between

the veteran Bund leadership and that of the youth. In this encounter
among the party leaders in the ghetto, the nature of the movement's
newspaper for youth was debated. The Tsukunft leaders wanted a
paper that would reach out to young people who had disengaged from
all forms of education and would speak in their language – a much
'folksier' newspaper than *Yugent Shtime*, which was packed with intellectual articles on historical and political themes. Thus, the Tsukunft
leaders proposed the establishment of an additional youth newspaper.
The party leadership, apprehensive about expanding the underground
work, ruled out the idea.[51] Consequently, *Yugent Shtime* became an
eclectic newspaper, carrying articles on and discussions of the history
of Marxist thought alongside reflections and thoughts of young people
about their lives in the ghetto. The latter items were published in special
departments called 'Letter to a Comrade', 'To a Comrade in Prison'
and 'Youth Speaks Out'. One of the newspapers told the story of young
Leybel, the oldest son in his family, who undertook to support the
family after his father died in the first year of the war.

In the summer of 1941 Leybel – described as a poorly young man
who toiled from dawn to dusk to support his family – was abducted by
a Jewish policeman and sent to a labour camp. He returned from the
camp about two months later, almost blind in one eye, hardly able to
stand, ill and bedraggled.

> Leybel tries to do something but cannot pull it off. He tries to
> peddle candy – they take his goods from him. He tries to sell rolls
> – a 'snatcher' comes along one day and swipes two rolls ... a whole
> day's earnings. But a miracle happens: he gets a job again. The
> wages are minuscule and the cost of living is high, but he makes
> do anyway. However, disaster strikes again: a policeman appears,
> clutching a note. Leybel has to go to a labour camp. Not wishing
> to go, he goes into hiding. For nights on end he moves like a nomad
> among lofts and cellars. He catches a cold and can no longer work.
> At home there is nothing that can be used to save him, even a
> spoonful of stew to place in his mouth. He ebbs like a candle, until
> one day at dusk he sets along with the sun. Nobody knows where
> he is buried. He was buried with all the others whom they buried
> at night, hundreds and hundreds of people in one grave.[52]

Many stories of this kind appeared in the Bund's youth newspaper.
'Leybel' was an archetype for many members of the movement – a
young man from the impoverished classes of the ghetto who, after

having to shoulder the burden of supporting himself and his family, was doomed to death by the hardships of ghetto life. The stories created a sense of identification; young Bundists in the ghetto found Leybel's story a familiar representation of ghetto life.

However, it would be wrong to consider Tsukunft in its ghetto metamorphosis only from the standpoint of cultural activity or dealing with its members' daily needs. Tsukunft was a political movement that preached a tough, uncompromising ideology and attacked its opponents and rivals with fierce polemical rhetoric. The polemics concerned Jewish nationalism, emigration from Poland, the goals of the current war and the role of the Soviet Union, to name only a few topics. One of the fiercest arguments pertained to a matter of direct concern in the lives of young people in the ghetto: the placement of young Jews in jobs on farms outside the ghetto.

Since the beginning of the occupation, the Polish agricultural countryside had been short of working hands on farms, especially when seasonal chores required many labourers. The main reason for the shortage was the deportation to Germany of Polish peasants for slave labour, starting in early 1940. The Polish farm-owners found an expedient solution: hire the Jews. The wages were minuscule and often were not paid at all, since the Jews contented themselves with foodstuffs that they brought home from their employers' farms. The movement of workers to the countryside, organized by Toporel – an association that encouraged Jews to do farm labour – was amazingly orderly. The groups were disciplined, ambitious and efficient. The Polish farmers prized their Jewish labourers. From standpoint of young Jews and youth-movement members who took these jobs, the gain was twofold. Instead of living behind ghetto walls that created isolation and doomed them to lives of deterioration, unemployment and poverty, they lived in the country, breathed fresh air, immersed themselves in an environment of productive labour and were assured of food and shelter. Above all, they could use the small amount of free time available to them, especially at night, for undisturbed educational movement work. It is no wonder that in 1941 the Zionist pioneering youth movements organized hundreds of members for agricultural work in the Polish countryside.[53]

The Tsukunft people attacked and fiercely criticized the youth movements for encouraging young Jews to accept work in the Polish countryside. The young Bundists considered the movement's policy a breach of solidarity on the part of the Jewish workers with their colleagues, the Polish workers and peasants. Tsukunft members monitored with concern the critical commentary in the Polish underground press about young Jews who accepted jobs in the countryside and thereby (it was argued) indirectly facilitated the deportation of Poles to Germany. Tsukunft leaders urged young people to avoid these 'training farms' and accused nationalist circles of encouraging young Jews to foster the illusion of emigration and evacuation, at the expense of Polish–Jewish solidarity in the struggle against Hitlerism.[54] The young people of Tsukunft were concerned that many youngsters were avoiding them because of their own organizational weakness and the scale of the other youth movements' activities, as they argued to the party leadership:

> To deal only with internal problems [of the Movement] means one thing – to abandon the great 'masses' of young people in Warsaw to the mercies of the Zionist organizations, which can operate more overtly because of their pro-emigration propaganda. Therefore, our work should be a combination of intensive and extensive efforts.[55]

The Tsukunft members activated their cultural settings in the ghetto by means of Yikor (Yidishe Kultur Organizatsye), the Yiddishist cultural organization. Yikor, established at the initiative of the Jewish intellectual Menachem Linder, attracted political and cultural circles of Yiddishists, Bundists, members of Left Po'aley Tsiyon such as Ringelblum and Shakhne Zagan, and miscellaneous cultural players. In January 1941 Tsukunft fell into discord about whether to take part in the activities of Yikor or to attempt to offer educational activity under its own auspices. Opponents of the Yikor option feared that Tsukunft would lose its ideological distinctiveness if it merged into a pan-Jewish cultural organization. Eventually, the movement decided to participate in Yikor activities, chiefly because by doing so it could extend its influence among children and teenagers.[56]

Tsukunft's underground cells were composed of 'quintets' 'septets' and 'dectets', and were usually staffed by employees of specific workplaces who came together for this purpose. In the first half of 1941 the Tsukunft leadership interacted with 36 groups, comprising 184 members who received underground newspapers. *Yugent Shtime* had a print-run of about 300 copies, of which 270 were circulated among young members of the movement and 25 were forwarded to movement leaders. In the estimation of the author of the party's underground diary, *Yugent Shtime* had a readership of some 3,000 people during January–March 1941.[57]

The Bund was the only political entity in the ghetto that sustained, at the practical level, the twin frameworks of a party and a youth movement. The party leadership did what all party leaders did in providing social assistance and sustaining an activist core; the young people of Tsukunft created a setting that functioned in underground ways similar to those of the Zionist youth movements. The party framework, which before the war had been a single functional entity with clearly defined functions, underwent a sweeping change when the occupation and the ghettoization ensued. An examination of the Bund's operating methods shows that two systems were actually at work – the party leadership and the old-time functionaries, and the young leadership of Tsukunft. Slowly the young Bundists abandoned the notion that, as the party's organization of young people, it was their duty to create a future cadre of party activists. Instead, they adopted the perspective of educational activity, maintenance of ideological values, and preservation of the movement's historical heritage and role for the future.

In 1941 the two flanks of the party leadership, the veteran and the young, evinced different trends of thought. The young people in Tsukunft displayed strong social sensitivity to the plight of children and teenagers and were eager to undertake the mission of educating them. In this sense, these leaders, like those of the other movements, wished to 'sell' the Bund's political ideology to larger numbers of youth. However, the pioneering youth movements were autonomous and independent of outside party leadership, whereas the Tsukunft leadership could not contravene decisions of the Bund Central Committee. This internecine tension was evident in the aforementioned March 1941 debate. For various reasons, the Central Committee refused to authorize the publication of another underground newspaper for young people, but the Bund began to publish its Polish-language newspaper, *Za Naszą i Waszą Wolność* (For Our Freedom and Yours) at that very time – evidently on the initiative of Maurycy Orzech, who wished thereby to strengthen relations between the Bund and the Polish socialist underground. This episode was typical of the differing trends of thought in the party: as the young people in the movement devoted their thinking to Jewish life in the ghetto, especially in regard to the travails of youth, the Bund leadership continued to follow its traditional pre-war political path.

Even though the Bund retained the considerable public sympathy that it had earned before ghettoization, its activist core remained small and was composed almost entirely of Tsukunft members. In its summarizing report for the period between July 1941 and March 1942,

Tsukunft reported having an activist cadre of about 400 members. These were the people who distributed the Bund underground press, participated in conferences and political and cultural evening events, and powered the movement's clandestine activity.[58] Thus, the activity of the Bund in the ghetto was actually that of Tsukunft. Tsukunft's solid relations with the ghetto masses and its involvement in their lives belonged to the social and political tradition of the Bund, which specifically targeted the impoverished stratum of Jewish society. Unlike several of the Zionist youth movements, Tsukunft did not confine itself to its own narrow bailiwick: its members mixed easily with the educated teenagers and young people of the downtrodden classes. This facility, the source of the movement's strength, also became the source of its weakness when the movement went underground. Organizational and educational activity for large numbers of young people does not sit easily with the needs of a political underground, and the mismatch was to prove detrimental to Tsukunft.

CENTRE AND PERIPHERY

From the onset of ghettoization, the youth movements and the Bund shared the wish to maintain contact between peripheral towns and the party in Warsaw. In late 1940 Bund activists in Warsaw began to make contact with other ghettos in Poland. Maurycy Orzech visited Kraków in November 1940 as an official in the Jewish Self-Help in Warsaw.[59] During these months, the party attempted to organize its activists in the peripheral towns in advance of a national conference of activists scheduled for November 1940 in Warsaw. Tselemenski, Yisrael Polak, Moshe Koyfman and Ya'akov Mendelsohn, the party's liaison officers, set out to organize the activists. When the Warsaw ghetto was quarantined, the conference had to be postponed until February 1941; when the Germans suddenly arrested Orzech, it was delayed again. Finally, the conference was called off altogether and deleted from the party agenda because of the conditions of the occupation.[60] This affair underscored the leadership's inability to fulfil its hope of maintaining a structure of coordinated countrywide activity. Thus, activists in peripheral localities created operational modalities tailored primarily to local conditions.

In areas of the *Generalgouvernement* outside of Warsaw, the Bund had underground committees that attempted to maintain some sort of organizational framework. This occurred in Łódź, Kraków, Piotrków-

Trybunalski, Tarnów, Częstochowa and Włocławek, and to a lesser extent in several other peripheral towns. In Kraków, activists convened in January 1940 and resolved to establish contact with towns in the vicinity. Thus Kraków became the centre that stayed in touch with Będzin, Sosnowiec, Tarnów and Chrzanów. Two Tsukunft liaison officers, Rachel Bari and Bluma Glickshtayn, maintained relations among various towns in Zagłębie and western Galicia.[61] Częstochowa became the hub through which contact with Radom was maintained. Mordechai Kushnir, one of two Bund activists in Częstochowa, visited Radom regularly and, as an activist in TOZ, met there with Bund members and gave them information and aid from Warsaw. Wilyam Fayvel, a Bundist in Radom, visited Częstochowa on behalf of his comrades and obtained information and assistance. Activists in Częstochowa also stayed in touch with Sosnowiec and Będzin, mainly through the services of Tselemenski and Artur Nunberg.[62]

The Bund began to organize its underground work in Częstochowa in November 1939, when members headed by Liber Brener and Mordechai Kushnir convened a meeting at the Jewish cemetery there. Those in attendance decided to organize the members of Tsukunft into seven-person groups, each group headed by a member of the town's Bund leadership.[63] According to Ya'akov Leber, a Bund member from Piotrków-Trybunalski who fled to Częstochowa in the summer of 1941 after his Bund colleagues in this town were thrown into prison, there were five such groups in 1941 and about 35 organized Bund members who stayed in touch mainly by passing around underground publications that arrived from Warsaw.[64] The activists met again in February 1940 – the last joint meeting of Bund members in Częstochowa.[65] There, as elsewhere, the members emphasized educational and cultural work for young people. This activity took place at the Medem Library, a large facility that had operated in Częstochowa before the war.[66] In a testimony given to his comrades in New York after the war, Kushnir stated that the Bund, in conjunction with activists of other parties, had co-published *Rada Starszych*, a satirical underground publication in the ghetto, edited by a former Jewish officer in the Polish army.[67]

In Piotrków-Trybunalski, the Bund underground was headed by Zalman Tenenberg, Ignacy Samsonowicz and Ya'akov Berliner. Tenenberg chaired the *Judenrat* that the Germans had established in Piotrków in September 1939. Piotrków was the only city in the *Generalgouvernement* in which the *Judenrat* leaders also established their parties' underground organizations. Thus, activity in the *Judenrat* and in the clandestine political underground became identical.[68] Various circles in the ghetto were concerned about the *Judenrat* leadership's underground pursuits. Ya'akov Kurts, a resident of Piotrków who reached Palestine in 1942, addressed himself to this matter in his memoirs:

> [Tenenberg] would engage secretly, as part of the *kehilla*, in party activity of the Bund. He and his comrades were in touch with the party in Warsaw and other cities and would receive contraband and distribute it among the members. Although we were rivals of the party, I stayed on good terms with them and they gave me their material to read. On several occasions, I remarked to them that they were wrong to engage in party activity within the *kehilla* framework at that time, because by doing so they were endangering the entire community. However, not only did they disregard my remarks, they also raised money from the members for propaganda, and this could no longer be kept totally secret.[69]

Organized movement activity also took place in Włocławek. Bund activists there, headed by Ya'akov-Leib Rosenthal – a Bund delegate to the town council and the *kehilla* board before the war – convened in September 1939 and decided to maintain a movement structure that would assist needy members and distribute reports on war developments. The Bund underground in Włocławek was comprised of 50 members, and alongside it was a Tsukunft committee headed by movement activist Leib Shnorbach. In the Włocławek ghetto, Tsukunft sponsored activity groups for youth and children and put out an underground news bulletin, *Wiadomości roktowskie*, mimeographed in about 80 copies. In Włocławek, as in other localities, Bund activists marked May Day and the party anniversary in October with special conferences, and in February 1941 Bund members there established a soup kitchen for their members.[70] A small amount of Bund activity also took place in Międzyrzec, in which the members established a workers' cooperative, and in Tomaszów-Mazowiecki, where the Bundists availed themselves of PPS members to help comrades who had been sent to labour camps. Bund members engaged in similar activity in the ghettos of Radom and Tarnów.[71]

The situation in Łódź was totally different from that in the *Generalgouvernement*. Bono Winer, the Tsukunft activist in the Łódź ghetto, recalls that he and his comrades were afraid to step out of their homes in early 1940 lest they be kidnapped and deported.[72] Contact between party activists in Warsaw and their comrades in Łódź had been slack even before ghettoization. In November 1939 the Łódź area became an administrative unit annexed to the Reich (the *Warthegau*); to reach it, one had to cross the border illegally – an action more dangerous than ordinary travel in the *Generalgouvernement*. Members in Warsaw remained in direct contact with activists in Łódź until summer 1940, when those who had fled from Łódź to Warsaw when the fighting erupted returned to their homes, bringing financial aid that the leadership in Warsaw had earmarked for people in Łódź.[73]

From early 1941, after the struggle with Rumkowski was crushed, the Tsukunft Central Committee in Łódź headed a group of about 20 young people who took part in movement work.[74] The young Bund leadership in Łódź devoted most of its attention to the plight of working teenagers, and even appealed to Rumkowski on their behalf.[75] They ran a small orphanage in the ghetto that took care of approximately 30 children, established a Jewish cultural society (Yidishe Kultur Gezelshaft in Litzmannstadt Geto) with Rumkowski's approval and, in conjunction with other youth organizations, participated in the training farm that had been established in Marisyn in the summer of 1940.[76] In this location, where Poles had cultivated small parcels of land before ghettoization, 23 agricultural societies affiliated with all political movements and organizations were established for 1,040 teenagers. One of these societies, with 60 young members, belonged to Tsukunft and SKIF.[77] The young Bundists, like members of the other movements, invested time in cultural and educational work in addition to farm labour. In the Łódź ghetto, as in Warsaw, the Bund had an extensive public infrastructure. Bono Winer wrote that, at a conference marking May Day in 1941, 1,087 Bundists took part: 514 party members, 390 members of Tsukunft and 185 members of the Sotsyalistishe kinder farband (SKIF). In the opinion of Nirenberg and Lederman, 800–950 people and members of their families were associated with the Bund activity, including 120 Bundists who had reached the ghetto in 1941–42 from towns near Łódź.[78]

POLISH SOCIALISTS AND THE BUND

The Polish Socialist Party disintegrated in late September 1939, after the surrender of Warsaw. The pre-war leadership of the PPS, affiliated with the party's right wing – headed by Kazimierz Pużak, Zygmunt Zaremba, Tomasz Arciszewski, Józef Dzięgielewski and others[79] – established a new entity for underground work and named it the Central Organization of the Movement of Workers' Masses in City and Village – Freedom–Equality–Independence (Centralne kierownictwo ruchu mas pracujacych miast i wsi – Wolność–Równość–Niepodległość) (PPS–WRN). This aside, various activists in the movement organized action groups of their own, published their own newspapers, and considered themselves a socialist underground with distinct characteristics. An example is the 'Freedom Barricade' (Barykada Wolności) group, headed by Stanisław Dubois, a member of the left flank of the PPS; Wacław Zagórski, who had returned from Wilno, and Zbigniew Mitzner established the 'Freedom' (Wolność) group, part of the WRN, and Norbert Barlicki, also a member of the left wing of the PPS, organized a group called 'Labourer and Peasant' (Robotnik i Chłop). In early 1940 Leszek Raabe, similarly a member of the left flank of the PPS, organized yet another underground group that attempted to reinstate the PPS doctrine of revolutionary and military struggle. The fragmentation among the Polish socialists escalated into an outright schism in September 1941, when the group of PPS leftist activists gathered and established an independent political underground named the Polish Socialists (Organizacja Polskich Socjalistów: PS). This group, which did not purport to be the core for a new party, featured a moderate pro-Soviet orientation and advocated cooperation with the Soviet Union in the war.[80]

The internal divisions that beset the socialist underground diminished its ability to function in that context; furthermore, the Nazis had imprisoned many leaders of the Polish Left, making the movement almost leaderless. Mieczysław Niedziałkowski, a leading figure in the PPS and the Polish trade unions who had helped to organize the labour brigade and conduct the fighting during the siege of Warsaw, was murdered in June 1940 along with dozens of Polish political activists and members of the intelligentsia in Palmiry, a village in the Kampinos forest some 30 miles from Warsaw.[81] Other leaders of the Polish Left – Kazimierz Czapiński, an editor of the PPS daily newspaper *Robotnik* and a delegate to the Sejm for the PPS before the war, and Barlicki and Dubois – were arrested in the summer of 1940 and sent to Auschwitz, where they perished. However, despite its losses and its severe internal fragmentation, the PPS lost none of its popularity and public support because of the valorous workers' resistance that it had organized during the siege of Warsaw. This action earned it the sympathy of Polish public opinion as the only defender of Polish national dignity after the government had fled and abandoned the capital to the invading Wehrmacht. Colonel Stefan Rowecki, commander of the Union for Armed Struggle (ZWZ), the armed Polish underground established in

November 1939, explained the party's great popularity in a report he sent to the Polish government-in-exile in February 1940:

> The PPS – a dominant political and social player among members of the working class – is indeed showing a great upturn in all of its political activity in this country at the present time. Thanks to the welcome and devoted work of Niedziałkowski and other socialist activists during the battle for Warsaw, the party's political 'capital' has expanded greatly ... The party apparatus has been revitalized and preserved despite the suffering they experienced in the areas annexed to the Reich and occupied by the Soviets.[82]

About two months after this report, in April 1940, Rowecki reported his assessment that the fractiousness and fragmentation in the PPS had prompted the party to turn inward and become insular, for which reason new members could not join the underground work and the party's strength in the underground diminished.[83]

The Bund was perplexed by the internecine dissension in the Polish socialist underground. In terms of ideology, the Bund was closer to the left wing, which had united in founding the PS in September 1941. In Britain and the United States by contrast, Bund activists were in close contact with Adam Ciołkosz, Wacław Komarnicki, Jan Stańczyk and other figures identified with the right flank, the WRN. The Bund stressed to its Polish counterparts that it did not identify with any particular faction, and expressed its hope that the merger of the PPS leftists would mark the beginning of a process that would unify the entire Polish socialist movement.[84]

In September 1940 the PPS–WRN underground issued a pamphlet that set forth the main principles of the Polish socialist perspective on the future complexion of Poland. The authors of this pamphlet reviewed the political and social struggle in Poland since the late nineteenth century between the national camp and the socialist movement, between conservative landowners and supporters of agrarian reform, and between fascist elements and supporters of democracy and social progress. On the matter of Poland's future, they wrote:

> The Third [Polish] Republic should begin its activity by executing the will of the first People's Government of Poland: social reform. The first duty of the new Poland is to revoke the excessive privileges of the gentry and to effect agrarian reform without compensation

[and] to eradicate the dominion of capitalism in industry and the financial system by introducing socialist management of industry and trade.[85]

The Bund fully embraced the vision of a post-war Poland based on principles of social justice and economic and political equality. As a Jewish party that had struggled for years for the rights of Jews in Poland and against political and social anti-Semitism, the Bund judged the Polish government and the Polish underground primarily by their attitudes toward the civil status of Polish Jewry after the war. The Bund was not fond of the Polish government-in-exile in London. From its perspective, this government was carrying on the political trends that had given the Polish regime its contours before the war. It included ministers from right-wing parties, and did not take vigorous action to stem the anti-Semitic campaign being waged both in London and among underground groups on the Right. *Za Naszą i Waszą Wolność* wrote the following in this matter:

> So who is in exile, especially in London? Most of them are representatives of the *ancien regime* ... Can one insist that representatives acquire an understanding of the new times that are coming? Are they capable of perceiving that the Polish masses, now fighting the invader in the trenches of the underground, are not struggling for just any Poland but for a democratic Poland, a socialist Poland, a peasants' and workers' Poland?[86]

The PPS–WRN took a different view of the Polish government-in-exile and its representatives in occupied Poland. The Polish socialists were part of this government and its allied auspice, the National Council (Rada Narodowa). The PPS was a participant in the Political Consultative Committee in the Underground (PKP), the highest-ranking political agency of most Polish underground circles that accepted the dominion of the government-in-exile in London. Even in autumn 1941, when the Polish left-wing factions fell into dispute over the government-in-exile's treaty with the Soviet Union, the WRN did not secede from the general Polish partnership.[87]

The acute dissension within the Polish political underground, like that among the exiles in London, turned on the question of how to treat the Soviet Union when it joined the war against Germany. Until the summer of 1941 the Polish Left and the Bund were unequivocal opponents of Soviet policy. The Red Army's invasion of eastern Poland at the beginning of the war, the Soviet alliance with Hitler, and the wave of arrests by the NKVD among Jewish and Polish socialists in the annexed areas had made the USSR, from their standpoint, an enemy in the anti-fascist struggle.[88] Polish socialists in the WRN camp were more staunchly anti-communist than Bund members. The leaders of the WRN – Zygmunt Zaremba or Kazimierz Pużak – held traditional anti-communist views, and the Soviet policies in 1939–41 merely stiffened their opposition to the USSR, which they considered the enemy of the Polish nation.[89] One of the socialist underground publications, *Wolność*, went so far as to assail the entire communist movement, for abandoning the anti-Nazi struggle by orders of Stalin.[90]

In late July 1941, the Polish government-in-exile signed an agreement with Stalin's regime. This denouement had been preceded by lengthy negotiations, during which the British had pressured the Polish government to reach terms with Moscow. The agreement sent a general shock-wave through the political constellation of London exiles. After several right-wing ministers resigned, Władysław Sikorski assembled a new government of a more liberal complexion, in which political forces of the pre-war liberal-democratic centre and the PPS were represented.[91] The Polish–Soviet accord also destabilized the socialist underground in Poland and prompted the left flank of the PPS to reorganize by establishing the PS in September 1941.

The Bund, which from the start had been more pragmatic towards the Soviet Union than the PPS–WRN, believed that by joining the war against Hitler the USSR had entered a new phase and taken on a new approach. The Bund also stressed the vast and important advantages of the Polish–Soviet accord for Poland. It nullified the Soviet–German territorial arrangements set forth at the beginning of the war, assured the formation of a Polish army on Soviet soil, and promised clemency for all Polish political prisoners whom the Soviets had arrested in the eastern territories. In this matter, the Bund stated the following:

> Since August 1941, the Soviet Union and Poland have no longer been enemies. Not only have they exchanged embassies, not only has the Soviet Union recognized Poland's independence, and not only have Molotov's terrible words on 17 September 1939 – 'Poland as a strong country no longer exists' – been revoked. The Soviet Union and Poland have promised to help each other in the struggle against Nazi Germany. The Sikorski Government did well this time by disregarding the demands and proposals of the former Sanacja groups, which demanded that Poland display

'hostile neutrality' toward the Bolsheviks and deemed the Soviets and Germany equal as enemies ...[92]

Despite the Bund's different views on political problems, especially with respect to the government-in-exile and the Soviet Union, and despite its criticism of the Polish socialist underground in the wake of its response to the anti-Semitism issue, there is no belittling the inter-relation between Bundist underground activists and some of their Polish counterparts. PPS members and former Polish trade-union activists sympathized with the Jewish cause. They were the most prominent Polish group that opposed the Nazis' anti-Jewish policies and the anti-Semitism of various segments of Polish society. The Polish socialists categorically rejected the Nazi policies toward Polish Jewry on both moral and pragmatic grounds. They considered the Nazis' anti-Semitic incitement an obstacle to the liberation of Polish society from the fetters of prejudice and reaction in order to build a democratic, free Poland. *Barykada Wolności* wrote about the decisions that were reached in this matter:

> The conference of Polish socialists thoroughly condemns all manifestations of solidarity with Hitlerism's bestial anti-Semitic policies as displayed by some Polish public elements. Denunciations of Jews are as much acts of national treason as are attempts to collaborate with the occupier. The conference states that the working class will vigorously oppose [such actions] ... Semi-Hitlerism cannot be a partner in the struggle against Hitlerism.[93]

Even though leftists and their groups condemned anti-Semitism and its backers in Poland, the Bund activists were dissatisfied with the extent of consistency and importance with which the socialist under-ground treated the matter. The Bundist underground press took the Polish socialists to task for their approach toward the anti-Semitism issue: 'Let us state frankly that most of the leftist and democratic underground Polish press has treated the anti-Semitic problems with silence. It has not given them the space they deserve. It has not warned the Polish public of sly ideological pitfalls.'[94]

The relationship that evolved between the Bund and activists in the Polish socialist underground, unmatched by any other Jewish underground group, furthered the party's clandestine activity. In the first few weeks of the German occupation of Kraków, PPS members, foremost Józef Cyrankiewicz, helped their Bund counterparts obtain

'Aryan' papers and provided them with 5,000 złoty to care for 25 children whose fathers had fled to the eastern, Soviet-occupied, areas.[95] Wacław Zagórski obtained 'Aryan' documents for David Klayn, the Bund's first liaison officer who operated on the non-Jewish side of Warsaw, and afterwards for Feiner and Fiszgrund.[96] Bund members in Sosnowiec, Lublin and Tomaszów-Mazowiecki also reported receiving limited financial assistance from members of the PPS.[97] Polish socialists were even more helpful in circulating the Bund's underground press. Zagórski, among the most prominent WRN activists who liaised with Bund members on the 'Aryan' side, wrote in his memoirs that the Bund leadership had asked PPS activists to transport newspapers to various towns in the *Generalgouvernement* and the publications were indeed forwarded to eight towns: Piotrków-Trybunalski, Częstochowa, Kraków, Tarnów, Kielce, Radom, Lublin and Siedlce.[98]

PPS operatives in various localities were sympathetic toward the Jews and tried to help them as best they could, not for political considerations but as part of a collectivity that opposed all anti-Semitic manifestations that the Jews were experiencing in Poland. Notably, during the war the Bund leaders in the underground neither met with any faction of the PPS leadership nor discussed or coordinated their views with them. The PPS people considered themselves an integral part of the Polish underground and were represented in its political and military organizations; the Bund pursued its underground activity on its own. However, Bundists availed themselves of personal connections with PPS activists to obtain assistance and information from the Polish underground, and other Jewish underground players found such sources difficult to access. From the standpoint of the socialist underground activists, there was no difference between helping Bundists and helping other Jews, but they, too, preferred – in view of the requirements of underground work and circumspection – to interact foremost with people they had known before the war. Apart from substantive assistance, which as stated was limited, this relationship had a psychological aspect of great consequence. The Bund underground emphasis on the proletarian fraternity that crossed ghetto ramparts was important not only ideologically; it was also crucial in showing that the Jews were not totally estranged from those segments of the Polish population that were sensitive to their suffering.

IDEOLOGY AND THE TEST OF TIME

Did the huge changes in the lives of Jews in the first years of the Nazi occupation prompt Bund activists to re-examine their movement's ideology? This question, which surfaced repeatedly – especially in the first few years of the occupation – is an important issue in understanding the actions of every movement and party during the Nazi era. Sometimes, the traditional ideology forced the movement to confront the issues that faced them in a somewhat anachronistic fashion. For Bundists, this ideology profoundly affected the way in which they dealt with the problem of the uniqueness of Nazi policy toward the Jews (i.e., how they faced the issue of the Jews' singular fate during the war).

In the first half of 1940 the hypothesis concerning the shared suffering of Jews and Poles under Nazi occupation seemed well founded. In January of that year, Reinhard Heydrich provided Hitler with details of plans to deport hundreds of thousands of Jews and Poles from the Wartheland. By that time, 87,000 Jews and Poles had been already removed from the Reich-annexed area in order to create settlement zones for ethnic Germans from eastern Poland. These plans – which were not fully implemented because of technical problems and because *Generalgouverneur,* Hans Frank objected to the resettlement of tens of thousands of Jews in his territory – were part of an extensive plan of forced changes in the demographic and settlement structure of all of Eastern Europe in reflection of the principles of the Nazi racial doctrine. In the first half of 1940, a special SS team, directly subordinate to Himmler in his function as *Reichskommissar für die Festigung des Deutsches Volkstum* (Reich commissar for reinforcement of the German national element), began to elaborate the *Generalplan Ost* (the grand scheme for the east). The deportations from western Poland in 1940 were part of this plan, which took until late 1941 to evolve in detail. The *Generalplan Ost* envisaged the dislocation and deportation to eastern Russia of 60 per cent of Poles and 70 per cent of Ukrainians and Belarus, whose vast land-holdings would be resettled with members of the German race.[99] At that time, deportations, arrests, murder, hardship and deprivation in food and living conditions were the lot of Jews and Poles alike.

The ghettoization in Warsaw erected a buffer between Bund members and their Polish counterparts in the PPS, and entailed the creation of new underground channels of communication. The ghetto, established in the heart of the Polish capital and populated by 450,000 Jews, forced the Bund to tackle the question of uniqueness of the Nazi policy toward the Jews and the difference between it and the Germans' repressive policy toward the Polish population.

The Bund contemplated the ghetto in Warsaw from a dual Jewish and Polish point of view. The severe hardship and high mortality rate experienced in the first winter of the ghetto left no doubt about the uniqueness of the Jewish suffering and fate. The underground journal of the young Bundists, *Yugent Shtime*, described the realities of the ghetto in December 1940: 'It takes only one glance at the people in the ghetto, at their lives, to realize that Hitler has made up his mind to destroy – physically, literally destroy – half a million human beings. Is it not amazing that the people are neither physically nor morally shattered?'[100]

Evidently, some Bundists already realized in those months that the intensity of the repression, brutality and totality of the German measures toward the Jews differed from any policy of terrorism and violence against Polish population groups. However, true to its tradition of examining historical processes from a class point of view, the Bund stressed that the ghetto represented Germany's attempt to sow disunity among the working class in Poland, to inflame anti-Semitic urges and to drive a wedge between the starving Jewish population in the ghetto and the Polish population outside it.[101]

In the first few years of the war, the Bund devoted much attention to the role of Britain and the Soviet Union in the conflict. Before the Germans invaded the USSR, as Britain, led by Churchill, withstood Hitler alone and the might of the Soviet Union was shackled by the Soviet–German non-aggression pact, the Bund needed to give this situation an ideological and political interpretation. The party's underground press drew a clear distinction of values among the fascist dictatorship, bourgeois democracy and the socialist world of tomorrow. In the struggle against the Fascist dictatorship, the Bund prescribed cooperation with bourgeois democracy. If British imperialism were liquidated, as Left Po'aley Tsiyon and HaShomer haTsa'ir counselled as a prime objective of the proletariat, a murderous fascist empire would come into being and obliterate the rights of the working class.[102] The Bund categorically rejected Soviet neutrality in the war between Britain and Nazi Germany. HaShomer haTsa'ir, Dror (a youth pioneer socialist Zionist movement) and Left Po'aley Tsiyon, by contrast, accepted the Soviet interpretation of the war as a clash between 'ruling British imperialism and starving German imperialism',[103] and since the future of the working class was bound up with that of the Soviet Union, neutrality should be maintained in the struggle between the 'two imperialisms'.[104]

However, since the Soviet Union and Germany went to war in the summer of 1941 and the United States entered the fray in early 1942, the Bund believed that a combined anti-fascist struggle involving the bourgeois democracies and the Soviet superpower would herald the creation of a world of freedom and social justice.[105] The Bund favoured maximum assistance for the military effort of the Soviet Union; what is more, the Polish government-in-exile concluded an agreement with Stalin's government in late July 1941. This does not imply, however, that the Bund's support affirmed the Soviet claim to sovereignty in eastern Polish territory.

In the ghetto, the Bund continued unremittingly to cross swords with its opponents. Ideology reinforced the faith of all parts of Jewish underground, staunch to begin with, in a better future after the war. However, it was overshadowed by a life typified by extreme fear of the unknown and slow but steady annihilation. A painstaking review of the role of movement ideology in ghetto activity reveals a constant gap between ideology and daily life. The ideology spoke of the uniqueness of the path being taken, and explained how all the movements were distinct and different from each other. It offered solutions for the future of Jewry, the Jewish community in Palestine, the future of Poland, the future of socialism and the international labour movement, and the future of Zionism. In daily life, all underground activists were preoccupied with obtaining the necessities of life, taking care of friends, educating the young and maintaining a semblance of a support system. Tsukunft, like every movement, focused on sustaining a remnant of the massive system of education and cultural endeavour that had existed before the war. As for actions, the movements were almost indistinguishable and they cooperated extensively, e.g., in the mutual-aid institutions and cultural organizations that came into being in the ghetto.

Just as the heritage of agricultural training, pioneering, settlement in Palestine, Hebrew culture and the ideal of the social revolution sustained the Zionist youth movements, so did the heritage of the Bund struggle against tyranny and fascism sustain Tsukunft. Heritage was the foundation on which the ideologies of all movements and parties in the ghetto rested. It was the lens through which the future was viewed, irrespective of a present in which the Germans marched from victory to military victory and steadily annihilated the ghetto population. From the ideological standpoint, the Bund adhered to its worldview and clashed with its rivals, sometimes no less fiercely than in interwar Poland. In the daily work, the restrictions that the ideology imposed on its carriers diminished, showing that these carriers had more in common than they had not.

NOTES

1. Arad *et al.* (eds), *Documents on the Holocaust*, pp. 191–2.
2. I. Trunk, *Judenrat:The Jewish Councils in Eastern Europe Under Nazi Occupation* (New York: Macmillan, 1972), p. 34.
3. Blatman, 'The Bund in Poland 1935–1939', *Polin*, 9 (1996), pp. 62–3.
4. R. Hilberg, S. Staron and J. Kermisz (eds) *The Warsaw Diary of Adam Czerniaków: Prelude to Doom* (New York: Stein & Day, 1979), p. 74; A. Hartglas, *Na pograniczu dwóch światów* (Warsaw: Oficyna Wydawnicza, 1996), pp. 281–4.
5. T. Szarota, *Okupowanej Warszawy dzień powszedni* (Warsaw: Czytelńik, 1988), pp. 21–2.
6. Hilberg *et al.* (eds), *The Warsaw Diary of Adam Czerniaków*, p. 77.
7. Hertz (ed.), *Doyres Bundistn*, Vol. 3, pp. 27–8.
8. Hilberg *et al.* (eds), *The Warsaw Diary of Adam Czerniaków*, pp. 87–8; Hartglas, *Na pograniczu*, pp. 301–4; C. Shashkes, *Bletter fun a Geto Togbukh* (New York: C.H. Glants, 1943), pp. 13–15.
9. Y. S. Hertz (ed.), *Zygielbojm Bukh* (New York: Unser Tsayt, 1947), p. 13; Shashkes, *Bletter fun*, p. 18.
10. Testimony of Bernard Goldstein, 2 April 1946, BA, ME-18/46.
11. Hilberg *et al.* (eds), *The Warsaw Diary of Adam Czerniaków*, pp. 152, 166.
12. *Biuletyn*, June 1940, *Itonut* (1), p. 19.
13. *Yugent Shtime*, April 1941, *Itonut* (3), p. 284; *Yugent Shtime*, September 1941, *Itonut* (3), pp. 308–9; Biuletyn, 20 December 1941, *Itonut* (2), p. 237.
14. *Biuletyn*, February 1941, *Itonut* (2), pp. 17–18.
15. Y. Kurts, *Sefer Edut* (Tel Aviv: Am Oved, 1944), p. 54; Hertz (ed.), *Doyres Bundistn*, Vol. 2, p. 274; Dambrowska and Wein (eds), *Pinkas HaKehillot – Polin*, 1, p. 196.
16. Meltz and Levi-Landan (eds), *Piotrkow-Trybunalski vehaSeviva*, p. 161; Dambrowska and Wein (eds), *Pinkas HaKehillot–Polin*.
17. *Piotrków-Tribunalski vehaSeviva*, p. 712; Hertz (ed.), *Doyres Bundistn*, Vol. 2, p. 319; memoirs of Mordechai Kotkowski, Yad Vasham Archives (YVA), Jerusalem, 033/1794.
18. Tselemenski, *Mitn Farshnitenem Folk*, p. 104; testimony of Naphtali Lau-Lavie, May 1975, ODC 8 (26).
19. Kurts, *Sefer Edut*, pp. 138–9.
20. Ibid.; testimony of Chaya (Hella) Ginsburg-Staszewski, YVA, 03/524; testimony of Yehoshua Grinboym, YVA, M-1/E 1914/1761.
21. Goldstein, testimony, BA, ME-18/46.
22. Letters from members of the Central Committee in Warsaw to members of the American representation of the Bund and the heads of the JLC in New York, BA, MG-1/29.
23. Tselemenski, *Mitn Farshnitenem Folk*, p. 100.
24. Ibid., pp. 92–3; N. Blumental (ed.), *Te'udot meGeto Lublin – Yudenrat lelo Derech* (Jerusalem: Yad Vashem, 1967), p. 31.
25. According to Tselemenski, *Mitn Farshnitenem Folk*, (p. 83), there were no Bund members on the *Judenrat* when he visited Międzynzec. Evidently he was mistaken in this matter or did not realize that Stein had joined the council. Report of Bund secretariat in Miedrzyzec to the Central Committee in Warsaw concerning party activity during the occupation, 16 June 1946, AAN–KC PZPR, 30/IV-2, file 2.

26. Dambrowska and Wein (eds), *Pinkas HaKehillot – Polin*, Vol. 1, p. 218.
27. A. Blayvays, 'Geto Epizodn …'. *Unser Tsayt*, 4/5 (1967), p. 28.
28. Tselemenski, *Mitn Farshnitenem Folk*, pp. 55–6, 58, 124–5; Hertz (ed.), *Doyres Bundistn*, Vol. 1, p. 267.
29. Wolf-Yasni, *Di Geshikhte*, p. 273.
30. Testimony of Moshe Lederman, YVA, P-5/14; Winer, interview (see note 32, Ch. 1).
31. B. Winer, *Dos Togbukh fun Lodzer Geto,1940, 1943–1944*, ed. Na'khum and Henya Raynharts, Perets Zilberberg, Hava Rozenfarb, private publication, 21, 24 June, 4, 12 July 1940.
32. G. Fogel, 'O działalności Bundu a getcie łódzkim w 1940r', *Biuletyn Żydowskiego Instytutu Historycznego*, 54 (1965), p. 106.
33. On 25 August and 3 and 7 September 1940 advertisements urged workers in the *ressortes* to strike and demonstrate for larger food rations. BA, MG-7/7.
34. Nirenberg, 'Di Geshikhte fun Lodzer Geto', p. 227; Wolf-Yasni, *Di Geshikhte*, p. 320.
35. Fogel, 'O dzialalności Bundu', pp. 107, 109–10; Nirenberg, 'Di Geshikte fun Lodzer Geto', p. 229.
36. A. Ben-Menahem and Y. Rab (eds) *Chronika Shel Geto Lodź*, Vol. 1 (Jerusalem: Yad Vashem, 1986), pp. 25–6.
37. Nirenberg, 'Di Geshikhte fun Lodzer Geto', pp. 229–30.
38. Ben-Menahem and Rab, *Chronika*, pp. 39-72; I. Trunk, *Lodzer Geto* (New York: YIVO, 1962), pp. 384–5.
39. *Konferents Partay Aktiv in Kukh*, 29 September 1940, BA, MG-7/7.
40. Goldstein, *Finf Yor*, pp. 117–22. One of the Bund members evidently engaged in gathering archive material for the party. The Bund did not provide material for Ringelblum's Oneg Shabbat archives, and its members were not active in that project.Y. Zuckerman, *BaGeto uvaMered* (Tel Aviv: Beit Lohamei haGeta'ot and Hakibuts haMeh'uhad, 1985), p. 43.
41. A list of members of the Bund, Tsukunft and SKIF central committees in the Warsaw ghetto is provided in *Folkstsaytung* 16–17 (25–6), 15 November 1947; and Hertz (ed.), *Doyres Bundistn*, Vol. 2, pp. 82–3.
42. M. Waychert, *Yidishe Aleynhilf, 1939–1945* (Tel Aviv: Menora Farlag, 1962), pp. 328–9; Goldstein, *Finf Yor*, p. 186.
43. I. Gutman, *The Jews of Warsaw,1939–1943: Ghetto, Underground, Revolt* (Bloomington, IND: Indiana University Press, 1982), pp. 122–32; remarks by Yitzhak Zuckerman on 26 February 1973, MA, A.580.
44. Hertz (ed.), *In di Yorn*, p. 34.
45. A. A. Berman, *BaMakom asher Ya'ad li haGoral* (Tel Aviv: HaKibuts HaMe'uhad, 1978), p. 207; M. Edelman, *Getto walczy* (Warsaw: C.K. Bund, 1946), p. 17. According to the Tsukunft diary, 1,105 young people enrolled in a series of Bund-sponsored academies in January 1941.Togbukh Tsukunft, 28 January 1941, AAN, Cukunft, 229/2.
46. *Yugent Shtime*, October 1940, *Itonut* (1), p. 117.
47. *Yugent Shtime*, December 1940, *Itonut* (1), p. 221.
48. *Yugent Shtime*, September 1941, *Itonut* (3), pp. 294–7.
49. Togbukh Tsukunft, 15 January 1941, AAN, Cukunft, 229/2.
50. Togbukh Tsukunft, 30 March 1942, AAN, Cukunft, 229/2.
51. Togbukh Tsukunft, 26 March 1941, AAN, Cukunft, 229/2.
52. *Yugent Shtime*, November 1941, *Itonut* (4), p. 63.
53. Gutman,*The Jews*, pp. 138–41.
54. *Yugent Shtime*, March 1941, *Itonut* (2), pp. 109–11; *Yugent Shtime*, October 1941, *Itonut* (3), pp. 464–5; Togbukh Tsukunft, 26 January 1941.
55. Togbukh Tsukunft, 26 March 1941, AAN, Cukunft, 229/2.

56. Togbukh Tsukunft, 7 January 1941, AAN, Cukunft, 229/2.
57. Togbukh Tsukunft, 21 January and 9 March 1941, AAN, Cukunft, 229/2.
58. 'Barikht fun der Yugent fun der tsayt fun Yuli 1941 biz Merts 1942', AAN, Cukunft, 229/1.
59. Tselemenski, *Mitn Farshnitenem Folk*, p. 40; Orzech to Nowogrodzki, 23 November 1940, BA ME-17/11.
60. Tselemenski, *Mitn Farshnitenem Folk*, pp. 41, 131–2.
61. A. Nunberg, 'Mit a Kav durkh der "Griner Grenets"', *Unser Tsayt*, 4 (1953), pp. 26–7.
62. Kushnir to Bund Secretariat in New York, 18 September 1946, AAN, KC PZPR, 30/IV-18.
63. L. Brener, *Vidershtand un Umkum in Tsenstachower Geto* (Warsaw: Yidisher Historische Institut in Poyln, 1950), pp. 59-60; Hertz (ed.), *In di Yorn*, p. 308.
64. Interview with Ya'akov Leber, 27 January 1988.
65. Brener, *Vidershtand un Umkum*, pp. 59–60.
66. Hertz (ed.), *In di Yorn*, p. 308.
67. Kushnir to Bund Secretariat in New York, 18 September 1946, AAN, KC PZPR, 30/IV-18.
68. Tselemenski, *Mitn Farshnitenem Folk*, pp. 100–5.
69. Kurts, *Sefer Edut*, p. 139.
70. *Historishe Zamelbukh, Materyalen un Dokumenten tsu der Geshikhte fun Algemaynem Yidishn Arbeter-Bund* (Warsaw: Ringen, 1947), pp. 99–104; I. Trunk, 'Kultur Arbet in Shatn fun Toyt', *Yugent Veker*, 3(4), April 1947, p. 19.
71. Tselemenski, *Mitn Farshnitenem Folk*, pp. 83–4, 112–22, 125–6.
72. Winer, interview (see note 32, Ch. 1).
73. Y. Nirenberg, 'In Lodzer Geto', *Unser Tsayt*, 12 (1947), p. 141; L. Lewinski, 'Działalność Bundu w Łódzi w latach 1939–1944', *Biuletyn Żydowskiego Instytutu Historycznego*, 54 (1965), p. 113.
74. Nirenberg to Bund Secretariat in New York, 23 May 1945, YIVO, RG-116, Poland (1939-1945), 6.4; Zilberberg to Bund Secretariat in New York, 22 September 1945, BA, M-7/20.
75. Nirenberg, 'Di Geshikhte fun Lodzer Geto', p. 249.
76. Wolf-Yasni, *Di Geshikhte*, pp. 272–4.
77. Ibid., p. 274; Lewinski, 'Działalność Bundu, p. 113.
78. 'Bona', 'Jak Bund święcił 1 maja 1941r. w getcie łódzkim?', *Biuletyn Żydowskiego Instytutu Historycznego*, 54 (1965), p. 115; Lederman to Bund Secretariat in New York, 26 October 1945, and Nirenberg to Bund Secretariat, 24 May 1945, BA M-7/20.
79. T. Sierocki, 'Polski ruch socjalistyczny w latach wojny i okupacji', in W. Góra (ed.), *Wojna i okpacja na ziemiach polskich 1939-1945* (Warsaw: Książka i Wiedza, 1984), pp. 176–7; J. Holzer, *PPS szkic dziejów* (Warsaw: Wiedza Powszechna, 1977), p. 174; Pużak, 'Wspomnienia', p. 18.
80. W. Zagórski, *Wolność w niewoli* (London: Nakładem Autora, 1971), pp. 97–9, 105–8; Sierocki, 'Polski ruch socjalistyczny', pp. 180–1, 189.
81. Rowecki to Sosnkowski, 30 January 1941, *Armia krajowa w dokumentech [AKWD]* 1939–1945 (London: Studium Polski Podziemnej, 1970–72), 1, p. 431.
82. Rowecki to Sosnkowski, 8 February 1940, ibid., p. 116.
83. Rowecki to Sosnkowski, 10 April 1940, ibid., p. 200.
84. *Za Naszą i Waszą Wolność*, October 1941, *Itonut* (3), p. 508.
85. *Yugent Shtime*, December 1940, *Itonut* (1), p. 221.
86. *Za Naszą i Waszą Wolność*, March 1942, *Itonut* (2), p. 124.
87. Delegat rządu to Mikołajczyk, 7 September 1941, *AKWD*, 2, pp. 55–6.
88. *Yugent Shtime*, October 1940, *Itonut* (1), p. 124.

89. Sierocki, 'Polski ruch socjalistyczny', p. 109.
90. *Yugent Shtime*, April 1941, *Itonut* (2), p. 210.
91. G. U. Kacewicz, *Great Britain, the Soviet Union, and the Polish Government in Exile (1939–1945)* (The Hague: M. Nijhoff, 1979), pp. 89–91; J. Coutouvidis and J. Reynolds, *Poland 1939–1947* (Leicester: Leicester University Press, 1986), pp. 61–77; *Biuletyn*, September 1941, *Itonut* (3), p. 282.
92. *Biuletyn*, August 1941, *Itonut* (3), p. 134.
93. *Yugent Shtime*, October 1941, *Itonut* (3), p. 462.
94. *Za Naszą i Waszą Wolność*, August 1941, *Itonut* (3), p. 253.
95. Tselemenski, *Mitn Farshnitenem Folk*, pp. 34–5.
96. Zagórski, *Wolność* pp. 191–2; Klayn, *Mitn Malach Hamaves*, pp. 78, 85–6.
97. Tselemenski, *Mitn Farshnitenem Folk*, pp. 54, 94–5, 109.
98. Zagórski, *Wolność*, pp. 161–3; Hertz (ed.), *In di Yorn*, p. 334; Hertz (ed.), *Doyres bundistn*, Vol. 2, p. 426.
99. R. Breitman, *The Architect of Genocide* (New York: Alfred A. Knopf, 1991), pp. 95-100; C. Madajczyk, *Polityka III Rzeszy w okupowanej Polsce*, Vol. 1 (Warsaw: Państwowe Wydawnictwo Naukowe, 1970), pp. 306ff ; G. Aly, *Final Solution: Nazi Population Policy and the Murder of the European Jews* (London and New York: Arnold, 1999), pp. 33–58.
100. *Yugent Shtime*, December 1940, *Itonut* (1), p. 222.
101. *Yugent Shtime*, November 1940, *Itonut* (1), p. 154.
102. *Yugent Shtime*, January–February 1941, *Itonut* (1), p. 433.
103. *Płomienie*, October 1940, *Itonut* (1), p. 133.
104. *Biuletyn*, April 1941, *Itonut* (2), p. 194.
105. *Tsayt Fragnn*, December 1941, *Itonut*, (4), pp. 254–5.

3

The Erlich–Alter Affair

IMPRISONMENTS AND LIBERATION EFFORTS

The imprisonment, release, re-imprisonment and death in prison of Henryk Erlich and Wiktor Alter, perpetrated by the Soviet authorities, kept Bund activists in Poland, the Soviet Union and the Free World preoccupied until 1943. When their deaths were reported in February 1943, and from then until the end of the war, the affair cast a dark shadow over the Bundists' attitude toward the Soviet regime.

Erlich and Alter left Warsaw a week after the war began. Most leaders of Jewish parties left at this time, and many Bund members joined them. Alter attempted to reach Lublin in the company of a group of party members, but when he realized that Lublin would soon fall to the Germans, he changed direction and headed to Kowel, where many refugees from Poland – including Jewish trade unionists and Polish socialists – gathered in September 1939. Evidently Alter wished to reach Brześć nad Bugiem and join the group of members that had left Warsaw with Erlich, including several members of the Bund Central Committee. Alter, together with a member of the PPS (probably Mieczysław Mastek, a PPS delegate to the Sejm and head of the railroad workers' union), wrote a memorandum to the Soviet ruling authorities expressing three main points: gratitude to the Soviet Union for its assistance in sparing the Polish population in the eastern part of the country from German occupation; hope that the future disposition of eastern Poland would be decided in view of its inhabitants' wishes; and a request that the Soviet authorities assure the political and general freedom of the workers' and peasants' parties. When the authors decided to send the memorandum to the Soviets, Polish workers and members of the railroad workers' union asked Alter to stay in hiding from the authorities. On 26 September 1939 NKVD police arrested all members of the group as they waited in their apartment in Kowel for the answer they had been promised.[1] Alter was taken before a military tribunal, and on 14 July 1941 was sentenced to death for anti-Soviet activity. Erlich reached Brześć nad Bugiem with several members of the Bund Central

Committee. In late September 1939, as the Soviet authorities swept up
Bund activists in the occupied Polish areas, those who had gone to Brześć
nad Bugiem decided to leave this town and attempt to reach Wilno via
Białystok. On 4 October 1939, as Erlich waited for a train at Brześć nad
Bugiem station, Jewish communists identified him and turned him in
to the railroad police.[2] After spending four days in the local prison, he
endured a two-year ordeal of incarceration and numerous interrogations.
The NKVD agents subjected Erlich and Alter to lengthy interrogations.
Minutes from these sessions show that Erlich, for example, was questioned
from 5 October 1939 to 26 June 1941 on many matters, such as the
Polish Communist Party, Polish trade unions, the Bund's political and
organizational endeavours in interwar Poland, and general political
activity in Poland. It seems that the Soviet authorities deemed Erlich
to be the highest-ranking Polish political leader whom they had captured, so they used their interrogation to extract maximum information
about the prewar political system in Poland. In the Soviets' estimation,
Erlich had attained a respected status in the American and Western
European political community, mainly because of his connections with
Western socialist leaders who belonged to the Socialist International.[3]

Erlich and Alter were accused of reactionary activity, conspiracy
with the international bourgeoisie, collaboration with opponents of the
Soviet regime and contact with Westerners. Their sentence was handed
down under paragraph 54(13) of the Criminal Law, which prescribed
the death penalty for any alien whose own actions, or those of the insti-
tution with which he was affiliated, might expose the Soviet Union to
war and imperil the structure of the Soviet state.[4] On 2 August 1941
Erlich was sentenced to death by a Soviet military tribunal. Three weeks
afterwards, his sentence was commuted to ten years in prison. At the
beginning of September he was brought to Moscow, and few days after
that (on 12 September), he was released from prison. Alter was sentenced
to death at the same time, but he too was released from captivity on
13 September.[5] After his liberation, Alter described his experiences in
a letter to comrades in the United States:

> I was arrested on 26 September 1939, in Kowel. I was moved to
> Łuck six weeks later and to Moscow on 8 December 1939. The
> investigation lasted 20 months. I was not abused, but I resisted
> and went on hunger strikes. (In all, I conducted a full or partial
> hunger strike for four and a half months.) On 20 July 1941, the
> military tribunal sentenced me to death on the basis of the accusa-
> tion that, as a member of the executive committee of the Socialist

International for several years, I had engaged in anti-Soviet activity
and masterminded the Bund's illegal activity in the Soviet Union
on behalf of the Polish police. Ten days afterwards, my sentence was
reduced to only ten years, and on 14 September I was released.[6]

The secretary of the Bund mission in New York, Emanuel
Nowogrodzki, did not become aware of the imprisonment of Erlich and
Alter until 6 October 1939. Immediately after this, Bund members in
America began efforts to marshal the support of leaders of Western
labour parties for a mobilization of world opinion that would apply
pressure for their release. Nowogrodzki reported the imprisonment of
the two Bund leaders to all member parties in the Socialist International,
advertised it in the American press, and asked American labour leaders
(William Green and Norman Thomas) to persuade the State Department to intervene on Erlich's and Alter's behalf through the American
Embassy in Moscow. Nowogrodzki also contacted leaders of the British
Labour Party and prepared documents showing that the two Bundists
were Polish citizens who held the status of war refugees.[7] However, the
British Foreign Office firmly opposed both his efforts and those of
pro-Bund Polish politicians in exile, on the grounds that the imprisonment of Erlich and Alter was no different from Soviet incarcerations
of other Polish public figures.[8] Wanda Wasilewska – a leading figure
in the pro-Soviet faction of the PPS who had moved to Moscow and
was well connected with the Soviet authorities – also intervened on
behalf of the two Bundists, as did Polish journalists who had acquain-
tances among government officials in the Soviet capital. After a month
of intensive activity, Nowogrodzki had to advise the Central Committee
members who were in Wilno at this time that his efforts had not paid
off, and that the political agencies whom he had contacted admitted
that there was little they could do for either of them.[9]

It was clear from the outset that the imprisonment of Erlich and
Alter was different from the Soviet incarcerations of other Jewish
political leaders. The two Bundists were members of the executive
committee of the Socialist International and were well connected with
labour parties in the West; thus, the Soviet authorities considered them
'heavyweights' in contrast to other political leaders who spent those
months in prison for opposing the Soviet regime. In the political realities of 1939–41, one could hardly expect the Soviet government to
agree to release them and let them head for the West, as the Bund
activists in the United States wished. The Polish government-in-exile
had no diplomatic relations with the Soviet Union because the latter

had occupied and annexed parts of eastern Poland. The British government, in turn, was striving to establish sound relations with the USSR despite the latter's August 1939 agreement with Germany, and there was no likelihood of British pressure on Moscow in the matter of the two interned Bund leaders.[10]

In the summer of 1941, however, the aftermath of the German invasion of the Soviet Union reversed the political realities and created a chance to effect their release. An agreement concluded between the Polish government-in-exile and the Soviet Union, to which Great Britain was a party, stipulated that all Polish war prisoners who held Polish citizenship as of November 1939 and had been exiled to the Soviet interior would be released and recognized by the Soviet government as Polish citizens. It was further stipulated that the Polish government would be allowed to assist them by means of a Polish diplomatic mission to be established on Soviet soil.[11]

On 27 July 1941 the British Foreign Office sent its embassy in Moscow a list bearing the names of eight Polish socialist leaders whose immediate release was sought by the Polish prime minister, Władysław Sikorski. On the list were six members of the PPS and the two Bund leaders.[12] In early August 1941 Nowogrodzki contacted Walter Citrine, the British trade union leader and the possessor of considerable influence in the labour movement in the West, and requested that he ask the British Foreign Secretary, Anthony Eden, to instruct his ambassador in Moscow to intercede with the authorities for the release of Erlich and Alter. In his response to Citrine, Eden replied that the Polish government, assisted by the British Embassy in Moscow, was striving to have them released.[13] The instructions that the British Foreign Office forwarded to the ambassador in Moscow, Stafford Cripps, in July 1941, were to make all efforts needed to convince the Soviet government that the release of the two Bund leaders would help reinforce Sikorski's standing *vis-à-vis* his critics in the Polish exile in London, who opposed the conclusion of an accord with the Soviet Union until the latter revoked the annexation arrangements in eastern Poland.[14]

Sikorski, whose government fell in the aftermath of its agreement with the Soviet Union, needed the strong support of the PPS and the Peasants' Party at that time. The first desideratum of these parties was the release all labour leaders in Poland whom the Soviets had imprisoned at the beginning of the war. Sikorski contacted Britain, which, wishing to maintain its status in order to settle the Soviet–Polish conflict, girded itself for an effort to liberate the Polish political prisoners. This intervention on behalf of major activists of the Polish socialist movement was consistent with the views of the British Foreign Office at the time, and this explains the appearance of the two Bund leaders, who were among the most prominent of these prisoners on the short list deposited with the British Embassy in Moscow. The Bund leaders in the United States, of course, were unaware that Erlich and Alter had just been sentenced to death, but they understood correctly that the more politically important they became, the harder the Soviets would find it to continue to keep them behind bars. They also understood the importance that the Polish government attributed to the support of American Jewish labour organizations in its efforts to mobilize American public opinion in the Polish cause. In early September 1941, Nowogrodzki cabled the Minister of Labour and Social Affairs in the Polish government-in-exile, Jan Stańczyk of the PPS:

> I have just cabled the Polish government, Sikorski and Mikołajczyk, and advised [them] that the Bund in Poland wishes to appoint Henryk Erlich and Wiktor Alter, who will probably be released from prison in Russia, to the National Council ... Please do everything within your power to ensure the acceptance of these candidates. The Jewish masses in Poland, your partners in resisting the occupation, await these actions on the part of the Polish Government. The Jewish workers in America will derive satisfaction from such a measure, which would attest to a change in the government's stance ...[15]

For the Soviet Union, September and October 1941 were two of the most difficult months of the war. The Red Army was on the verge of disintegration; Moscow was about to fall to the Germans. Stalin needed help from the Western powers, and to attain it he had to enhance the image of the Soviet Union in American and British eyes. Thus, the Soviet authorities decided to release Erlich and Alter, who, in the opinion of Lavrenty P. Beria (head of the NKVD), had an influence on American Jewish public opinion.[16] Shortly after their release on 15 October 1941, the two Bundists moved, along with the Polish Embassy in Moscow and other diplomatic missions, to Kuybyshev, where the Soviet Government had established its provisional capital.

POLITICAL ACTIVITY IN A SNARE

For the next three months – until they were imprisoned again – Alter and Erlich stood at the forefront of political and propaganda activity in Kuybyshev on behalf of the Jewish cause. Since they were the most prominent politicians among the Jews whom the Soviets released from prison camps in the summer of 1941, they inadvertently became involved in the Soviet regime's efforts to establish a Jewish committee that would help mobilize Western Jewish public opinion for the Soviet war effort. They also played a role in the social relief activity that the Polish Embassy had begun to organize and in the tempest that erupted concerning anti-Jewish discrimination in recruitment for the Polish army that General Władysław Anders was establishing on Soviet soil.

Immediately after Alter and Erlich were released, the American Bundists wished to remove them from the Soviet Union. To accomplish this, members of the Bund mission in New York stepped up their efforts to have them admitted as delegates to the new Polish National Council that the government-in-exile in London had set up. Nowogrodzki and his comrades demanded that both party leaders be co-opted onto the council, even though the Polish government agreed to one Bund representative at the most.[17] In October 1941 members of the American Bund mission contacted Erlich and asked for his consent to be the party's candidate for the National Council,[18] but an unexpected difficulty arose. That month, Erlich was busy setting up the Jewish anti-Hitlerist Committee (Żydowski Komitet Antyhitlerlowski: ŻKA). Erlich and Alter had been striving to get this committee under way even before they reached Kuybyshev, and shortly after they arrived they wrote letters to Beria and to Stalin himself, in an attempt to move the initiative ahead.[19] Accordingly, the two of them evidently preferred to have Alter go to London first, to serve as the Bund representative on the National Council. In a letter sent in October 1941 to Adam Ciołkosz, a PPS delegate to the National Council who maintained close relations with Bund members in the United States, Erlich explained:

> Approximately ten days ago, I forwarded a letter to the ambassador [Kot] concerning our participation in the National Council. I noted the stance of our comrades in America, who wished to see two Bund representatives on the council … but for the moment, one may speak of only one representative (myself or Alter) … Thus I officially announced, in the name of our party, that Comrade Alter is a candidate for the National Council.[20]

The plan to bring Alter to London clashed with the intention of Stanisław Kot, the Polish ambassador in Kuybyshev, to mobilize the Bund leadership for action sponsored by the Polish Embassy. In

October–November of 1941, the Polish Embassy began preparations to establish relief centres for Polish citizens whose liberation from labour camps and other incarceration facilities, pursuant to the Soviet–Polish agreement, had begun. Concurrently, the first relief parcels from miscellaneous welfare organizations, foremost in the United States, started to reach the liberated refugees, many of whom were Jewish. According to the Polish Embassy's summarizing report on relief actions for Polish citizens – completed in Teheran in August 1943, after Soviet–Polish relations fell apart – 39.3 per cent of Polish citizens who had received relief from delegates appointed by the Polish Embassy for this purpose were Jews.[21] Kot was making an effort to downscale the anti-Jewish discrimination that was taking place in many of the embassy relief centres. He was afraid that Poland would be criticized by Jewish players in the West. For this purpose he wished to send Alter, as the embassy's representative, on a tour of various centres in the Soviet Union where Polish citizens had gathered. After discussing the matter with Kot in early November 1941, Alter turned down the ambassador's offer for the following reasons:

> Several days ago, I received a cable from New York [informing me] that the Polish Government has decided to make efforts to facilitate my departure to London as quickly as possible. I believe this trip will take place in the next few weeks, and I do not think I can begin a round that might last for several weeks … The offer to undertake the outing as the embassy's emissary is undoubtedly proof of trust, which I greatly appreciate. However, the emissary's powers and its possibilities in arranging substantive assistance for the refugees are so modest that the candidate whom I have proposed as my substitute would be no less effective than I in carrying out this work.[22]

Kot responded harshly to Alter's refusal to work for the embassy. In a letter he sent Alter after he was first apprised of the rationale for the refusal, the ambassador wrote:

> We are working under such difficult conditions, the possibility of sending representatives is encountering such severe difficulties, that we must consider obstacles placed in our path by people from whom, in our estimation, we are entitled to expect assistance, as an unpleasant surprise and nothing more. Furthermore, I regard as groundless the reasons you offer for refusing to make the trip.[23]

In Kot's estimation, Alter's mobilization on behalf of the embassy would facilitate the opening of relief missions for Polish citizens in the Soviet Union – an operation that the Soviet authorities severely hindered by denying these missions any kind of diplomatic status. Alter realized that Kot needed his assistance not because of his special abilities but because of his personal background and his connections with public figures in the American and British labour movements.

The Soviets also understood the potential advantages of co-opting the two Bund leaders into their activities, and released them mainly to enable them to help establish the ŻKA and promote the Soviet cause among members of the American Jewish labour movement. Colonel Arkady Volkovyski, assisted by several additional high-ranking officers in the NKVD, was in charge of relations with Erlich and Alter. Volkovyski, of Jewish origin, met with additional Bund members who had gathered in Kuybyshev in the autumn of 1941 and informed them that the Soviet government was very interested in their two leaders' relations with Western actors and had released them so they could be partners of the USSR in the anti-fascist struggle.[24]

In the middle of October 1941 Erlich and Alter sent a memorandum to Stalin and Beria spelling out the goals and *modus operandi* of the ŻKA. They considered the committee an instrument for the attainment of goals beyond propaganda activity in the anti-Nazi struggle and marshalling assistance for the Soviet Union in its war against the Germans. They sought to turn the ŻKA into an organization that would provide Jewish refugees from Poland who were in the Soviet Union with relief, recruit American Jewish volunteers for a legion that would help fight the Germans on Soviet soil, assist the Jewish underground in Poland and act on behalf of Jews in the German-occupied countries. Generally speaking, they regarded the ŻKA as a Jewish socialist mission with quasi-diplomatic status that would operate alongside foreign embassies and cooperate with the anti-fascist countries. The idea of establishing the new organization marked the inception of a volte-face in the traditional stance of the two Bund leaders and the party they headed. Erlich and Alter, among the most prominent activists in the Second Socialist International in the 1930s, never contemplated the formation of a representative Jewish organization in which Jewish labour circles in various countries would collaborate on behalf of Jewish interests. The Anti-Hitlerist Committee should not be regarded as a national Jewish association, of course, but one may consider it a first step toward the formation of a world Jewish-socialist association. During the war, the needs were defined as appropriate in view of the vicissitudes of the time, but for the long term, and especially after the war, the idea bruited by the two Bund leaders contained a kernel that could grow into the establishment of a broad and united Jewish-socialist movement.

According to their proposal, the organization should be headed by a ten-person committee – seven Polish and Soviet Jews and one representative each from the Soviet government, the British Embassy and the American Embassy. The chairman, deputy chairman and secretary would be Erlich, Shlome Mikhoels (the famous Jewish artist) and Alter, respectively. Before this, in August 1941, Erlich and Alter met with prominent Jewish figures including the Jewish poets Peretz Markish and Itzik Fefer, and Mikhoels himself.[25]

Kot was worried about the developing relationship between the Bund leaders and the Soviet leadership, suspecting that it would infringe on Polish interests. In October 1941 he reported the following to his government in London:

> The Bund emissaries informed me that the Soviet government (the NKVD) had contacted them about propaganda services, especially in America … I stressed to them that they should be very cautious in this matter and tolerate no exploitation of Polish citizens without the government's knowledge and contrary to its intentions. In the meantime, the NKVD has been treating the Bundists very sympathetically and is looking for other leaders to release before the end of their terms (Avraham Faynzilber, a member of the Wilno town council, arrived three days ago), whereas thus far I have not seen even one Jew from other parties …[26]

Kot's impression about the importance the NKVD attributed to the Bundist influence in the United States was correct. In the first few months, dozens of Bund activists were released from detention camps on the basis of a list that the Bund mission in New York had forwarded to Erlich and Alter.[27] The two leaders evidently handed the list to the Soviets so they would be released for participation in the ŻKA's work.[28] In his memoirs, Jerzy Glicksman wrote that the Soviets had released him from a labour camp in August 1941, given him food and money for travel, and told him that he was entitled to visit most Soviet cities.[29] Better known personalities affiliated with the party leadership, such as Tsukunft leaders Lucjan Blit and Leon Oller, went to Kuybyshev after their release and established a Bundist committee – in which Erlich and Alter participated – that centralized the efforts to locate members as they were released from the camps and distributed relief supplies that had been sent from the United States.

At that time Erlich and Alter had a hand in almost every Jewish issue on the Soviet political agenda. Apart from the matters described above, they engaged in recruiting Jews for the Polish army that Anders was establishing on Soviet soil (Polskie Siły Zbrojne w ZSSR) and involved themselves in the question of establishing a Jewish legion within this force. Anders and his officers – as well as the Polish government in London – were distressed about the large numbers of Jews who thronged the induction centres that received volunteers for this army. They responded by applying a policy of conscious discrimination and rejected many Jews rudely and on insulting grounds. However, they also accused the Soviet authorities of creating difficulties in the mobilization of Jews by refusing to recognize them as Polish citizens.[30]

In October 1941 Anders, Kot, Erlich, Alter, Otto Pehr of the PPS and the Jewish Affairs officer at the Polish Embassy in Kuybyshev, Ludwig Zeidenmann, met to discuss this matter. Anders argued that it was difficult to recruit Jewish volunteers because many of them – especially those who had given the Red Army an enthusiastic welcome as it invaded eastern Poland – were of dubious loyalty to Poland. Anders also ruled out the establishment of a separate Jewish unit, as proposed by two Revisionist-Zionist functionaries, because he would also have to form special units for Ukrainians and Byelorussians, too, and then his army would lose its national complexion. Erlich vehemently rejected the accusation concerning Jewish sympathies for the invading Red Army, defining such manifestations as trivial. Anders said they were anything but trivial.[31] Erlich took exception to all of Anders' accusations, stated that they were merely one more instance of the rampant anti-Semitism that characterized pre-war Poland, and stressed that Polish citizens had been guilty of anti-Semitic behaviour towards Jewish compatriots during their sojourn in Soviet labour camps. However, Erlich and Anders agreed with respect to the Jewish legion: 'The Bund totally accepts General Anders' view. We Jews are fighting and wish to fight not for Palestine but for Poland.'[32]

The three Bund activists – Oller, Blit and Faynzilber – expressed a similar view in a memorandum that they presented in December 1941 in the name of the party to the Polish prime minister, Sikorski, who had come to Kuybyshev for talks with Stalin. Instead of forming a separate Jewish unit, they argued, the Polish government should encourage physical-fitness and military-training programmes for Jews so that they could join regular units of the newly formed Polish army.[33] In his memoirs, Anders recorded Erlich's and Alter's remarks in their meeting with him:

> Our view, like that of General Anders, is that the Polish army should be homogeneous, a common organization in which all citizens are equally privileged irrespective of religion and nationality, and its major function [should be] military struggle for a democratic Poland, a homeland for all its inhabitants.[34]

The Bund leaders' attempts to smooth relations between Jews and Poles in the Polish army did not pay off. Although they were pro-Polish, and although they shared Anders' views on the formation of a separate Jewish legion, Erlich and Alter encountered the anti-Semitism that was rampant among members of the Polish leadership – the very factor that had thwarted the integration of Jews into the Polish army.

In the meantime, the heads of the NKVD had become concerned about the political relations and independent activity that Erlich and Alter had formed.[35] In early December 1941 these officials realized that the recruitment of the two Bund leaders for the Soviet propaganda campaign offered more risks than opportunities. The two Jews were in constant touch with the British ambassador in Moscow, Stafford Cripps; they had been named by the editorial board of the New York Jewish daily newspaper *Forverts* as its correspondents in the Soviet Union;[36] moreover, they had reported to the West on developments in the Soviet Union in contravention of Soviet wishes. In late September 1941, about two weeks after he was released from prison, Alter sent his American comrades, and Walter Citrine in Britain, a detailed written account of the realities he had found during his incarceration and suggested ways in which the Western countries could put pressure on the Soviet government:

> The political results of this lunacy: despair and discouragement among tens of millions of people and disorder in all areas of life. The finest and most experienced experts are languishing in prisons and camps, not to mention those who were shot to death. Here is the basis for Hitler's military victories. The real focal point of the counterrevolution is the NKVD and its operations. From the perspective of humanity and victory over Hitler, this pus has to be removed before it consumes the Soviet Union ... The following slogan should be disseminated in the press, public opinion and

institutions of the United States: political amnesty in the Soviet
Union – an essential condition for victory over Hitler.[37]

In early December 1941 the Soviet Union reversed its position on
the citizenship of Jewish refugees from Poland. On 1 December Foreign
Minister Molotov stated that the USSR did not deem Jews and members
of other non-Polish minorities to be citizens of Poland. The release of
Jews from labour camps slowed immediately after he made this statement and came to a virtual halt a short time later.[38] Initial contacts toward
the formation of the pro-Soviet Polish organization, the Union of
Polish Patriots (Związek Patriotów Polskich: ZPP) began at this time.
Concurrently, the Soviets' military situation improved after the Red
Army halted the German offensive on various fronts and freed Moscow
from the menace of occupation. In the political arena, the Soviet Union
concluded a friendship agreement with the Polish government after
Stalin's talks with Sikorski in Moscow, and American Lend-Lease ship-
ments began to arrive. Therefore, the NKVD officials reassessed the
two Bund leaders' activities and decided that they were not only no
longer essential for Soviet interests but possibly harmful. Shortly after
midnight on 4 December 1941, Officer Kazanovich of the NKVD tele-
phoned the two Bundists at their hotel in Kuybyshev and summoned
them to an urgent meeting. Erlich and Alter left the hotel and were
never seen again. Blit and Oller, who had been with them at the hotel,
cabled the Polish Embassy that day:

> On 4 December, at 00.30 hours, Messrs Henryk Erlich and
> Engineer Wiktor Alter were in the restaurant of the Grand Hotel
> ... An employee of Intourist [the Soviet Tourism Agency]
> approached them and called Mr Alter to the telephone. A moment
> later, Alter returned to the table and told Mr Erlich that they had
> to go somewhere at once. When Mr Blit asked him about it, Alter
> replied that they would return soon. Although more than 13 hours
> have passed since the two gentlemen left, we have received no
> word concerning what happened to them and why they have not
> returned to their hotel room thus far. We are forwarding this
> report to the embassy to ask it to take action to ascertain the
> whereabouts of Messrs Erlich and Alter.[39]

Four days later, the Polish Embassy reported the contents of the
Bund members' cable to the Soviet Foreign Ministry and asked the
ministry to locate the two Jewish leaders.[40] About three weeks later,

Andrei Vyshinsky (Molotov's pro-tem at the Soviet Foreign Ministry) advised the embassy that the two men were being investigated and added vehemently that, in any event, both of them were considered Soviet citizens under Soviet law.[41] In fact, the two Bundists were not the subjects of any investigation during those weeks. Instead, they were in the prison in Kuybyshev, where they would be kept in total isolation for many months. Evidently the NKVD had made up its mind to terminate both men's activities because their continued independent work was risky for the Soviet Union, but without murdering them because such an action, in view of their prominence and their relations with the West, would create a great international scandal. In a letter to the Supreme Soviet Presidium (dated 27 December 1941) written from his prison cell in Kuybyshev, Erlich stated that as they were leaving the hotel on the night of 4 December 1941, he and Alter were told that they were to meet with a special emissary of the NKVD. After waiting for about 20 hours, they were informed that an explicit order to imprison them had been handed down.[42]

This time, Erlich and Alter would not leave prison alive. The two Bund leaders had attempted to create a framework for Jewish political activity that would influence the new political reality created by the changes in the international situation in the summer of 1941, but their efforts were dashed by interests and forces much stronger than they.

POLITICAL INTEREST AND INTERFERENCE

Once informed about the re-internment of Erlich and Alter, the American mission of the Bund in New York decided to take a series of measures to involve all related political players in the affair. A Bund delegation met with the Soviet ambassador in Washington, Maxim Litvinov. The Polish ambassador was asked to assure the intervention of the Polish government. Letters were sent to PPS officials in the Polish government-in-exile and the National Council, Stańczyk and Ciołkosz, and to the prominent British trade unionist Walter Citrine. Finally, the matter was given wide exposure in the American press with the help of American labour leaders (William Green and Norman Thomas).[43] Because the affair was politically sensitive, the Bund activists who toiled for their leaders' release had to contend with players whose considerations and interests differed from and clashed with their own.

The Labour activists in Britain oscillated between conflicting interests. On the one hand, the arrest of two leading members of the

Socialist International evinced fury and protest, especially since the detainees had been labouring to establish a Jewish organization that would take part in the war effort against Nazi Germany. On the other hand, the British government had adopted a policy of strict non-intervention in internal Soviet affairs and refrained from criticizing Stalin's regime in order to deny the Nazis grist for their anti-Soviet propaganda. The British government was also apprehensive about taking its own stance without American concurrence. The major Labour activists did not manage to act on the arrested Bundists' behalf, and they were under strong pressure from communist and pro-Soviet circles in the British labour movement that considered any criticism of the Soviet Union harmful to the overall war effort against Hitler. For them, the fate of the two Bund leaders was a trifling matter.[44] Similarly, when Walter Citrine spoke with Anthony Eden about Erlich and Alter in May 1942, Eden replied that the matter was an internal Soviet issue on which His Majesty's Government would not express a view.[45]

The British Foreign Office accepted the Soviet argument that, since the two Bundists were Soviet citizens, it was indeed an internal Soviet affair. Evidence that the issue of Erlich's and Alter's citizenship was related to the Soviet posture was provided in a letter from the Soviet Foreign Ministry to the Polish Embassy in Kuybyshev on 1 December 1941, to the effect that recognition of inhabitants of western Ukraine and Byelorussia as Polish citizens applied only to Poles and not to Ukrainians, Byelorussians and Jews.[46] On 26 January 1942 the Soviet Foreign Ministry, in response to an enquiry from the Polish Embassy in the matter of Erlich and Alter, replied that the two men were Soviet citizens since they were not of Polish origin.[47] In January 1942, when Kot and Vyshinsky met for a talk, the Polish ambassador again brought up the Erlich–Alter matter with the acting Soviet Foreign Minister. The minutes of this meeting contain the following remarks:

> AMBASSADOR [Kot]: There is, Mr Chairman, one more question which has been raised several times by the Embassy. It concerns Erlich and Alter, both Polish citizens and Warsaw town councillors who are kept in prison by you ... do this for me and allow us to take these men away. I shall take full responsibility for their not engaging in anti-Soviet agitation abroad ... Nobody will believe that those men were implicated in pro-Nazi activity ... Who may need it? Will the common struggle against Germany benefit by it?

VYSHINSKI: I understand your intentions and feelings, Mr Ambassador, but I cannot discuss the case of Erlich and Alter with you because, as you know, in the view of the Soviet government those men are Soviet citizens.[48]

The government of Poland resisted any change in the matter of the Polish citizenship of inhabitants of the eastern areas that the USSR had annexed in 1939. The Polish citizenship of Jews in these areas may have been a marginal issue from the perspective of the Polish government, but the latter took a vehement and unequivocal stance on the issue of the Polish citizenship of Ukrainians and Byelorussians. A retreat in this matter was tantamount to the forfeit of these territories and recognition of the Soviet annexation. Indirectly, then, the struggle over the Polish citizenship of Erlich and Alter was a struggle against recognition of the arrangements that the Soviets had made in eastern Poland – arrangements to which they adhered even after their relations with the Polish government thawed.

The Polish government-in-exile also kept American Jewish public opinion in mind. It hoped to exploit the disgruntlement and anger that the American Jewish trade unions, and public opinion in general, evinced after the two Bund leaders were incarcerated – especially after their deaths were reported in February 1943 – to maximize Jewish and general American public support for the Polish cause, especially as the Soviets were increasing their information efforts among American Jews. Here, too, as with the case of the two Bundists' Polish citizenship, the Polish government turned the Erlich–Alter affair into a political tool with which they attempted to promote interests that were pronouncedly Polish.[49]

The Bund activists in New York could only stand by helplessly as the Polish and Soviet governments turned the Erlich–Alter affair into a political football. Faithful to their policy of avoiding policy positions that might endanger Bund members or general Jewish interests, they did not take a public stance in the dispute about their leaders' citizenship and focused their efforts on frustrating and hopeless intercessionary activity. From the outset, the Bund members understood that their two leaders were doomed and the prospects of their release were nil. Frantz Kurski, the veteran Bundist, said as much to his colleague John Mill back in January 1942, shortly after they were re-arrested.

According to unofficial reports, the situation is grave. I personally understand (and no one informed me of this) that they were arrested

for 'anti-Soviet provocations' outside the Soviet Union. It is true
that they were released in September 1941, but they were never
forgiven. We do not know the meaning of their re-imprisonment.
But it stands to reason that the situation is grave, terrible ...[50]

The Bund mission's efforts to make contact with Erlich and Alter
or, in any event, to obtain information about their fate, began in the
autumn of 1941. The Bundists in the United States met with the
acting Polish Foreign Minister, Edward Raczyński, who told them that
only one person could expedite the handling of the affair: Averell W.
Harriman, a member of the Soviet–American–British military committee that operated in Moscow in late September 1941. Harriman was
on good terms with the Kremlin leadership, but his intervention
required approval of the State Department in Washington.[51] Therefore, the leaders of the *Arbeter Ring*, Yosef Waynberg and Yosef Baskin,
petitioned Secretary of State Cordell Hull,[52] and Alexander Erlich
(Henryk's son) wrote to the First Lady, Eleanor Roosevelt, to ask for
her help.[53] It was all to no avail.

Szmuel Zygielbojm, having joined the National Council in London
in April 1942, appealed that month to General Anders, who was visiting London. Anders seemed to lack accurate information about the two
Bund leaders. He informed Zygielbojm that, in his opinion, vigorous
diplomatic action might be of use. Zygielbojm reported Anders' opinion
to Sikorski, who said that the Polish Embassy in the Soviet Union was
dealing with the matter steadily and was giving it special attention.[54]

As this devils' dance of political players continued, Erlich and Alter
languished for months in the Kuybyshev prison, their fate unknown to
anyone. Now, unlike their first term of incarceration, they were not
interrogated but were kept in total isolation and denied all contact with
the world. On 15 May 1942 Henryk Erlich, the older of the two (about
sixty and in poor health after the imprisonment and intensive interrogations he had endured during 1939–41), committed suicide by hanging
himself on the bars of his prison cell. The NKVD officials who were
responsible for Erlich were dismayed. They issued orders to prevent
information about the suicide from reaching the ears of foreign enquirers
and, above all, of Alter himself, lest he do something similar.[55]

In August and September 1942, the Bund members in New York
believed that Erlich and Alter were no longer alive – incorrectly in
Alter's case. In the middle of August 1942, a Bundist who had made
his way to Teheran with Anders' army advised London of a rumour to
the effect that Alter had been executed and that a similar fate might be

awaiting Erlich.[56] Zygielbojm took up the matter with the First Secretary at the Polish Embassy in Kuybyshev, Wysław Arlet, who had spent some time with both Bund leaders in Kuybyshev before they were arrested. Arlet claimed that both men were doomed. Their indictment for espionage on behalf of Germany, and allusions that Kot had picked up from Vyshinsky in July 1942, shortly before he completed his term as Polish ambassador to the Soviet Union, indicated that neither was still alive.[57] Tadeusz Romar, who succeeded Kot in the summer of 1942, expressed his opinion that the two men were still alive, but the Bundists derived little confidence and hope from this source.[58]

It seems that the senior NKVD officialdom had decided in February 1943 to wind up the Erlich–Alter affair once and for all. A military tribunal in Kuybyshev reaffirmed the 1941 verdict and sentenced Wiktor Alter to death. He was executed by a firing squad at 2 a.m. on 17 February 1943. On the day of the murder, the chief NKVD officer in Kuybyshev, expressed the following in a top-secret memorandum to the Deputy Commissar of Internal Affairs:

> Your order to execute by shooting the prisoner no. 41 was carried out on 17 February. A certificate has been drawn up which I am enclosing together with the personal file. I withdrew all documents and records relating to the prisoner no. 41 … His belongings have been burned.[59]

On 23 February 1943 the Soviet Ambassador to the United States, Maxim Litvinov, handed a terse letter to William Green, president of the American Federation of Labour. The missive contained an official announcement of the deaths of Erlich and Alter. Litvinov stressed that the matter concerned two Soviet citizens who had been sentenced to death for acting against the Red Army and attempting to conclude peace with Nazi Germany.[60]

This disclosure of the death of the two men at that time, like most actions in the Erlich–Alter affair, actually originated in a political calculus. It occurred shortly after the battle of Stalingrad, when the Red Army was riding a tide of sympathy in the West for its heroic conduct in the war. The Soviet government was not concerned about the waves of protest that the report would generate, and it was right: the protests ebbed several weeks later. The Soviet authorities' insensitivity and cynicism toward the fate of the two Bund leaders was symbolically expressed in a bill that Intourist presented to the Polish Embassy in Kuybyshev in the middle of April 1943, about six weeks after the report of the Bundists' death appeared. Intourist asked the Embassy to remit 2,577 roubles for Erlich's and Alter's stay in a Moscow hotel on 13–19 October 1941, before they moved on to Kuybyshev.[61]

The Erlich–Alter affair left the Bund members feeling bitter and helpless. The murder of the two Party leaders marked the end of an era in Bund history. It was Erlich and Alter who had elevated the Bund to the position of a leading political movement among Polish Jewry and led an insular and introverted party (as the Bund had been in the 1920s) into the mainstream of socialist activity in Europe. This endeavour is expressed in an account of Bund history that Erlich wrote during his first term in prison – the annals of the party's struggle on behalf of the Jewish working class, the story of its relations with parties of the Polish Left in the 1920s and the 1930s, and its extensive activity for the Jewish cause in Poland.[62]

The imprisonment of Erlich and Alter, and the desperate efforts to release them, occurred as the Final Solution was being set in motion in Eastern Europe. In their consciousness, the Bundists linked these events and interpreted them as the beginning of the end of Polish Jewry and the liquidation of the party and its members. Baruch Shefner expressed these feelings in the *Forverts*:

> One concurrently sheds tears over the two harsh revelations of the time: The huge mass grave in Poland and the small grave in Russia. You feel that the eyes of the persons who were shot, alone, in the small grave in Russia reflect the entire tragedy of the millions buried in the mass grave in Poland …[63]

Throughout this period – from the first imprisonment of Erlich and Alter until their death – one could perceive the gap between the Bund's actual influence in international political circles and the influence attributed to it by Soviet and Polish officials. The NKVD quickly realized that the party actually had little real ability to sway American working-class attitudes in the direction of support of the Soviet cause. It also transpired that Jewish influence in the United States – in which various Soviet players and figures in the Polish government-in-exile believed – was a paper tiger. Erlich and Alter, two Jewish leaders of the Jewish working class in Poland, had absolutely no political influence on the world stage and were abandoned by all of its actors. The Polish government exploited their cause for its needs, the Soviet government understood that it did not need them and that their independent activities only harmed its interests; and the governments of Britain and the United

States took no interest whatsoever in their fate. As the political game surrounding the fate of their two comrades developed, the Bund members stood by helplessly, unable to thwart the progression of events that led to their deaths.

NOTES

 1. Portnoy, *Henryk Erlich and Victor Alter*, pp. 71–2; Gliksman, *Tell the West*, pp. 29–30; diary of Ignacy Schwartzbart, 17 October 1941, YVA, M-2/765.
 2. Gertrud Pickhan, 'Das NKVD-Dossier über Henryk Erlich und Wiktor Alter', *Berliner Jahrbuch für osteuropäische Geschichte*, 2 (1994), p. 162; *Henryk Erlich and Victor Alter*, pp. 73–5; T. Yarnushkewits, 'Mit H. Erlichn in Sovietisher Tefise', *Unser Tsayt*, 1 (1957), p. 21.
 3. Pickhan, 'Das NKVD-Dossier', pp. 160–61.
 4. E. Yapou, 'Lama Hutsu Erlich ve-Alter LaHoreg?' *Gesher*, 111/12 (1985), p. 101.
 5. Kot to Polish Embassy in Washington, 16 September 1941, BA MG-2/28; P. Korzec, 'The Riddle of the Murder of Henryk Erlich and Wiktor Alter by the Soviets', *Gal-Ed*, 10 (1987), p. 285; S. Redlich, *War, Holocaust and Stalinism* (Luxemburg: Harwood, 1995), pp. 9–10.
 6. Alter to Bund members in the United States, 21 September 1941, Korzec, 'The Riddle of the Murder', p. 241.
 7. Nowogrodzki to Mendelsohn, 15 November 1939, BA, MG-1/17; Nowogrodzki to Thomas, 30 October 1939, BA, M-12/8-A.
 8. I. Tombs, 'Erlich and Alter, "The Sacco and Vanzetti of the USSR": An Episode in the Wartime History of International Socialism', *Journal of Contemporary History*, 23-4 (1988), pp. 532–4.
 9. Nowogrodzki to Mendelsohn, 15 November 1939, BA, MG-1/17.
10. Kacewicz, *Great Britain*, pp. 49–50; Tombs, 'Erlich and Alter', pp. 532–4.
11. Coutouvidis and Reynolds, *Poland 1939–1947*, p. 62.
12. British Foreign Office to British Embassy in Moscow, 26 July 1941, BA, MG-4/28.
13. Eden to Citrine, 11 August 1941, BA, MG-4/20.
14. British Foreign Office to British Embassy in Moscow, 26 July 1941, BA, MG-4/28.
15. Nowogrodzki to Stańczyk, 5 September 1941, BA, ME-18/34.
16. Redlich, *War, Holocaust and Stalinism*, pp. 10–11.
17. D. Blatman, 'On a Mission against All Odds; Szmuel Zygielbojm in London (April 1942–May 1943)', *Yad Vashem Studies*, 20 (1990), pp. 239–40.
18. Nowogrodzki to Erlich, 5 and 6 October 1941, BA, ME-18/34.
19. Erlich and Alter to head of the NKVD in Kuybyshev, 21 October 1941, L. Hirszowicz, 'NKVD Documents Shed New Light on Fate of Erlich and Alter', *East European Jewish Affairs*, 22 (2), 1992, p. 69; Letters from Erlich and Alter to Beria and Stalin, October 1941, Redlich, *War, Holocaust and Stalinism*, pp. 165–6.
20. Erlich to Ciołkosz, 23 October 1941, BA, MG-4/45-A.
21. Report on the Relief Accorded to Polish Citizens by the Polish Embassy in the USSR, September 1941–April 1943, BA, MG-9/155, p. 4.
22. Alter to Kot, 12 November 1941, Korzec, 'The Riddle of the Murder', p. 301.
23. Kot to Alter, 12 November 1941, ibid., p. 301.
24. Testimony of Avraham Faynzilber, 3 August 1976, ODC, 17 (93).
25. Memorandum from Erlich and Alter to Stalin and Beria concerning the formation of the ŻKA, 10 October 1941, BA, MG-4/51-B; Erlich to the Presidium of the

USSR Supreme Soviet, 27 December 1941, Redlich, *War, Holocaust and Stalinism*, p. 167.

26. Report from Kot to Polish government in London, 3 October 1941, Korzec, 'The Riddle of the Murder', p. 299.
27. Nowogrodzki to Erlich and Alter, 8 November 1941, BA, M-7/20.
28. Portnoy (ed.), *Henryk Erlich and Victor Alter*, pp. 104–5.
29. Glicksman, *Tell the West*, p. 343.
30. I. Gutman, 'The Jews in Anders' Army in the Soviet Union', *Yad Vashem Studies* 12 (1977), pp. 236–46.
31. Minutes of meeting at the Polish Embassy in Kuybyshev, 24 October 1941, BA, MG-4/51-B.
32. Ibid.
33. Memorandum from Blit, Faynzilber to Sikorski, 9 December 1941, YVA, 025/228.
34. W. Anders, *Bez Ostatniego Rozdziału, Wspomnienia z lat 1939–1946* (Newtown, Wales: Montgomeryshire Printing, 1950), pp. 99–100.
35. A report of the heads of the NKVD in Kuybyshev to the Soviet Foreign Ministry, 14 December 1941, Hirszowicz, 'NKVD Documents', pp. 70–72.
36. Report of the American ambassador in Kuybyshev to the State Department in Washington, 9 December 1941, BA, MG-4/28.
37. Alter to Bund members in the United States, 21 September 1941, Korzec, 'The Riddle of the Murder', p. 295; letter from Alter to Citrine, 26 September 1941, ibid., pp. 297–8.
38. Sikorski's memorandum to Churchill, 5 March 1942, PRO, FO-371/31079.
39. Blit and Oller to the Polish Embassy in Kuybyshev, 4 December 1941, Korzec, 'The Riddle of the Murder', p. 304.
40. Polish Embassy in Kuybyshev to Soviet Foreign Ministry, 8 December 1941, YVA, 025/226.
41. Cables from Soviet Foreign Ministry to Polish Embassy in Kuybyshev, 23 and 26 December 1941, Korzec, 'The Riddle of the Murder', p. 305.
42. Erlich to the Soviet Presidium of the USSR Supreme Soviet, 27 December 1941, Redlich, *War, Holocaust and Stalinism*, p. 168.
43. Minutes of Bund American mission meeting, 18 December 1941, BA, ME-18/32 and 20 January 1942, BA, ME-18/35.
44. Tombs, 'Erlich and Alter', pp. 538–45.
45. Zygielbojm to Nowogrodzki, 8 May and 29 May 1942, BA, MG-2/5.
46. Soviet Foreign Ministry to Polish Embassy in Kuybyshev, 1 December 1941, *Documents on Soviet–Polish Relations, 1939–45 (DSPR)*, Vol. I (London: Heinemann, 1961), pp. 227–8.
47. Soviet Foreign Ministry to Polish Embassy in Kuybyshev, 26 January, 1942, ibid., p. 681.
48. Minutes of meeting between Vyshinsky and Kot, ibid., p. 363.
49. D. Engel, *Facing a Holocaust: The Polish Government-in-Exile and the Jews 1943–1945* (Chapel Hill, NC and London: University of North Carolina Press, 1993), pp. 55–62.
50. Kurski to Mill, 2 January 1942, BA, ME-40/80.
51. Minutes of Bund American mission meeting, 16 March 1942, BA, ME-18/35.
52. Waynberg and Baskin to Hull, December 1941, BA, MG-4/28.
53. Alexander Erlich to the White House, 24 December 1941, BA, MG-4/28.
54. Zygielbojm to Sikorski, 30 April 1942, YVA, 025/246.
55. Report on Erlich's suicide, 18 May 1942, Redlich, *War, Holocaust and Stalinism*, p. 169; correspondence among Soviet officials in the aftermath of Erlich's suicide, Hirszowicz, 'NKVD Documents', pp. 75–81.
56. Zygielbojm to Nowogrodzki, 30 August 1942, BA, MG-2/5.

57. Ibid.
58. Zygielbojm to Nowogrodzki, 28 January 1943, BA, MG-2/26; Zygielbojm to Yiveneska, 1 February 1943, BA, M-16/151-D.
59. Report on Alter's execution, 17 February 1943, Redlich, *War, Holocaust and Stalinism*, p. 170.
60. Portnoy (ed.), *Henryk Erlich and Wiktor Alter*, pp. 166–7.
61. Polish Embassy in Kuybyshev to Polish Foreign Ministry in London, 15 April 1943, YVA, 025/259.
62. Pickhan, 'Das NKVD-Dossier', pp. 168–86.
63. Portnoy (ed.), *Henryk Erlich und Wiktor Alter*, p. 227.

4

The Bund and the Jewish
Fighting Organization

FACING THE FINAL SOLUTION

The first murder of Jewish civilians – the onset of the mass murder of Lithuanian, Byelorussians and Ukrainian Jewry by the *Einsatzgruppen* – took place on 24 June 1941, only two days or so after the great German invasion of the Soviet Union began. Two hundred and one Jews were massacred in the Lithuanian border town of Gargzdai by a unit (*kommando*) of the Security Police (*Sicherheitspolizei*). The murder operations quickly spread throughout the occupied areas. The implementation of a policy of systematic annihilation ensued in late July 1941, in daily planned *Selektionen* including the mobilization of the Lithuanian civilian population as auxiliaries. In these actions, tens of thousands of Jewish men, women and children were selected and executed at hundreds of murder sites.[1] The Nazi Final Solution of the Jewish problem had begun.

The first information on the mass murders in Wilno and the eastern territories of Poland, which started in July–August 1941, reached Warsaw in the autumn of 1941, evidently by means of a member of the Polish Scouts, Henryk Grabowski, who interacted closely with the youth movements in the ghetto, especially HaShomer haTsa'ir. Grabowski visited Wilno, met with members of the Zionist pioneering youth movements there, and delivered the harsh tidings of what was happening there upon his return to Warsaw. Liaisons and members of the movements who circulated between the two ghettos created an influx of further reports. The information that reached Warsaw at that time corroborated the initial reports, delivered several months earlier, to the effect that the Germans were perpetrating mass murder of the Jewish population in eastern Poland. In early February 1942, Ya'acov Grojnowski, a young Jew from Izbica, reached Warsaw after having fled from the Chełmno extermination camp, where he had been working in a *Sonderkommando* group. In Chełmno, a village 60 kilometres from Łódź, a murder squad had gone into action in December 1941 under Hauptsturmführer-SS Herbert Lange. The mass murder of Jews at the Chełmno site, which had been intended for Jews from Łódź and its vicinity, was carried out by means of sealed gas vans – a method already applied in the Minsk area. Grojnowski's reports from Chełmno and reports delivered to members of the Oneg Shabbat underground archive in the Warsaw Ghetto,[2] in addition to earlier reports on the events in Wilno and eastern Poland, painted a picture that came into greater and greater focus: the Germans had embarked on a planned campaign of mass destruction of Polish Jewry.[3]

In October 1941 information on the murders in the east began to appear in the Bund press and the other underground newspapers. In its October 1941 issue, *Biuletyn* reported the following details:

> A growing number of horrifying reports are coming in on Hitlerist atrocities against Jews in the newly occupied areas in White Russia, Lithuania and the vicinity of Białystok. Thousands of Jews have been shot in Wilno … Jews have been taken from a series of cities, ostensibly for labour, and shot to death. Women and elderly have also been shot. There are towns in which 80–90 per cent of the Jewish population have perished. Jews from Białystok are being sent to Pruzhany and villages in that area. Jewish property is being looted systematically. The nightmare of bloodshed has shrouded the Jewish localities in the newly occupied areas in stark agony.[4]

That month, the *Yugent Shtime* reported detailed information, including some inaccurate details, on murders in a number of cities and towns including Lwów, Pińsk, Włodzimierz-Wołyński, Brześć nad Bugiem, Janów and other small localities, and summarized the matter: 'Such atrocities are unprecedented in Jewish history. The shed blood of tens of thousands of innocent victims will yet arise and demand [vengeance]. The requiting of this blood will yet come.'[5]

Did the Bund leaders, foremost those of Tsukunft, understand the significance of the massacres in the east? Did they understand that in one stroke they must transform their *modus operandi* and gird for armed struggle as a response to the Jews' impending extinction? Examination of the processes that the Bund underwent during those months shows that diverse and conflicting trends prevented the leaders realizing the dreadful but inexorable fact that the Jews faced total destruction.

During November 1941–April 1942 reports of murder throughout Poland steadily multiplied in the Bund newspapers, as in the underground newspapers of the other movements. The Bund members, although shocked, drew no explicit conclusions from these events, and a few continued to regard them as part of an inclusive process initiated by the Nazi state to eradicate large population groups in Poland.[6] In early 1942 the Bund was inclined to step up its activity among young people and strengthen relations between the young leadership and members of the Central Committee. In other words, its aim was to reinforce and strengthen the bonds of the party framework. Activists of the other movements' underground organizations shared this goal. However, activist leanings became dominant among the Tsukunft activists during those months, and they regarded the need to organize for armed struggle as an immediate imperative. According to Marek Edelman, the Bund established a fighting organization with the participation of Polish socialists in early 1942, headed by Bernard Goldstein, Abrasha Blum and Avraham 'Berek' Shneidmil.[7] It is doubtful, however, that this embryonic agency amounted to a fighting organization. In January 1942 Tsukunft in the Warsaw ghetto maintained 21 groups of teenagers and young people who were organized in cells of five and seven – 140 members in all. In a meeting of group leaders on 8 January 1942, it was agreed that the groups would hold an internal debate on the desired course of action in the future and would attempt to establish deeper relationships with additional youth groups in the ghetto, foremost among young people who had finished high school.[8] The concerted organizational work by members of Tsukunft early that year became manifest about two months later. In a meeting of activists held in early March 1942, it was reported that the number of groups had risen to 22 and the number of members to 160.[9] On 14 January 1942, at a meeting of the Tsukunft Central Committee, it was decided to reactivate the Tsukunft defence groups ('Tsukunft-Shturm') along lines similar to the pre-war groups that protected party assemblies from anti-Semitic thugs.[10] However, there is no evidence that these groups made preparations for armed struggle. It seems that the organizational effort of the Tsukunft leadership during these months was aimed at expanding the infrastructure of movement activity and co-opting as many young people as possible. The leaders did discuss the matter of armed resistance, but the debate was hesitant and the members were of many minds. On 15 April 1942, at a meeting among 30 Tsukunft activists and members of the Bund leadership, a debate was held on the question of Jewish armed uprising in view of the reports of murders in Poland. The movement adopted the following conclusions:

Our task is to urge youth at mortal risk and the young Jewish masses not to entertain false hope and to die with dignity as human beings; not to let [themselves] be led like lambs to the slaughter. To call today for active self-defence, as several irresponsible organizations have done, is to call for mass suicide. In contrast, we should urge them to behave wisely, and if it be death – then in dignity, as dignified people.[11]

It is difficult to get an accurate sense of the regnant trends of thought among young Bundists in view of these remarks. Their inner contradiction is perceptible. The Tsukunft members seemed to understand that armed self-defence was an essential alternative response to the genocide campaign, but they did not believe the time for it had come. To organize for action at that time, they believed, was an irresponsible and hasty act that placed the entire ghetto in existential danger.

In January 1942 members of the Zionist pioneering youth movements, under Yitzhak ('Antek') Zuckerman, made an initial attempt to enter into dialogue with Bundists and other ghetto political players to promote the formation of a Jewish fighting organization. The youth movement underground deemed it especially important to recruit the Bund for this organization, believing that its connections with Polish socialists outside the ghetto could be used to communicate with the Polish underground.[12] Indeed, the Bund used its connections with the PPS not only to secure sources of weapons and assistance but also to forward, through Polish underground channels, information to the government-in-exile in Poland and to Bund members in the United States. The leadership of the youth movements was very hopeful in early 1942 that the Polish government and the Western powers would act vigorously to halt the genocide as soon as they received accurate information on the developments in Poland.

The first attempts in January 1942 to conduct a joint meeting with the Bund did not work out well. As Zuckerman describes it, the Bund refused to meet with members of heHaluts because its activists did not regard this movement as a partner in political dialogue. Only when the leaders of Po'aley Tsiyon contacted the leaders of the Bund in March 1942 did Orzech and Blum agree to attend the joint parley.[13] Apart from Zuckerman, who represented heHaluts, several leaders of labour parties in the ghetto took part in the meeting: Lazar Levine and Stefan Grayek of Right Po'aley Tsiyon (a Zionist socialist party), Melech Faynkind and Hersh Berlinski of Left Po'aley Tsiyon and Orzech and Blum of the Bund. Zuckerman apprised the participants of the most recent information that had arrived on murders in various parts of Poland and proposed that a general Jewish fighting organization be formed. He also proposed that a joint representation of all parties and youth organizations be established – to represent the fighting organization *vis-à-vis* the Polish authorities – and spoke of organizing in the 'Aryan' sector of Warsaw to procure arms. The delegates from Po'aley Tsiyon favoured Zuckerman's proposal.[14] Hersh Berlinski, in his memoirs, describes Orzech's attitude in the following words:

> The Bund has always favoured self-defence. The history of the Bund attests to this. Were we not living in the wretched conditions of the ghetto, we would not be seated around one table with this political grouping. Only in the ghetto can such things happen. The ghetto is but a little world unto itself. The elimination of the ghetto depends on outside political players. The Bund is bound by fetters to international political actors. Their decisions apply to it and commit it. Therefore, the Bund will not belong to an entity whose tactics and action may clash with the general tactic. The Bund has struggle groups of its own. Other parties also have struggle groups of their own. From the conspiratorial point of view, the entire underground may collapse if a united organization is established. The Bund's struggle groups will not reveal its form of organization, its goals in this struggle, to the general fighting organization, because these are military secrets that have to be kept secret. For the reasons spelled out, the Bund will not participate in the general fighting organization.[15]

It was Zuckerman's impression that the Bund leaders were of two minds about participating in a joint fighting organization. Orzech presented a rigid, uncompromising stance, but Blum spoke with greater openness and willingness, even though he too ruled out the formation of such an organization under the conditions that prevailed in March 1942.[16]

The initiative to establish a joint fighting organization having failed, the left-Zionist organizations in the ghetto, in conjunction with communist activists, established the Anti-Fascist Bloc.[17] The Bund leaders refused to join this organization too, even though it was less strongly identified with Zionist parties because of the Communists' central role in forming it. Adolf Berman, an activist in Left Po'aley Tsiyon, asked Abrasha Blum why the Bund refrained from joining the Anti-fascist Bloc in view of its traditional anti-fascist posture. Blum replied that various political circumstances were to blame. It was inconvenient for the Bund to participate in an underground organization that included the Communists, who were isolated and poorly regarded by most Polish underground circles, including the right wing of the PPS. It was Berman's impression that Blum was discomforted about discussing the matter and that, personally, he favoured the Bund's participation.[18]

The Bund's opposition to joining a joint Jewish organization nipped in the bud the attempt to establish such an entity for armed resistance. In fact, only after the great deportation to Treblinka in September–October 1942 did an organization with genuine operational ability come into being in the ghetto. The Bund's posture in the March 1942 meeting also affected internal processes in the party, chiefly relations between the veteran leadership and the young leaders in Tsukunft.

Unlike other parties in the ghetto, which ruled out the idea of fighting on principle and as an existentially hazardous adventure, the Bund did not categorically dismiss the notion of warfare. Indeed, Orzech stressed that all underground entities should gird for armed struggle but ruled that they should do so separately.[19] He objected to a joint organization because 'The Bund practises socialist politics, not pan-Jewish politics.'[20] According to Edelman – the only Bundist in the Warsaw ghetto who mentioned these intermovement contacts in 1942 in his post-war memoirs – Orzech and Blum stressed at the meeting that the armed struggle should be coordinated with the Polish underground, for without its assistance a Jewish uprising could not possibly succeed.[21] The Bund's posture should probably be examined not only from the ideological standpoint but also, and foremost, from the practical point of view, in an attempt to understand the internal processes that the Bund experienced during those months.

Leon Feiner, the Bund's main liaison officer on the 'Aryan' side, laboured desperately during that time to strengthen relations with activists in the PPS and use them to acquire arms for the members of Tsukunft – a quest from which he came away empty-handed.[22] The participants in that meeting, all of whom were members of Zionist movements and parties, observed Orzech's resistance to a joint Jewish organization and considered it ideological. However, his objections also stemmed from pragmatic considerations. Orzech knew that the prospects of forming a fighting organization in the ghetto were nil without assistance from the Polish underground. Only through its connections with the Polish underground at that time – connections that no other Jewish player in the underground could match – was the Bund leadership able to appeal to the Free World and plead for its intervention as the murder campaign in Poland continued.[23] Indeed, a report by Feiner was sent to London in May 1942, containing detailed information on the genocide of the Jews throughout Poland and a vehement demand for Polish government and Western intervention to halt the murders by taking punitive actions against their perpetrators.[24]

Orzech sensed no contradiction between his view of the meaning of the Final Solution and his attitude as a socialist who regarded Poland as his home. He and other Bund leaders realized that the destruction of the Jews was unparalleled in the Nazi regime's panoply of repression, but they continued to number themselves among the Polish socialist underground movement that sought to inaugurate a new world for the state and the inhabitants of post-war Poland. Among the young Bundists, by contrast, a perceptible change was occurring. They saw, the idea of pan-Jewish struggle as the proper response, as the Nazis' murderous actions steadily gathered momentum. Even they, however, did not regard their cause as pronouncedly Jewish. Instead, they deemed it a struggle against fascism and on behalf of a free and egalitarian Poland – a struggle that the Jews were as duty-bound to prosecute as were the other progressive underground movements in Poland. In its edition of February–March 1942, *Yugent Shtime* urged the Jewish to struggle jointly with the young Polish socialists against the Nazi 'vandalism'. The goal of the struggle was to fulfil 'the idea of a free Poland and the liberation of the Jewish masses and all of humanity'.[25]

At that time, Tsukunft elected five group leaders: Avraham Fayner, Zalman Freidrich, Szmuel Kostrinski, Leyb Speichler and Marek Edelman.[26] Even these young Bundists, however, found it hard to take the final step and cross the bridge to general Jewish partnership in warfare against the Germans. They may have been inhibited by the party leadership; they may have believed it possible to recruit young forces among the Polish socialist underground for their struggle. Be this as it may, their agreement in principle to embark on joint Jewish warfare against the Nazis originated not in an ideological transformation but, in the main, in the tradition of anti-fascist struggle on which these young people had been raised for years. The Jewish tragedy merely motivated them to move toward application of the idea of organizing for war. For this purpose, they were willing to collaborate with other young people in the ghetto and with young Poles. The young Bundists entertained vain hopes about the ability of their counterparts on the Polish Left outside the ghetto to help. Contrary to the estimation of Zuckerman and members of the pioneering youth movements, the Bund lacked the kind of relations with the socialist underground that could result in substantial assistance in procuring arms. Sufficient quantities of weapons could be provided only by the leadership of the armed Polish underground, the Home Army (Armia Krajowa: AK) and few members of the PPS underground who interacted with the Bund had any influence among them.

CRISES AND COLLAPSE

In early May 1941, the Bund underground was dealt a severe blow – the first in a series of crises that would last until the summer of 1942. Hennoch Rus described the event in his Tsukunft diary:

> A young Jew came to Saba's house and asked about her, saying that a friend of hers wanted to see her urgently in the street. Since Saba was not at home, the young man asked where she could be found. Since they did not suspect a thing, they gave him the address of Saba's workplace. At the factory they met with Saba, examined her, and sent her to the hospital ... Saba had come down with a dangerous illness ... Because of her severe illness ... and because of the fear that she would infect others, they put her brothers and sisters into quarantine. That brought the activity to a halt.[27]

Seventeen-year-old Alter Bas (known as 'Saba' in the underground) was captured with Bund underground newspapers in his possession. According to Rus's account, Bas was the victim of prior searches and surveillance; there may also have been a denunciation. He was interned in the terrifying Gestapo prison in Warsaw, the Pawiak Prison, along with several PPS activists in the Polish resistance. His Bund comrades, fearing that the Germans would force him to reveal details about the movement and its activists, removed people who had been in close contact with Bas from Warsaw. This paralysed Tsukunft's underground activity for some time, until the storm blew over and it became evident that Bas had told his interrogators nothing of substance about the Tsukunft underground. Young Bas was eventually sent to Auschwitz as a political prisoner; his comrades in Warsaw received the report of his death in April 1942.[28]

The Bund's underground infrastructure in the *Generalgouvernement*, which relied heavily on PPS liaison officers, collapsed again in the summer of 1941. In June of that year, Tselemenski handed the Polish liaison Jadwiga Wyszyńska, whose name Maurycy Orzech had received from PPS activists, a parcel of Bund underground newspapers for delivery to members in Częstochowa, Piotrków-Trybunalski, Tomaszów-Mazowiecki, Kraków and Radom. On the train to Częstochowa, the Gestapo captured the Polish liaison officer, and Tselemenski, who was aboard the train, rushed back to Warsaw and gave the party leadership the bad news.[29] After capturing Wyszyńska, the Gestapo began to arrest Bund members in various towns, including all Bund leaders who were active in the *Judenrat* of Piotrków.

Eleven Bund members in Piotrków were arrested and, on 13 September 1941, were deported to Auschwitz and murdered. Ignacy Samsonowicz and Leon Kimelman managed to escape to Warsaw; Ya'acov Leber fled to Częstochowa. Before banishing them to Auschwitz, the Gestapo interrogated several activists, especially Tanchum Fraynd, to obtain the names of the Bund undergrounders in Warsaw who had sent the newspapers.[30] Bund activists were also arrested in Kraków, Tomaszów-Mazowiecki and Częstochowa.[31] To all intents and purposes, this marked the end of the party's underground work outside of Warsaw. Tselemenski, the most important liaison officer of the Central Committee in Warsaw, refrained from leaving the ghetto for about a year lest he be captured and interned.[32] For fear that the Gestapo would also begin to arrest members of the leadership in Warsaw, party activists occasionally swapped places of residence in the ghetto. Sonya Nowogrodzki apprised her husband in New York of this development: 'I've written to you that many members of our family [party members] have moved because of the new situation that has come about.'[33]

PPS members mediated between the Bund leadership in Warsaw and movement members in Wilno after the Germans occupied the latter town in the summer of 1941. In July of that year, Klayn met with Władysław Ryńca, a Polish socialist who lived in Wilno. Ryńca brought with him from Wilno several letters from Bund activists there – Grisha Yaszunski and Herman Kruk. Relations between Bund leaders and PPS members in Wilno were established by Irena Liszczyńska, a young PPS member who was acquainted with several Bundists employed in workshops in that town. At her initiative, Ryńca met with Bund activists and agreed to deliver their letters to fellow Bundists in Warsaw. Ryńca, a friend of Zagórski's, received money and letters from David Klayn in Warsaw and forwarded them to Bund members in Wilno. Contact between the Bund leadership in Warsaw and members in Wilno, by means of Ryńca, continued until April 1942, when the Germans embarked on genocidal *Atkionen* in the Warsaw ghetto. In addition to letters and money, the Polish liaison officer provided the

Bund leadership with first reports on murders in the Wilno area and eastern Poland. He even entered the ghetto in February–March 1942 and met with members of the party's Central Committee.[34]

On the night of 18 April 1942 the Germans carried out a planned murder raid in the Warsaw ghetto. SS men entered the ghetto and availed themselves of the Jewish *Ordnungdienst* to locate the homes of various underground activists and several of 'the Thirteen', a group of Gestapo agents under Avraham Gantsvaych. The Germans raided their homes and murdered 52 people, including the economist and demographer Menachem Linder, who had been working with Emanuel Ringelblum and was one of the most important cultural activists in the ghetto,[35] and several activists in the Tsukunft underground – Yosl Laroch, Moshe Goldberg, Moshe and Esther Shklar and Pesach Zuckerman.[36] Sonya Nowogrodzki and Lozer Klog, an editor and publisher in the Bund's underground press, spent that night away from their apartments after having been tipped off about the raid.[37]

The Gestapo informed Adam Czerniaków that the murders were meant as a punishment for illegal activity and for issuing underground publications. Czerniaków summoned public activists who were involved in these publications, evidently including Orzech, and asked them to take action to squelch the underground press. Czerniaków stated with emphasis that the continued activity of the underground press was placing the entire ghetto in existential danger.[38]

From the undergrounders' standpoint, the murder *Aktion* in the ghetto was a preliminary phase in the planned murder of all the interned Jews. At this time, shortly before the large deportation from the *Generalgouvernement*, the Nazis were murdering political activists and party members in other ghettos as well. On the night of 27–28 April 1942, approximately 70 members of various parties were arrested in Radom, including two who belonged to the Bund. Ringelblum reported murders in Kraków, Tarnów, Ostrowiec, Częstochowa, Kielce and other localities.[39] The Germans evidently wished to wipe out the political and underground leadership in the ghetto, lest it inspire the Jews to rebel and put up resistance to the impending deportations. *Za Naszą i Waszą Wolność* responded to the events of 18 April as follows:

> The Germans shot Jews who dealt in matters contrary to their interests, who dealt in politics, and who published underground literature in the ghetto. Socialists were shot. Who is spreading these rumours in the ghetto? Everyone who's benefiting from ghetto life, from the plenitude that they've been given … What

about the murdered people in Radom, several of whom were sent
to Auschwitz? [What about] the destruction of the Jews in Lublin,
Łódź, the Kolo district, the murder of 50 thousand Jews in Wilno?
… That night of bloodshed in the ghetto is but a small link in a
lengthy chain of savage murders of Jews by Hitler's people. The
Hitlerist criminals have already totally dispossessed the Jews with
their looting, but they cannot plunder our aspiration to liberty, our
will to struggle. Therefore, let us unite the ranks for struggle.[40]

The events of 18 April marked a further stage in the undermining
of the underground structure of the Bund, which had already been dealt
a severe blow in 1941. Tsukunft activists were bewildered about the
presence of a relatively large group of Bundists on the list of wanted
persons. The climate of suspicion and fear, prompted by the belief that
denunciation had led to the inclusion of Tsukunft activists among the
victims, gave rise to an internal investigation by the Tsukunft leadership against Leon Dyamant, a member of the five-person cell to which
one of the victims, Moshe Goldberg, had belonged. Dyamant, an eccen-
tric and unstable person, was a barber who had joined a cell whose
members, including Goldberg, were all barbers. These members, all
closely associated with the Bund even though some were not actively
involved in underground work, knew that Goldberg took part in
circulating the underground press and had occasionally obtained from
him copies to read. The Bundists' suspicions targeted Dyamant after
two additional members of the cell were murdered in the events of 18
April. In their surveillance of the suspect, they saw Dyamant convers-
ing openly with known Gestapo informers in the ghetto.[41]

In June 1942 the Tsukunft members who investigated the 18 April
events wrote a detailed report on their suspicions concerning Dyamant.
This document was meant for the Bund Central Committee but does
not seem to have reached it. The veteran leaders of the Bund, like other
underground activists, had gone into hiding and moved from place to
place to forestall a further provocation. Orzech himself spent some
time in hiding on the 'Aryan' side of Warsaw.[42] In their report, the
Tsukunft members express the conclusion that Dyamant had indeed
denounced Goldberg and his comrades. He consorted with Gestapo
informers, led an ostentatious and wasteful life, absented himself for
many days without informing anyone of his whereabouts, and routinely
spread reports in the ghetto that he was receiving the Bund underground
press. The members recommended that he be punished in a manner
befitting the crime of provocation.[43] The murders on the night of blood-

shed in April 1942 were the third blow that the Bund underground absorbed. The organizational weakness of the Bund underground became evident again. It is true that the Tsukunft and Bund leaders were spared, because they, like the heads of the other parties and organizations, knew how to prepare for an expected German provocation, went deep into the underground, and were less familiar to the ghetto population at large. However, the factor that actually impaired the Bund's underground activity was the capture of rank-and-file members. Tsukunft was less resistant than the pioneering youth movements to the penetration of provocateurs and Gestapo agents. In early 1942 of all times, as reports of genocide came in, Tsukunft attempted to recruit additional members for the movement and its various settings. It seems that in disseminating the underground press, Tsukunft also abandoned all precautions. The members of Tsukunft's underground cells worked at one location, sometimes lacked a shared background in movement activity, and felt no sense of collective responsibility to the movement framework specifically.

The fact that Tsunkunft and the Bund generally predicated their underground actions on outside aid and support from the PPS also proved, after the fact, to be dangerous. In two cases, the abduction of Alter Bas and the capture of the Bund's underground publications several months later, the Gestapo manhunt was aimed not at the Bundist underground but at underground activities of Polish circles. Bas was treated as a Polish political prisoner and the Bund underground publications were seized in the possession of a young woman member of the Polish socialist resistance. However, the Bund's relations with these socialist underground circles led indirectly to the uncovering of the movement's underground activists, for otherwise the Gestapo would not have reached them at all. The Germans took no interest whatsoever in the Jews and their forbidden political activity, of course.

Thus, at this critical juncture in the formation of a Jewish fighting organization in the ghetto, Tsukunft toppled into organizational disarray. Unlike the Tsukunft underground, the Zionist pioneering youth movements managed to preserve their organizational strength almost without disruption. They were deployed in smaller social units than an open folk movement such as the Bund. The Zionist youth movements had an intimate, relatively closed structure that did not rely on broad circles of support and hardly availed itself of activists in the Polish resistance. This characteristic ultimately protected these movements and their members as the great deportation from the Warsaw Ghetto loomed.

THE ROAD TO JOINT JEWISH WARFARE

The Germans began to deport the Jews of Warsaw on 22 July 1942. From then until 10 September 1942, with brief respites, 300,000 Jews were removed from the ghetto and sent to death in the gas chambers of Treblinka.[44] As soon as the *Aktion* in the ghetto began, the underground public agencies convened to devise methods of response. Participating in the meeting, which evidently took place on 23 July, were representatives of Left Po'aley Tsiyon Agudath Israel, the Communists, the General Zionists, Right Po'aley Tsiyon and the Bund. Alongside them were leaders of the the Zionist youth movements. The youth movement members and the delegates from the leftist parties insisted that the deportations warranted an active response. Edelman wrote that Bund activists consulted several times during the first days of the deportation (22 or 23 July) and that on one such occasion the leaders of the Bund's five underground groups met. According to Edelman, they decided that an immediate attempt should be made to spare the activists from the deportation, because they could not embark on active self-defence. At these meetings, the Bund leaders had met with the main activists in Tsukunft and also a member of the PPS. The participants in the 23 July meeting expressed their support of resistance to the *Aktion* and expected assistance from socialist underground circles to arrive at any moment, allowing the Tsukunft underground to respond to the manhunt taking place in the ghetto streets.[45] Apart from these meetings, no attempts were made to convene the activist corps of the party for consultations. Important Bund activists left the ghetto during the deportation and went into hiding on the 'Aryan' side. Abrasha Blum asked Goldstein and Tselemenski to do the same in order to assist Feiner in his efforts to arrange sources of assistance for the Bund. Orzech joined his family, which had already gone into hiding outside the ghetto. Sonya Nowogrodzki was captured in the middle of August 1942 and perished in Treblinka.[46] Two hundred and fifty children were sent to Treblinka for extermination that month, as was the entire staff of the Bund orphanage that had been set up in the building occupied before the war by the Medem Sanitorium in Miedzeszyn, a short distance from Warsaw. The Bund lost almost all of its activists during the months of the great deportation. Among approximately 500 activists and confidantes with whom underground liaison had been maintained, only 20–25 young activists remained in late September 1942, when they gathered in a jointly held apartment on Franciszkańska Street. There, they sank into a gloomy and utterly despairing frame of mind in view of the loss of their families and their movement comrades.[47]

In late July 1942 (or early August), Bund member Zygmunt (Zalman) Friedrich was dispatched from Warsaw to find out where the deportation trains were being sent. Using connections with a railroad employee who belonged to the PPS, he travelled to Sokołow, where he met with Bund member Azriel Wallach, who had escaped from Treblinka.[48] Wallach apprised Friedrich of events in the camp, and on the basis of the information that Friedrich brought back to the ghetto, the 20 September 1942 edition of the Bund newspaper *Oyf der Vakh* (On the Rampart) ran an article under the headline, 'Warsaw Jews Being Murdered in Treblinka'. The article refuted the lies that the Germans had been disseminating in the ghetto, by means of postcards sent by deportees, to the effect that the Jews of Warsaw were being sent to Brześć nad Bugiem, Pińsk, Białystok and other locations. Then the article stated:

> It was all a lie! ... All of the trains carrying Warsaw Jews went to Treblinka, where the Jews were murdered in a horrifying fashion. What was the actual fate of the deported Jews? ... Treblinka is the first stop on the Małkinia–Siedlce line ... The camp at Treblinka is 1–2 square kilometres in area ... The newly arrived people ... were undressed, [gathered] in groups of 200, and sent to a 'shower' ... from which no one emerged ...[49]

On 28 July 1942 members of HaShomer haTsa'ir, Dror-heHaluts and Akiva (a non-socialist Zionist youth organization) established the ŻOB (Żydowska Organizacja Bojowa), the Jewish Fighting Organization. The members of its command were Shmuel Braslav, Yitzhak Zuckerman, Zivia Lubetkin, Mordechai Tenenbaum and Yosef Kaplan. The group selected four representatives (Tosia Altman, Frumka Plotnicka, Leah Perlstein and Arie Wilner) to operate on the 'Aryan' side and to attempt to obtain weapons for the organization.[50] The deportations, however, progressively eradicated all political frameworks apart from the youth movements. Practically speaking, this front did not undertake any joint activity, as major activists went into hiding and many members were captured and sent to Treblinka. The Bund members, realizing that they would not be able to organize any real self-defence in the ghetto, decided to urge the ghetto Jews – in a poster written by Orzech – not to report to the transports and to resist deportation.[51]

The Zionist youth movements performed more successfully than the veteran parties' activists in their efforts to spare their members from the deportation. The young people, who had left their families and formed groups, lived together and worked in German workshops in the ghetto, which gave them some immunity from deportation. Tsukunft, as part of a party organization, suffered from the weakness of the party framework. Only at the end of the great deportation, when the veteran leadership was no longer operative in the ghetto, did the leaders of Tsukunft assume leadership of the vestiges of the movement and adopt the *modus operandi* of the youth movements.

When the great deportation ended, the Tsukunft leadership began to try to organize the surviving young members of the movement and to bring the Bund into the ŻOB. In late October 1942, members of HaShomer haTsa'ir, heHaluts-Dror and Left Po'aley Tsiyon met to devise the organization's operating methods. The senior party people wished to establish a political framework as an adjunct to the fighting organization. The need for such a framework, which would provide appropriate representation in contacts with political players outside the ghetto, led to the formation of the Jewish National Committee (Żydowski Komitet Narodowy: ŻKN) alongside the ŻOB.

As soon as the political and organizational structures of the ŻOB were formed, the members of the organization attempted to co-opt the Bund. After the war, Edelman recalled that the Tsukunft leadership had held lengthy debates on whether or not to join the ŻOB, and the proponents and opponents of this move commanded equal numbers. The issue was resolved when Hennoch Rus, who initially objected to joining, changed his mind.[52]

In November 1942 Mordechai Anielewicz, Yitzhak Zuckerman, Hersh Berlinski and Yochanan Morgenstern (Right Po'aley Tsiyon) met with Tsukunft leaders Blum and Shneidmil. The Bund refused to join the ŻKN because by so doing, it believed, it would renounce its autonomous representation *vis-à-vis* the Polish government. However, it agreed to join the ŻOB. At this meeting, a decision was made to establish a coordinating committee (Komitet Koordynacyjny) through which the Bund would interface with the National Committee. After this meeting, Shneidmil was annexed to the ŻOB staff and Abrasha Blum was posted to the coordinating committee. A short time later, Edelman replaced Shneidmil as the Bund's representative on the ŻOB staff. Hersh Berlinski considered this an indication that the Bund was uninterested in becoming active in the ŻOB, and Zuckerman believed that Shneidmil, who at approximately forty was older than the other staff members, felt ill at ease in the company of the young people who collaborated with him on the joint staff.[53]

Edelman made further reference to his appointment as the Bund representative to the ŻOB joint command in his conversation with Hanna Krall:

> I wasn't the one who was suppose to be there. It should have been ... Well, it doesn't matter. Let's call him 'Adam'. He graduated before the war from military college and took part in September 1939 campaign ... One day the two of us were walking together along Leszno Street, there were crowds of people, and all of a sudden some SS men started shooting. The crowd scrambled away desperately. And so did he ... It all actually happened without a single word, from one day to the next: he simply quit all activity. And when the first meeting of the command group was about to be held, he was useless for participating in it. So I went instead.[54]

It is hard to determine exactly why Shneidmil was replaced by Edelman. It seems that apart from the reasons mentioned, Blum and his comrades decided that Shneidmil, a man with military experience, would invest his time in the immensely difficult task of organizing the Bund's fighting groups. Abrasha Blum was the key figure in revitalizing the remnants of the movement after a political arrangement that allowed him to join the ŻOB was worked out.[55] Vladka Mid described the prevailing trend of thought among young members of the Bund that month:

> Comrade Abrasha told us that another general Jewish coordinating committee had been formed in the ghetto, made up of representatives of various political organizations. Its function is to gather up the surviving forces and organize armed resistance ... And he spoke as though he were answering my question: 'Yes, it's true, we are few, most of our comrades and functionaries have been deported. But we're not alone. Other groups and organizations have also begun to make preparations. Now we have to go about our work with the help of the comrades who survived in the workshops ... We have to organize the groups and prepare them for active struggle.'[56]

In accordance with decisions made upon the establishment of the ŻOB, each movement and party was tasked with creating its own fighting groups. According to Edelman, groups that lived together were formed in late October – in the main ghetto under the command of Baruch Pelts and Yitzhak Goldstein, in the 'brush-makers' shops' area under Yorek Blons and Yanek Bilak, and in the Többens and Schulz shops under Avraham Feiner, Nachum Chmielnicki and Velvel Rozowski.[57] These organizational measures were dauntingly difficult because the Tsukunft leadership in the ghetto had to locate surviving members and restore, *ex nihilo*, the movement framework that had disintegrated during the deportation.

In late 1942 and early 1943 Jews were transferred from the Többens and Schulz shops to the Trawniki and Poniatowa labour camps near Lublin. Walther Többens attempted to persuade his workers to report for deportation and explained that they were being relocated not for extermination but for labour (as indeed was the case). However, the intended deportees perceived this as another case of German deceit.[58]

The Jews listed for deportation to the camps in Lublin included several Tsukunft activists in the ŻOB, such as Velvel Rozowski and Moshe Kaufman – who, according to Edelman, managed to escape from the train and remain in the ghetto.[59] The Bund activists in the ŻOB fiercely criticized the party leadership on the 'Aryan' side for not having done enough to equip the Bund fighting groups with essential weapons. The leaders of Tsukunft and the movement's activists in the ŻOB – Blum, Shneidmil, Edelman, Avraham Feiner, Khazkel Filozof, Hennoch Rus and Moshe Kaufman, along with Tselemenski, who liaised between the ghetto and the 'Aryan' side – held a meeting in January 1943. At this meeting, Edelman said that the party leadership was not doing enough to encourage young people to join the ŻOB. The Bund did not have enough fighting groups, he said, and pro-Bund young people who worked in the Többens and Schulz workshops could not be mobilized for the Bund fighting groups for lack of arms. In contrast, the youth movements' fighting groups, Edelman alleged, were easier to join because of their sources of weapons.[60]

In the period between January and April 1943, the Bund, like the other movements in the ŻOB, made a desperate effort to secure sources of arms outside the ghetto. Apart from Blum, Shneidmil and Edelman, other Tsukunft activists who were members of the ŻOB joined the senior Bund leadership on the 'Aryan' side. Bund operatives outside the ghetto at this time included Zalman Friedrich, Michael Klepfisz, Tselemenski and Vladka Mid, who was sent by Blum to liaise with underground leaders outside the ghetto.[61] Orzech and Goldstein, members of the veteran Bund leadership, went into hiding outside the ghetto and played almost no role in the party's efforts to obtain weapons; the same may be said about Salo Fiszgrund and Leon Feiner, who represented the Bund on the coordinating committee.[62]

During those months, the Bund persisted in its efforts to secure sources of arms through its connections with members of the PPS. Feiner contacted PPS member Janek Kolikowski, who promised to obtain three handguns and several bricks of dynamite. In the end, a PPS man was captured with the handguns in his possession and Kolikowski was able to procure the dynamite only.[63] Michael Klepfisz managed to obtain, with PPS assistance, a formula for the preparation of firebombs and a small quantity of fuel to prepare them, which he brought to the ghetto.[64] However, Feiner swiftly realized how little assistance the PPS members were able to offer.[65] The major group within the PPS – composed of members of the WRN – identified with the Jews' struggle and favoured supplying the ghetto with arms but objected to meaningful participation in anti-Nazi warfare at the time that the Jews were planning armed resistance.

When the news of the mass murders at Katyń forest of Polish officers by the Soviets leaked out (during April–May 1943) there was much anger toward the Soviet Union in Polish underground circles and public opinion – even members of the pro-Soviet political organization in the Polish underground hesitated to call for armed resistance. The Polish masses, they knew, would construe such a message as a call to assist the murderers of the Polish officers and since their declared pro-Soviet attitudes had made them quite unpopular in Polish underground circles to begin with, they sought to soft-pedal their views.[66] To have advocated a joint Polish–Jewish rebellion in the spring of 1943, when the Warsaw ghetto uprising began, would have been unpopular both for strategic reasons and because of the prevailing political conditions in Poland. The Bundists realized that even the Polish socialists, their allies and partners in the class struggle, would not join them in armed resistance. In his memoirs, Tselemenski wrote that – as he had been told by friends in the PPS – members of the leftist underground had discussed the matter several times but ruled out participation in the rebellion unless the Germans began to perpetrate mass murder among the Polish population.[67] Ringelblum also made note of impressions he had acquired in the streets of Warsaw from PPS supporters. PPS members sympathized with the Jews' struggle and felt ill at ease about the business-as-usual ambiance of life in Polish Warsaw in the midst of the Jewish tragedy, but the socialist underground believed that emotions were no substitute for cold political and military calculus. A military uprising, the socialist underground ruled, should be launched when the conditions for this were ripe, as they were not in the spring of 1943.[68]

The process of Bund enlistment in the underground and in fighting organizations was different elsewhere in the *Generalgouvernement*
than in Warsaw. This is best illustrated in Częstochowa. Between March
and June 1942, youth movement members Yosef Kaplan, Arie Wilner,
Mordechai Anielewicz and Frumke Plotnicka brought reports about
the mass murders in eastern Poland to the Częstochowa ghetto. The
news did not prompt the movements to organize jointly for self-defence,
in part because the Częstochowa *Judenrat* informed the Jews soothingly,
in the name of the Germans, that they were an essential labour force
and therefore would not be harmed.[69] Large-scale *Aktionen* in the ghetto
began on 22 September 1942 and lasted until 8 October. During that
time about 40,000 Jews from Częstochowa were taken to Treblinka in
several series of transports; the 6,000 or so who remained were gathered
in a small ghetto that became a labour camp.

In late December 1942, after liaison officer Rivka Glants of Dror
delivered several handguns and some money from the ŻOB command
in Warsaw, a joint fighting organization was established in Częstochowa.
It embraced members of the leftist youth movements and groups, the
Communists, the Bund, Left Po'aley Tsiyon and the non-partisans.
The few Bund activists in Częstochowa did not deliberate about whether
or not to join the united command, perhaps because by that time the
Bund had already integrated into the Jewish fighting organization in
Warsaw, or perhaps because of the different circumstances in the
Częstochowa ghetto, where the fighting organization was not estab-
lished until after the large-scale deportation of Jews to Treblinka had
been completed. Mordechai Zilberberg of HaShomer haTsa'ir was
installed at the head of the fighting organization; Somek Abramowicz of
the PPR was chosen as his deputy. The Bund delegate to the expanded
ŻOB command was Mordechai Kushnir.[70]

In Piotrków-Trybunalski the Bund continued to engage in underground activity even after its underground had more or less collapsed
in the summer of 1941. This activity was coordinated by three members
of Tsukunft. In April 1943 they established, along with Communists
and youth movement members, an underground organization that
contacted the ŻOB in order to lead a group of fighters to the forest[71]
– an initiative that did not succeed. In July 1943 the small ghetto established in Piotrków-Trybunalski after the large deportation to Treblinka
in October 1942 was liquidated. Some 1,700 Jews remained in and
around the city in several labour camps established by enterprises that
had factories there. The workers who remained in the small ghetto
and, subsequently, in the labour camps included several Bund members.

1. Jews being transferred into the Warsaw ghetto.

2. Jews selling armbands with the Star of David in the Warsaw ghetto.

3. Beggars in the streets of the Warsaw ghetto

4. A sweetshop in the Warsaw ghetto.

5. A coffee shop in the Warsaw ghetto.

6. Selling potatoes in the Warsaw ghetto.

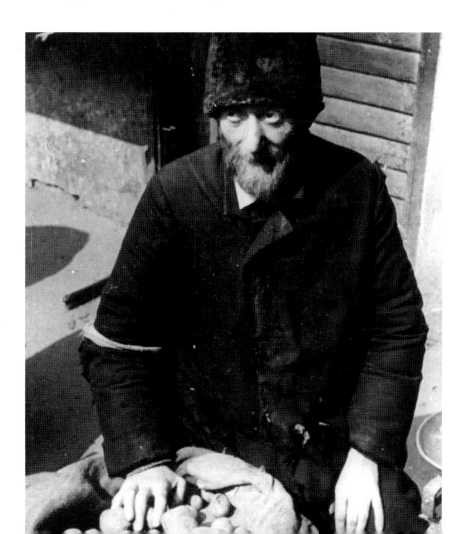

№ 038944

LEBENSMITTELKARTE
KARTA ŻYWNOŚCIOWA

Gültig für den Monat Oktober 1941 — Ważna na miesiąc październik 1941

Kreis
Name
Wohnort
Strasse

Nicht übertragbar — Bez prawa odstąpienia
Der Verlust hält Gewalt
W razie zagubienia duplikat wydany nie będzie!

KUNDEN(LISTEN)NUMMERN — NUMERY LIST KONSUMENTÓW

I Nr		II Nr	
III Nr		IV Nr	

96. 300 Kalorien täglich wurden pro Kopf der Bevölkerung im Warschauer Getto offiziell zuerkannt. Ein Mensch braucht täglich mindestens 2400 Kalorien.

7. A ration card, issued by the *Judenrat* in the Warsaw ghetto.

8. One of the street markets in the Warsaw ghetto.

9. Smugglers bringing goods into the Warsaw ghetto.

10. The Jewish police in the Warsaw ghetto.

11. Jews about to be deported, Umschlagplatz.

12. Henryk
Erlich.

13. Wiktor Alter.

14. Abrasha Blum and his wife, Luba.

They made contact with PPS underground activists, who provided them with publications of the Polish socialist underground and reports on the Jewish uprisings in Warsaw in January and April 1943.[72]

In the Łódź ghetto the wave of transports that began in late 1941 did not lead to the establishment of a fighting organization, as happened in Warsaw and other localities. The special conditions there did not allow the young movement and party members in the ghetto to take any step toward armed resistance, and the matter did not figure in their discussions. In September 1942, thousands of elderly, sick and children were deported from the Łódź ghetto to extermination in Chełmno in the great *shpere*. The Jews of the ghetto did not deduce the true meaning of the Final Solution from this traumatic event; rather they continued to believe that the productive elements in the ghetto would survive. Furthermore, the ghetto remained relatively calm from September 1942 until its liquidation in August 1944; this reinforced the feeling that the ghetto population was not in danger as long as it maintained a strict regime of labour.[73] This does not mean that the reports on mass murder of Jews in other parts of occupied Poland did not reach the ghetto, including the activists in Tsukunft. On 15 April 1943 Bono Winer recorded in his diary 'the report about Treblinka. A terrifying feeling. But the time of revenge will come.'[74] However, Tsukunft members in the ghetto, like the rest of the ghetto population, were convinced that holding a job would render them immune from the deportation that they expected and that they would survive by the simple expedient of obtaining jobs at the workshops.[75] In August 1943 approximately 70 members of Tsukunft groups in the ghetto worked in various places, as did some 50 teenagers who belonged to SKIF, for whom separate groups had been established. The framework of underground operations, which included lectures, talks and cultural activity, was transferred to the workshops. Groups for young people met once a month; group coordinators' events in activists' apartments took place less frequently.[76] The activists' efforts to maximize the number of young people and party members who held jobs caused an increase in the number of members who toiled in the workshops. In September 1943 there were 118 members in Tsukunft and SKIF groups;[77] by November 1943 the numbers had reached 145 and 69 respectively.[78] This upturn in membership of Bund groups was not motivated by ideological decisions, since although the group members were Bund sympathizers, as Winer explained, they joined mainly because of the relative security that participation in a political organization conferred. The decisive considerations pertained to personal security, not to ideology.[79]

During the final deportations from Łódź in the summer of 1944, the Bund leadership, in concert with other political actors, tried to urge the remaining Jews to put up passive resistance. In August 1944 Moshe Lederman and Ya'acov Nirenberg, the longest-tenured Bund leaders in the ghetto, along with leaders of the Communists, Left Po'aley Tsiyon and the Zionists, met with Rumkowski. The issue of the Jews' response to the liquidation of the ghetto and the deportation to Auschwitz was brought up at the meeting. Nirenberg's memoirs state that the participants could not agree whether to urge the Jews to resist the deportation passively.[80] This remained the situation until the tragic denouement of the ghetto, and the deportation of its population to Auschwitz, indicated that the party leaders were unable to inspire the remnants of Łódź Jewry to offer resistance during the last weeks of the ghetto.

WILNO AND BIAŁYSTOK

By early 1941, after the Soviets carried out a spate of arrests of Bund members and Jewish trade union activists in 1939, and after the party leadership went to the United States in early 1941, the party's presence in Wilno had diminished to a small group only. When the German invasion began on 22 June 1941, many Jews fled from Wilno for their lives. They included several party members, such as Shlomo Hirszhorn (a Bund activist from Lublin), Yankl Tropyansky and Mordechai and Lena Yevzerov. The Yevzerovs returned to Wilno about two weeks later, after finding the retreat routes to the east blocked by the rapid advance of the Wehrmacht. Herman Kruk described the acute indecision he experienced at that time – whether to stay in Wilno, which was about to fall to the Germans, or to head eastward with the fleeing convoys. As Kruk explains it, he decided to remain in Wilno despite the impending danger of the Germans because he lacked the strength to resume migrating after having left Warsaw at the beginning of the war and having been a refugee. Paty Kremer, the 75-year-old widow of Arkady Kremer, one of the founders of the Bund in 1897, also decided to stay in Wilno.[81] Most Bund members who stayed in Wilno were refugees from Warsaw who had reached Wilno after the war began; along with them was a small group of indigenous members of Tsukunft and SKIF. Because they were not well known in Wilno, the Soviet regime did not discover and arrest them as it did other members of the party. On 4 July 1941 the first *Judenrat*, a ten-member panel, was established in Wilno.

Shortly before this, public activists and members of Jewish parties convened for a meeting in which Bund activists took part: Grisza Jaszunski of Warsaw; Yoel Fischmann, an activist in the local association of artisans and a member of the former *kehillah* council; Berel Vidman, also a member of the Wilno *kehillah* council representing the Bund; and Nachum Wapner. Bund members were not, however, represented on this *Judenrat*, which was chaired by Shaul Trotsky. Only when the *Judenrat* expanded to 24 members on 24 July 1942, did Grisza Jaszunski and Yoel Fischmann join, evidently after negotiations between the *Judenrat* and these Bund members.[82]

On 24 September 1941, when the Germans dissolved the Wilno *Judenrat*, Jaszunski and Fischmann were thrown into prison. After the Wilno Jews who remained alive following the mass murders in Ponar were rounded up into two ghettos, the two officials were released and joined the five-member *Judenrat* that was established in Ghetto A. Shortly after the ghettoization, Bund activists convened and discussed the party's areas of activity in view of the new realities. Participating in the meeting, apart from Fischmann and Jaszunski, were Paty Kramer, Hirsch Gotgeshtalt and his wife (Bund members from Warsaw), Herman Kruk and Avraham Chwoynik, the most prominent member of Tsukunft and a perceived leader of young Bundists in the ghetto. Those in attendance assigned Kruk to organize the public library in the ghetto, Gotgeshtalt to work for the *Judenrat* labour department and his wife Miriam in the education department, and Chwoynik to work for the housing department. Evidently the Bund members also wished to name Kruk their representative *vis-à-vis* the *Ordnungsdienst* (the Jewish police), but Kruk objected to this when it became apparent that the *Ordnungsdienst* was controlled by Ya'acov Gens and colleagues from the Zionist Revisionist party.[83]

In Wilno, the Bund and its activists experienced a totally different process from that in Warsaw and in other ghettos in the *General-gouvernement*. The cadre of party activists in this town, nearly all of whom were refugees as opposed to long-time residents, rose for the first time under the occupation to major positions of influence and public life in the ghetto. In view of the events that befell the Jews of Wilno, especially the liquidation of Ghetto B (where Jews who were not able-bodied, mainly the sick and elderly, had been concentrated) in October 1941, party activists began to hold Bund leaders who had ranking positions in the *Judenrat* in lesser esteem. At this time, various stances and attitudes concerning the party's course of action rose to the fore among Bund members in Wilno. Members of the veteran leadership, especially those who had belonged to the *Judenrat* or who had worked in its departments, spared no effort in the first six months of 1942 to maintain the positions of power and influence that they had claimed in the ghetto as a counterweight to the rising star of Gens and his police force. However, a turning point occurred in July 1942, when Gens was named the representative of the ghetto, which was to culminate in April 1943 in the total ousting of Jaszunski from the *Judenrat*. The veteran leadership, which attempted without great success to mobilize activists in other parties – Communists and members of Po'aley Tsiyon – for its struggle against Gens, found itself steadily banished from all the positions of influence that it had attained at the beginning of the ghetto era.[84] The Bund members in the ghetto argued to Gens and the activists of the Zionist parties that they had been discriminated against in the apportionment of basic living needs and jobs in the *Judenrat* institutions.[85] The diminishing status of the Bund leaders in the ghetto was also reflected in fierce disputes and a schism within the Bund in early 1942 between the young members and the veteran leadership as to whether the party should join the newly founded United Partisan Organization, the FPO (Faraynikte Partizaner Organizatsye).

The Wilno ghetto was the first in which a Jewish fighting organization came into being. At the end of January 1942, about three weeks after the Zionist youth group published its call for resistance, members of HaShomer haTsa'ir, Ha-No'ar ha-Tsiyoni, the Communists and Betar (the youth organization of the Zionist Revisionists) established the FPO. No Bund members participated in the inter-movement contacts that led to this action. In early 1942 the young Bundists were not yet cohesive enough to join the other movements in the fighting organization that had been formed, whereas the party's senior leadership in the ghetto, which functioned within the ambit of the *Judenrat*, categorically ruled out Bund enlistment in any fighting entity.[86] At that time, the Bund in the ghetto had not yet begun regular underground activity, and at the first large party meeting held in the ghetto at the late date of February 1942, with the participation of 13 activists including two from Tsukunft, Avraham Chwojnik and Shmuel Kaplinski, the Bund leaders, Jaszunski and Fischmann, rejected the idea of joining the FPO. The young Bundists opposed the party leaders' stance in this matter and began, on their own counsel, to negotiate with the FPO leadership in order to join the organization.[87]

The decision to establish the joint fighting organization was made in the course of talks between members of HaShomer haTsa'ir and various political players in Wilno, including the Communists. Evidently

Kovner and his comrades hesitated to appeal to the young Bund members in the expectation that they would reject the idea of participating in a pan-Jewish fighting entity. In Kovner's opinion, the Bund had taken a strong anti-communist turn in January 1942 because of the heavy and terrible residue of the murder of Alter and Erlich, and this was an obstacle to the enlistment of young Tsukunft members in the organization.[88]

However, it was not the murder of Erlich and Alter that kept the young Bundists from joining the FPO. In January 1942 Erlich and Alter were still alive; one doubts whether the Bund members of the ghetto knew that they had been re-arrested in December 1941.[89] The resistance and hesitancy in the matter of joining the FPO originated mainly in internal problems and disagreements between the young Bundists and the veteran leadership.

About half a year after the FPO was established, the young Bund members joined it and Chwoynik became a member of the joint command. The internal disputes between the young Bundists and the veterans, who were active in the *Judenrat*, lasted into the summer of 1942. On 3 July 1942 the Bund members held another meeting at which, according to Kruk, they fell into two groups: 'passive' and 'active'. Kruk seems to be referring to members who participated in Bund activity in *Judenrat* institutions or in organizing the party's underground activity, as against the sort who were merely deemed sympathizers or fellow-travellers. The young members gathered momentum during those months as Gens' takeover of the ghetto, as noted, steadily weakened the source of the party leadership's influence in the *Judenrat*. As soon as the Bund in Wilno elected a new leadership in July 1942, party leaders Jaszunski and Vidman were ousted from the new Central Committee,[90] and the more activist group gradually assumed the positions of activists who had ruled out Bund participation in the FPO and resisted the consent and cooperation that the Tsukunft leaders had achieved with the heads of the other constituent movements in the FPO.

The struggle against the FPO waged in June 1943 by Gens and Salek Dessler, chief of the ghetto police, reverberated among Bund members, too. The young Bundists favoured any decision to respond with force if Gens and his police attempted to harm the FPO. The veteran Bund members objected to this and urged the young activists to rule out any action that might, in their estimation, endanger the ghetto. However, the young faction won this dispute, the Bund leadership resolving that the party would lend the FPO its *de facto* support.[91] In July 1943, in the course of the struggle between the FPO and Gens concerning the

capture of Yitzhak Wittenberg, the FPO commander, Chwoynik proposed, in discussions among members of the joint command, that FPO
members respond by committing suicide to any attempt by Gens and
his police to hand Wittenberg over to the Germans.[92]

Practically speaking, the Bund in the ghetto operated within two
separate frameworks after it joined the FPO. One framework was
comprised of the young members, whose loyalty to the goals and *modus
operandi* of the FPO transcended every party consideration; the other
was composed of the veteran leadership, which integrated itself into
the work of the *Judenrat* and wished that its young members in the
FPO would remain faithful to its policies and avoid actions that might
endanger the ghetto. The young and the veteran members in Wilno
disagreed not about the principle of joining the FPO, as had been the
case in Warsaw, but about the very existence of the organization, which,
in the opinion of the Bund leaders and many political activists in the
ghetto, placed the ghetto in palpable mortal jeopardy. Although Gens'
authoritarian personality made him unpopular, his policies were
amenable to most of the Jewish population, which believed that through
them the productive part of the ghetto had a slight chance of survival.

The young Bundists, like the Communists and members of Zionist
youth movements, ruled out the *Judenrat*'s policies and bruited war as
the only response to the Germans' genocidal actions against the Jews.
They obtained the trust of the other constituents of the FPO and
steered clear of ideological disputation. In September 1943, when the
ghetto was liquidated and its last survivors sent to labour camps in
Estonia, the FPO leadership decided to evacuate the remaining fighters
in the ghetto to the forest to carry on with the warfare. Shortly before
the evacuation, the Bundists debated the question of resorting to the
forests. The veteran leadership decided to join the rest of the Jews in
the camps; the young Bundists who belonged to the FPO, about 25 in
number,[93] decided to join their FPO comrades in the forest.[94] Almost
all of the Bund leaders in Wilno, including Fischmann, Gotgeshtalt,
Vidman and Kruk, perished in the labour camps in Estonia.[95] Chwoynik,
who for reasons of disability hesitated to join those who went to the
forest lest he become a burden to his comrades, was captured by the
Germans along with his girlfriend, Assia Bik, on 24 September 1943
as they passed through the sewers. Both were hanged.[96]

When contacts toward forming a fighting organization got under
way in the Białystok ghetto in the summer of 1942, members of
HaShomer haTsa'ir turned to the Communists and the Bundists in
the ghetto to establish a united Jewish front. Shalom Poports, aged 32,

a SKIF leader in Wilno who had relocated to Białystok before the war, participated in these meetings. He headed a group of ten young Bundists that did not hesitate to join other movements in Białystok to create a pan-Jewish fighting organization.[97]

Other young members of Tsukunft, along with several veteran Bund members who remained in Białystok, did not join Poports and his comrades when they became members of the fighting organization. The oppositionist group was headed by Yerahmiel Kostin, the de facto leader of the Bund in Białystok after the veterans had been imprisoned by the Soviets or left town.[98] Mordechai Rubinstein – a *Judenrat* functionary, principal of the Tshisho school before the war, and a Bund sympathizer – shared his attitude.

The internal dispute among Bund members on whether or not to join the fighting organization persisted even after Mordechai Tenenbaum-Tamaroff reached Białystok in November 1942 to establish such an organization in the ghetto. Tenenbaum aimed to create a shared organizational framework and to co-opt political groups that had not joined the 'A Front' of HaShomer haTsa'ir, the Communists and the aforementioned faction of the Bund. He discussed this matter with Bund members who objected to the formation of a joint fighting organization and criticized them sharply.[99] Tenenbaum was well acquainted with the contacts that had taken place in Warsaw in the spring of 1942 and the Bund's opposition to a joint Jewish fighting organization. There is no doubt that his criticism of the Bundists in Białystok was affected by this, even though these Bundists were not of the same mind as their comrades in Warsaw. Rubinstein and Kostin, two Bund leaders in Białystok who came out against the idea of warfare in January 1943, did not hold views identical to those of Orzech in Warsaw, who ruled out the possibility of a pan-Jewish partnership in anti-Nazi struggle on ideological and practical grounds. In Białystok, because it was clear that the Germans did not intend to kill all the Jews in the *Aktion* that began in February 1943, Rubinstein feared that an uprising launched in response to the foreseen *Aktion* would endanger the Jews left behind. Tenenbaum himself adopted the attitude of Efraim Barasz, the acting chairman of the *Judenrat*, that if the Germans deported 'only' six thousand Jews in the course of the February 1943 *Aktion*, as Barasz had been assured, the ŻOB would not respond with resistance.[100]

In Białystok the Bund underwent a process similar to that experienced by its members in Wilno. The young members, those active in SKIF and Tsukunft, did not hesitate to enlist in the initiative to create a fighting organization in conjunction with other political movements. The veteran group vacillated, not for ideological reasons but because of the realities of life in Białystok. This was a working, productive ghetto, possible in terms of its living conditions, and endowed with a leadership that the public liked and trusted. Therefore, the Jews in Białystok hoped, especially after the prospects of the war turned around in 1943, that the Germans would soon be defeated and the Red Army would reach Białystok before they could liquidate the ghetto.

Even now, memory of the spring of 1942, and the failure to establish a joint Jewish fighting organization in Warsaw at that time, makes it difficult to accurately assess the Bund's contribution towards establishing a Jewish fighting organization in the ghetto. Apart from the dispute about whether Orzech's refusal to participate in the youth movement members' initiative to establish a Jewish fighting organization truly caused no such organization to come into being in March–April 1942, it is necessary to examine the role of the Bund in the fighting organizations from a broad perspective that takes realities in other ghettos into account.

The response of Bund members to the question of joining a Jewish fighting organization was, as in other areas of Jewish existence at this time, not uniform. However, once the young Bund members decided to participate in a pan-Jewish uprising against the Nazis, the importance of ideological emphases and academic disputes diminished. The Zionist youth movements lent the uprising an historical significance that combined the Jewish aspiration for a national home with the struggle to defeat fascism and ordain a future of freedom and socialism; the Bund regarded the uprising as a step on the path to a free, socialist and democratic Poland in which Jews would be equally empowered citizens, and as a phase in the struggle of freedom-loving people to shake off the fascist yoke. In their very decision to take part in the Jewish fighting organizations, the members of Tsukunft made a momentous ideological choice and created a clear Jewish consensus on the historical meaning of the anti-Nazi Jewish uprising.[101]

From the time they decided to join the ŻOB and participate in pan-Jewish warfare against the Nazis, the young Bundists became a significant force in the history of the movement. Once the Bund abandoned its demand for joint Jewish–Polish struggle against the Nazis and soft-pedalled its protest against the absence of Polish underground participation in the Jewish uprising, the main foundation of its political philosophy was undermined. However, Tsukunft underground activists joined the ŻOB not because the estrangement of the Polish underground, which did not help the Jewish fighters to obtain arms, had extinguished their faith in the Jewish–Polish partnership of fate, but because the issue had become irrelevant. Leon Feiner understood the process that the young members of the ŻOB, irrespective of their party or movement affiliations, had undergone – from the moment these young people had decided to fight, ideological disputes lost their importance:

> The participants in the uprising were ideologues who swam in different currents. An exemplary fraternity of arms exists among Bundists, Zionist pioneers, members of HaShomer haTsa'ir, and others. It is a steadfast spirit … an *esprit de guerre*, a spirit of sacrifice, courage, revenge and dignity. The battles … are not only manifestations of the wish to avenge the unpunished murder of an entire people, not only a war against the deprivation of rights, but a manifestation of the will to atone with dignity for having been ensnared by the Nazis' deceits … Many of the fighters had an opportunity to remove themselves from the ghetto and save their lives, but they did not exploit it, feeling it their destiny to avenge themselves of the enemy … to fight for dignity and to fight uncompromisingly against fascism, on behalf of a new world.[102]

In 1942–43, having fathomed the genocidal intent of the Germans' actions, the young Bundists took an obvious step toward the conclusion that the fate of the Jews is of particularistic significance amidst the generality of fateful historical events that befell the peoples of Europe in their struggle against fascist repression and tyranny. The process at issue was not powered by ideational probings and the adduction of inescapable conclusions in a new historical reality. The time and the setting were not fit for an exploration of the traditional ideology, and it is not the nature of political movements to reconstruct their ideological underpinnings in times of crisis. Neither the post-war Bundist interpretation of the part played by the Bund in the ghetto uprisings (and its attempt to inflate the party's role in the armed Jewish struggle) on the one hand, nor the polemics of members of the Zionist youth movements against the anti-Zionist Bundist ideology on the other, can help us understand the immense and complex problems faced by underground activists from all political movements and in all the ghettos as they endeavoured to establish Jewish fighting organizations.

NOTES

1. C. Dieckmann, 'Der Krieg und die Ermordung der litauischen Juden', in U. Herbert (ed.) *Nationalsozialistische Vernichtungspolitik 1939–1945* (Frankfurt a.M.: Fisher Taschenbuch Verlag, 1998), pp. 292–3.
2. R. Sakowska, *Ludzie z dzielnicy zamkniętej* (Warsaw: Wydawnictwo Naukowe PWN, 1993), pp. 177–8.
3. Gutman, *The Jews of Warsaw*, pp. 162–70.
4. *Biuletyn*, October 1941, *Itonut* (3), pp. 420–21.
5. *Yugent Shtime*, October 1941, *Itonut* (3), pp. 459–61.
6. *Biuletyn*, 15 November 1941, *Itonut* (4), p. 41.
7. Edelman, *Getto walczy* p. 17; report by Leon Feiner, 24 May 1944, Hertz (ed.), *In di Yorn*, pp. 120–21.
8. Tsukunft, protokol Nr.1, 8 January 1942, AAN, Cukunft, 229/1.
9. Tsukunft, protokol Nr. 7, 4 March (?) 1942, AAN, Cukunft, 229/1.
10. Tsukunft, protokol Nr. 2, 14 January 1942, AAN, Cukunft 229/1.
11. Togbukh Tsukunft, 15 April 1942, AAN, Cukunft, 229/2.
12. Y. Zuckerman, *A Surplus of Memory: Chronical of the Warsaw Ghetto Uprising* (Berkeley, CA, Oxford: University of California Press, 1993), p. 175.
13. Interview with Yitzhak Zuckerman, Moreshet Archives (MA), Giv'ats Haviva, A. 661.1.
14. According to a report by Zuckerman, sent in March 1944 from Warsaw to London, in M. Neustadt (ed.), *Hurban vaMered shel Yehudei Varsha* (Tel Aviv: The General Federation of Labour, 1947), pp. 93–4.
15. *Dray – Andenkbukh* (Tel Aviv: Ringelblum Institut 1966), pp. 157–8.
16. Lecture by Zuckerman, 26 February 1973, MA, A. 580.
17. Gutman, *The Jews of Warsaw*, pp. 170–76.
18. Berman, *BaMakom*, p. 232.
19. Neustadt, *Khurban vaMered*, p. 94.
20. Ibid.
21. Edelman, *Getto walczy*, pp. 16–17.
22. Hertz (ed.), *In di Yorn*, p. 121.
23. Ibid.
24. Ibid., pp. 20–23.
25. *Yugent Shtime*, February–March 1942, *Itonut* (5), p. 232.
26. Edelman, *Getto walczy*, p. 17.
27. Ibid.
28. Tselemenski, *Mitn Farshnitenem Folk*, pp. 69–70, 141; Hertz (ed.), *Doyres Bundistn*, Vol. 2, p. 419; Togbukh Tsukunft, 7 April 1942, AAN, Cukunft, 229/2.
29. Tselemenski, *Mitn Farshnitenem Folk*, pp. 139–45, 147–8.
30. Ibid., pp. 178–9; Klayn, *Mitn Malach haMaves*, pp. 97–8.
31. Hertz (ed.), *Doyres Bundistn*, Vol. 2, pp. 460–62; Tselemenski, *Mitn Farshnitenem Folk*, pp. 150–1; Hertz (ed.), *In di Yorn*, pp. 309–11.
32. Tselemenski, *Mitn Farshnitenem Folk*, pp. 148, 153.
33. Sonya Nowogrodzki to Emanuel Nowogrodzki, 30 October 1941, BA, ME-16/80.
34. Kruk, *Togbukh*, p. xlii; on 16 February 1942, Kruk wrote about having received greetings from Abrasha Blum in Warsaw, ibid., p. 172; interview with David Klayn, Marek Edelman and Layka Jaszunski-Glazer (n.d.), BA, S–2/32; Zagórski, *Wolność*, p. 200.
35. Goldstein, *Finf Yor*, pp. 220–21; Tselemenski, *Mitn Farshnitenem Folk*, p. 154.
36. Feiner's report of 24 May 1944, Hertz (ed.), *In di Yorn*, p. 121; Hertz (ed.), *Doyres Bundistn*, Vol. 2, p. 438; 3, pp. 359–61.
37. Tselemenski, *Mitn Farshnitenem Folk*, p. 155.

38. E. Ringelblum, *Ksovim fun Geto*, Vol. 1 (Tel Aviv: Peretz Farlag, 1985), pp. 353–4; Hilberg et al. (eds), *Diary of Adam Czerniaków*, pp. 344–5; Tselemenski, *Mitn Farshnitenem Folk*, p. 155.
39. Ringelblum, *Ksovim*, pp. 347–8.
40. *Za Naszą i Waszą Wolność*, May 1942, *Itonut* (4), pp. 191–2.
41. Tsukunft report on the events of 18 April 1942, June 1942, AAN, KC PZPR, 30/III–2; internal memorandum by Tsukunft members on their surveillance of Dyamant, 10 June 1942, AAN, KC PZPR, 30/III–2. A report from the Polish underground (the Delegatura) in early 1943 mentions Leon Dyamant as an important Gestapo informer who operated a widespread network of informers. According to this report, he was eventually murdered by the Gestapo, AAN, KC PZPR, 202/II-8.
42. Hertz (ed.), *Doyres Bundistn*, II, pp. 55–6.
43. Tsukunft report on the events of 18 April 1942, AAN, KC PZPR, 30/III–2.
44. Gutman, *The Jews of Warsaw*, pp. 203–13.
45. Edelman, *Getto walczy* pp. 30–31; Goldstein, *Finf Yor*, pp. 247–8.
46. Edelman, *Getto walczy*, p. 39; Tselemenski, *Mitn Farshnitenem Folk*, pp. 164-5; Goldstein, *Finf Yor*, pp. 279–80. According to Edelman, Sonya Nowogrodzki was captured on 13 August 1942, in the Többens workshop, where she was employed, and was sent to Treblinka.
47. Edelman, *Getto walczy*, p. 40; Patt to Gilinski (undated), BA, M-12/4-A. The Medem Sanitorium workers could have avoided the deportation but chose to accompany their wards.
48. Hertz (ed.), *Doyres Bundistn*, Vol. 2, pp. 367–8; Edelman, *Getto walczy*, pp. 31–2.
49. *Oyf der Vakh*, 20 September 1942, *Itonut* (6), pp. 525–9.
50. Neustadt, *Hurban vaMered*, p. 98.
51. Edelman, *Getto walczy*, p. 31; Goldstein, *Finf Yor*, pp. 249–50.
52. H. Krall, *Shielding the Flame* (New York: Henry Holt, 1986) pp. 62–3.
53. *Dray – Andenkbukh*, p. 176; Zuckerman, *A Surplus of Memory*, p. 251.
54. Krall, *Shielding the Flame*, pp. 41–2.
55. Edelman, *Getto walczy*, p. 40.
56. Vladka, *Mishnei Evrei haHomah* (Tel Aviv: Hakibbutz Hameuhad, n.d.), pp. 77–8.
57. Edelman, *Getto walczy*, p. 45.
58. Gutman, *The Jews of Warsaw*, pp. 332–3.
59. Edelman, *Getto walczy*, p. 46.
60. Tselemenski, *Mitn Farshnitenem Folk*, pp. 204–5
61. Vladka, *Mishnei Evrei haHomah*, p. 78.
62. Ibid., pp. 86, 90.
63. Ibid., pp. 102–3; Tselemenski, *Mitn Farshnitenem Folk*, pp. 211–14.
64. Tselemenski, *Mitn Farshnitenem Folk*, p. 228; Krall, *Shielding the Flame*, pp. 93–4.
65. Vladka, *Mishnei Evrei haHomah*, p. 100; see also report by Feiner, 24 May 1944, in Hertz (ed.), *In di Yorn*, p. 121.
66. Sytuacja w Ruchu Wytrzymałość, AK report, May 1943, AAN, KC PZPR, 203/III-136.
67. Tselemenski, *Mitn Farshnitenem Folk*, pp. 231–2.
68. E. Ringelblum, *Stosunki polsko-żydowskie w czasie drugiej wojny światowej* (Warsaw: Czytelnik, 1988), p. 134.
69. R. Perlis, *Tenu'ot haNo'ar haHalutsiyot beFolin haKevushah* (Tel Aviv: Hakibuts HaMe'uhad, 1987), p. 241.
70. Ibid., p. 243.
71. Testimony of Mordechai Kotkowski, YVA, 03/522; Meltz and Levi-Landau (eds), *Piotrków Trybunalski ve'haSeviva*, pp. 790–91.
72. Memoirs of Mordechai Kotkowski, YVA, 033/1794.

73. Trunk, *Lodzer Geto*, pp. 464–71.
74. Winer, *Dos Togbukh*, 15 April 1943.
75. Winer, interview (see Ch. 1, note 33).
76. Protocol of meeting of Tsukunft group leaders, 27 August 1943, Winer, *Dos Togbukh*, p. 116.
77. Protocol of Tsukunft meetings, 10 September 1943, ibid., p. 120.
78. Protocol of Tsukunft meetings, 5 November 1943, ibid., p. 125.
79. Winer, interview (see Ch. 1, note 33).
80. Nirenberg, 'Di geshikhte fun Lodzer geto', in Hertz (ed.), *In die Yorn*, pp. 289–92.
81. Kruk, *Togbukh* , pp. 3–5; Hertz (ed.), *Doyres Bundistn*, Vol. 1, p. 136; Vol. 2, p. 130; Vol. 3, p. 470.
82. Kruk, *Togbukh*, pp. 26–7.
83. I. Arad, *Ghetto in Flames: The Struggle and Destruction of the Jews in Vilno in the Holocaust* (New York: Holocaust Library, 1982), pp. 237–8; Y. Musnik, 'Der Lebn un Likvidatsie fun Vilner Geto', in Hertz (ed.), *In di Yorn*, pp. 317–8; Kruk, *Togbukh*, pp. 77–8; Musnik to Schwartz, 22 October 1945, BA, M-7/20.
84. M. Balberyszski, *Shtarker fun Ayzn – Iberlebungen in der Hitler Tekufe* (Tel Aviv: Farlag Hamenora, 1967), pp. 210–11; Kruk, *Togbukh*, pp. 94, 140–41, 200–2, 251, 295–6, 298–9; M. Dworzecki, *Yerushalaym de-Lita in Kamf un Umkum* (Paris: Union Populaire Juive, 1948), p. 373.
85. These allegations were expressed in a letter sent by two Bund activists on the *Judenrat* to their counterparts in the Warsaw Ghetto: Glaser-Jaszunski and Gottgestalt, to Bund members in Warsaw, 29 June 1942, BA, S-2/32.
86. Testimony of Nisan Resnik, YVA, 03/3971; R. Korczak, *Lehavot baEfer* (Tel Aviv: Sifriyat Poalim, 1965), p. 98; her testimony of December 1944, MA, D.1.441.
87. Kruk, *Togbukh*, pp. 168–9.
88. L. A. Sarid, 'Teshuvat Abba Kovner leMastinav', *Yalkut Moreshet*, 47 (1989), p. 27.
89. Kruk's diary offers no details about the Erlich and Alter affair before 15 May 1943. From that date on, he recorded Polish radio reports of the murder of the two officials and the impact of the murders on party members in the ghetto. Kruk, *Togbukh*, pp. 474–7, 496–7.
90. Ibid., pp. 298–9; Musnik to Nowogrodzki, 17 August 1945, BA, M-7/20.
91. Kruk, *Togbukh*, pp. 563–4.
92. Dworzecki, *Yerushalaym de-Lita*, p. 444.
93. Polewski to Nowogrodzki, 15 July 1947, BA, M-7/20; S. Polewski, 'Bundishe Tetikayt in Vilner Geto', *Unser Tsayt*, 9 (1958), p. 25; testimony of Nisan Resnik, 8 November 1964, ODC 54 (12).
94. Testimony of Miryam Rubinzon, YVA, M-11/94.
95. Hertz (ed.), *Doyres Bundistn*, Vol. 2, pp. 334, 341.
96. Ibid., pp. 511, 515.
97. C. Grossman, *An'shei haMahteret* (Merhavia: Sifriat Poalim, 1965), p. 10; see also her testimony, MA, D.2.2.
98. Hertz (ed.), *Doyres Bundistn*, Vol. 2, p. 491.
99. M. Tenenbaum-Tamaroff, *Dapim min haDeleka* (Tel Aviv: Hakibuts HaMe'uhad, 1947), p. 45.
100. Ibid., pp. 67–8.
101. D. Blatman, 'No'ar Tsiyoni veBunda'i veHitgabshut Ra'ayon haMered', *Dapim leHeker Tekufat haShoa*, 12 (1995), pp. 153–7.
102. Hertz (ed.), *In di Yorn*, pp. 55–6.

5

Leadership in Exile

THE POLITICS OF RELIEF

The Bund had deep roots among members of the American Jewish working class. These roots had been planted in the late nineteenth century, when the United States absorbed throngs of Jewish immigrants from Europe. By the beginning of World War I, and *a fortiori* afterwards, the Jewish labour movement in the United States, especially in New York, was the solid economic spine of its counterpart in Poland. It supported the Yiddish-language school system, the youth movements, cultural activity, trade unions and the struggle against anti-Semitism. It was only natural that the Bund in Poland considered the Jewish Labour Committee (JLC), established in the 1930s, or the chapters of the *Arbeter Ring* as siblings of the party in Poland; in these American settings, as in the party branches in Warsaw or Łódź, Yiddish was the dominant *langauge* and the world of images and terms was the same. Often, too, activists in the American Jewish labour movement and those who remained 'back home' in Poland had kinship relations.

About a year before the war, three Bund members reached New York: Emanuel Nowogrodzki, secretary of the Bund Central Committee in Poland, and two colleagues, Jacob Pat and Benjamin Tabaczynski. Before the war, they dealt in fundraising for relief, education and youth organization activity for their party in Poland. When the war began, Tabaczynski and Pat began to work under the auspices of the JLC. Pat was named secretary-general of this highly influential organization; this circumstance had a far-reaching effect on the amounts of money that the committee forwarded to the Bund and proletariat circles in Poland during the war.[1] In September 1939 Nowogrodzki started a fundraising campaign for the Bund and raised $2,500 for the party within two weeks or so.[2] However, the most important change occurred in the political status of the Bund Representation. Until the war, the active members in New York regarded themselves as emissaries of the party in Warsaw or of Tsisho. Their activity centred on one goal, fundraising, and they did not regard themselves as having an independent political role in the party. When the war erupted, the activists in New York, together with the secretariat and the JLC, decided to merge the activity of the Bund mission with that of the JLC. This gave the Bund Representation an influence on events at the JLC and, indirectly, on the activities of Jewish organizations in which JLC members were active, such as the board of the JDC.[3] Nevertheless, the Bund activists, foremost Nowogrodzki, had the good sense to maintain some organizational independence. On 11 November 1939 Nowogrodzki and his colleagues established the American Representation of the Bund in Poland (Amerikaner repre-sentants fun algemaynem yidishn arbeter-Bund ['Bund'] in Poyln), a pronouncedly political entity and the long arm, so to speak, of the party in Poland. In a circular to members of the JLC and Jewish labour orga-nizations after the decision to establish the mission was made, Nowogrodzki wrote, 'This is a political mission that acts to obtain resources for the Bund movement in Poland – with authorization and permission of the political representation of the Bund in Poland.'[4]

The Representation had 11 members including Nowogrodzki, Tabaczynski, and Pat. In early December 1939, it held the first confer-ence of the Central Committee of Bund organizations and supporters that Nowogrodzki had established.[5] However, although the organizational structure of the party in New York had changed, its *modus operandi* and goals had not. The Bundists in New York were unsure about the stand-ing of the political agency that they had established within the party framework *vis-à-vis* the Central Committee in Poland. Nowogrodzki understood that once the Central Committee had left Warsaw and Poland had been occupied, a leadership had to be established elsewhere, and clearly this could be done only in New York. However, when it became apparent that most members of the leadership had reached Wilno in October and November 1939, the question of relations between the Representation and the Central Committee, which had congregated in Wilno, became current. Nowogrodzki tipped the scales in this matter, ruling that the Representation would not replace the Central Committee and that it would limit itself to representing the Bund's interests in the United States.[6] Practically speaking, it reserved only one function for itself: organizing relief operations and fundraising for the comrades in Europe. This division of powers persisted until the Central Committee members in Wilno reached the United States in 1941.

The members in New York knew full well that the movement activists in Poland were in danger and had to be removed from occupied Poland quickly. At the early date of 2 October 1939, Nowogrodzki and David Dubinsky, Jewish union leaders in New York, cabled the Labour

Party secretariat in London. They gave the leaders of the British party a list of prominent Bundists and their whereabouts, including Erlich, Portnoy, Kazden, Szerer and Gilinski. Nowogrodzki and Dubinsky asked the Labour leaders to spare no effort to extricate these men from Poland because of the danger they faced from both the Soviets and the Germans.[7] The members of the Representation in New York also attempted, at the very beginning of the war, to send money to their comrades in occupied Poland. Communications between Poland and New York was coordinated in the first two months of the war by Frantz Kurski (Szmuel Kahan), the veteran Bund journalist and one of the important activists in the Diaspora at the turn of the century. Kurski, who lived in Paris at the time, received money from the United States in September–October 1939 and forwarded it to Warsaw and Łódź by means of French banks. It was a paltry sum – $1,500 in all – and the entire arrangement was shortlived. In December 1939 Kurski was unable even to move $500 from Paris to Poland.[8]

From November 1939 on, the Bundists in New York sent via Wilno money that they had collected for colleagues who had gathered there and for comrades in Warsaw. Soon afterwards, Nowogrodzki sent $3,000 to Wilno and Kovno, no small matter for the collectivity of Bundist refugees that had just arrived from Poland.[9] This marked the onset of a large-scale relief operation that developed in 1940 at the initiative of Nowogrodzki and his comrades, with almost all of its funding from the JLC. The first few thousand dollars forwarded at the beginning of the war, too, were given to Bund activists by the secretariat of the JLC.

The *modus operandi* created by the Bundists in New York at the onset of the war did not change in any substantial way until the end of 1940. Throughout that year, Nowogrodzki continued to raise funds and send relief to members of the movement in Warsaw and Central Committee members who had settled in Wilno. At his initiative, Bund activists and sympathizers who resided in Zurich, Stockholm, Copenhagen and even Tangier, were mobilized for the relief effort as conduits for money and relief parcels to Poland and Wilno. In the main, the moneys gathered and transferred were small sums donated by relatives and friends of the party activists who had settled in the United States. The Bund Representation obtained additional contributions from the party's American sympathizers. The Bund representatives in New York found it difficult to raise substantial sums for their comrades in Poland during these months, mostly because the JLC was not yet geared for large-scale relief and fundraising work. In this regard, Pat wrote the following to the Central Committee members in Wilno: 'They [members of the

JLC] are unable to send more money to Poland. The Joint is handling that. [The JLC] is dealing only with a small group of labour-movement leaders and their families; as for others, they are unable to help.'[10]

One cannot state with confidence that all the moneys and relief addressed to Warsaw actually reached this city. In November 1940, after he left Wilno and reached Stockholm *en route* for the United States, Shloime Mendelsohn received confirmation from Sonya Nowogrodzki in Warsaw that $2,300 had been forwarded to activists in that city. A report that Leon Feiner sent to Britain in May 1942 containing a review of Bund operations in 1940–42, also confirms the receipt of money in 1940. Sonya Nowogrodzki confirmed the receipt of relief and food parcels that were sent during those months.[11] By 1940 however, the existential distress in Warsaw had rendered the sums raised abroad insufficient. In February 1940, the Central Committee members in Wilno asked their colleagues at the JLC to raise $15,000 urgently; in view of reports that they received from Poland, this was the sum they believed necessary for assistance and relief for movement members.[12] This sum was neither raised nor sent to Poland, but until the end of 1941 money and relief parcels from the United States continued to reach that country and the Bund underground activists in Warsaw and, via them, members in peripheral towns.[13]

A new phase in the work of the Bund Representation in New York began in September 1940. On the 25th of that month, the leading Bundists in New York – Nowogrodzki, Pat and Tabaczynski – held their first meeting with Szmuel Zygielbojm, who had reached the United States just then. It was especially important to co-opt Zygielbojm into the work of the American Representation because he was not only a well-known senior member of the Bund leadership but also the first leading member who reached New York after personally experiencing the horrors of the German occupation in Warsaw in its first few months. At this meeting, Zygielbojm described the Jews' lives in the occupied country and the operations undertaken by party members in the underground. The participants decided (1) not to establish an official Bund political mission in the United States before the Central Committee members came from Wilno; (2) to annex Zygielbojm to the Relief Committee of the JLC, a special assistance committee that raised funds for the members in Poland (established in late 1939 and run on a limited basis in the first year of the war); and (3) to leave the decision on how to apportion relief sent directly to Poland in the hands of the Central Committee members in Wilno, as long as the members of the committee remained in contact with the Bund underground activists in Warsaw.[14]

The secretariat of the Bund relief committee convened about ten days after this meeting. This committee was chaired by Joseph Weinberg, national president of the *Arbeter Ring*. In 1941, this Relief Committee raised $33,000 from Jewish workers and Jewish labour unions in the United States for Bund members in Poland and the Soviet Union. The money was used to buy a thousand food parcels to send to Poland, in order to provide relief for Bund-member refugees who reached the United States, and to support PPS-affiliated relief associations of Polish socialist refugees.[15]

The Bundists in the United States received confirmations about the arrival in Warsaw of moneys and parcels that had been sent to the Polish capital in 1941. By this time, the money was being forwarded by the Polish government-in-exile and by the Polish underground, and the relief parcels were sent mainly by Bund activists in Zurich, Copenhagen and the HIAS office in Lisbon.[16] Sonya Nowogrodzki wrote to her husband in New York on this matter: 'Five-kilogram food parcels that you sent via Copenhagen and Lisbon have arrived. These parcels have given the family [members of the movement] much delight and assistance.'[17]

The Bund members in the United States were also notably successful in rescuing their comrades in Europe. In addition to the members of the Central Committee, for whom the JLC obtained American entry visas, party members who had left Wilno and had reached Japan and congregated in Kobe or Tokyo as refugees – approximately 200 members in February 1941[18] – were extricated in a comprehensive operation. Nowogrodzki and his colleagues made a massive effort to provision them with entry visas for the United States or some other safe location. The success of the Bund activists in America in delivering their comrades to safe shores is noteworthy in view of the severe pressure applied to the US embassy in Tokyo by diverse political groups trying to get various fugitives into the United States. In March 1941, the American Representation sent the Bundists in Japan $1,800 for initial living needs; by the end of that year, most of them were given entry permits to the United States or Canada. Of approximately 900 Jews who were transferred by the Japanese to the Jewish centre in Shanghai in the autumn of 1941, only 46 were Bund members, and five of them obtained entry visas to Australia shortly afterwards.[19]

The members of the Bund Central Committee who had left Poland reached the United States in late 1941 and early 1942. At this time, too, the party completed the formation of its organizational structure in the United States. Main decisions about policy, apportionment of funds and organizational and political work would be made by the American Representation of the Bund in Poland. The mission was made up of 12 activists who belonged to the Bund Central Committee, along with Pat and Tabaczynski, activists in the JLC. The Central Committee of the Bund in Poland, a compact body of eight or nine members, mostly Central Committee members who had left Warsaw, was established alongside the mission. This Central Committee dealt mainly in matters of ideology and constituted the Bund's 'response team'. It publicized the Representation's political decisions and advertised manifestos in the Jewish and general press in the United States. Apart from these institutions, a Presidium of the American Representation of the Bund in Poland was established – a small entity composed of Frantz Kurski, Chayim Wasser, Shloime Mendelsohn, Emanuel Szerer, Emanuel Nowogrodzki, and Szmuel Zygielbojm. This small group of leading Bundists received underground material from Poland, maintained liaison with the Polish government-in-exile in London with regard to contacts with underground groups in occupied Poland, and coordinated political relations with non-Jewish entities in the United States. They were also the only Bundists in the United States who drew wages from the party exchequer.

As the Bund Representation, within its various settings, consolidated itself in New York, the Bund carved out a major leading position in the Jewish labour movement in America. This development traces to the growing influence in the JLC of the Bund activists who had come from Wilno. The JLC, established in 1934, took no *a priori* position for or against the Bund's political or ideological policies. Its principal duty, in its own perception, was to unify all Jewish working-class forces and supporters of Yiddish education in response to the Nazi accession to power in Germany and anti-Semitism in Eastern Europe. Although it defined itself neither as Zionist nor as anti-Zionist, it was strongly influenced by Bundism and many of its activists had identified with the Bund's political doctrine in Poland.

In January 1942 the internal ideological discord brought the JLC to the verge of rupture. The ascent of Zionist activity in the United States during those months on the one hand, and the consolidation of the activity of the Bund Representation on the other, prompted both the proponents and the opponents of Zionism on the JLC to demand that the committee make up its mind on the major questions that the Jewish people would confront after the war. In view of these disputes, a meeting was convened with the participation of various public figures: JLC activists, Bund members and personalities such as Uriel Weinreich, the director of YIVO. At this meeting, Shloime Mendelsohn argued that the JLC should avoid taking a stance on political questions such as Jewish emigration to Palestine, since the Jewish community there, half a million strong, was not very meaningful for the future of the world's 16 million Jews.[20]

At this meeting, the Bund achieved an important victory that elevated its standing in the JLC. Its triumph had far-reaching implications for the last few years of the war, especially with respect to financial relief activities. Mendelsohn and his colleagues, seasoned politicians who for years had engaged in party work in the harsh conditions of pre-war Poland, understood that one could not ask the JLC to repudiate publicly the Jewish community in Palestine; their sole desideratum was that the committee be induced to proclaim neutrality in the ideological dispute between the Bund and the Zionist activists. Adolph Held, the highly influential president of the JLC, stated at the meeting that his organization did not wish to intervene in any ideological dispute; instead, he said, it wished to remain loyal to the American Jewish public of which it was a part.[21] Jacob Pat, the Bund activist who by this time had become the secretary-general of the JLC, summarized the debate:

> The unwritten ideology of the JLC is concern for the future of the Jewish people wherever Jews live. This is the basis of its assistance to Jews and our struggle against fascism and anti-Semitism. We concern ourselves with Jews in all Diaspora countries ... A way in which everyone may find his place in the Labour Committee should be found ... As for Jewish self-rule in Palestine – everyone should keep his opinion to himself.[22]

By expressing matters in this fashion, Pat removed the issue of the Jewish national home from the JLC political agenda. Beyond ideology, however, a much more crucial question remained on the agenda: where to direct the relief money that the large Jewish labour organization was raising. The JLC's sources of funding grew steadily from 1942 on, and the Bund members made every effort to have these moneys referred primarily to the Jewish labour movement activists in occupied Poland. In their opinion, there was no reason to pledge funds to the Jewish national home because that enterprise, from their perspective, was not central in Jewish life. Moreover, the Jews in Palestine were neither in immediate existential danger nor under extreme hardship, as were the Jews in Poland. The Bundists' argument carried the day. In 1942–44, the Bund activists obtained positions of influence in the important decision-making centres of Jewish American labour organizations and claimed a large share of the JLC's relief funds.

The Bund's influence became evident at the time the money for Jewish refugees in the Soviet Union was being apportioned. For a year and a half, starting in late 1941, after the Polish–Soviet agreement of the summer of 1941 made it possible to offer these refugees more generous relief, the JLC forwarded more than $100,000 in cash and in material aid to Jewish refugees across the USSR. It is difficult to determine whether the money was given to Bund members only, but in view of the relationship between the Bund activists in New York and the JLC members who raised these donation funds, this seems to have been the case. In early 1942 the Bund Representation in New York stopped raising relief funds as it had during the first two years of the war. It earmarked most of the money that it collected in 1942 – about $30,000 – for information and propaganda activities, the movement's press in the United States and current activities.[23] The JLC assumed responsibility for relief money for members in Europe and forwarded this money to the Soviet Union on the basis of lists that the Bund Representation prepared and handed over to the JLC secretariat. These lists, including approximately 2,000 names of party members and associates, had been sent to the American Bund Representation by a small group of party activists in the Soviet Union – chiefly Blit, Faynzilber and Gliksman – who operated rather freely in the aftermath of the Polish–Soviet accord.[24] This small group of major members also received $1,000 per month in aid from the JLC through the mission of the Polish Ministry of Finance at the Polish Consulate in New York, which transferred the money to the Polish Embassy in Kuybyshev.[25] Practically speaking, the American Representation of the Bund became an intermediary between the JLC, which raised the relief funds, and the Jews who received the money. Since the lists of persons eligible for assistance were drawn up by the Bund members in Kuybyshev, who naturally were contacted mostly by party members, almost all of the money sent by members of the American Jewish working class to Jewish refugees in the Soviet Union, by means of the Jewish Labour Committee, reached refugees associated with the Bund.

SZMUEL ZYGIELBOJM: INITIATIVE, FRUSTRATION, SURRENDER

Since the beginning of the war, Bund leaders who operated outside occupied Poland wished to integrate into the centres of Polish political activity in exile – mainly the institutions of the Polish government-in-exile. These settings solidified steadily during the war years, and the Bund worked out a unique division of functions that was unparalleled in any other political entity or movement that had been active in Poland until the occupation: an underground leadership in the occupied country and a political leadership in exile. Although obviously each of these settings operated differently, they complemented each other and created a Jewish political movement with a unique structure that attempted to maintain its pre-war influence both among Jews in occupied Poland and within external political frameworks that would influence the fate of Polish Jewry during the war.

The Bund's political activity in exile began in France. In October–November 1939 a Polish government-in-exile was established in Angers, chiefly by members of the opposition to the Polish government that had fled to Romania at the beginning of the occupation. This government-in-exile was headed by Władysław Raczkiewicz (president) and Władysław Sikorski (prime minister). The figures who had served in the last Polish government (whom the Polish public had blamed for the country's traumatic defeat in September 1939) were not represented in the government-in-exile. Most of the new government's members originated in oppositionist and anti-Semitic right-wing circles, but some were from the PPS and others were centrists. Although it encountered legitimacy problems upon its formation, this government quickly won the support of underground political and military circles in Poland and became a state entity that represented the country *vis-à-vis* the Allies during the war.

From its first day, Sikorski's government endeavoured to portray itself as one of Polish national unity. The Sanacja camp, which in its various manifestations had ruled Poland from 1926 to the German invasion, was represented, as were the National Democratic camp (Endecja) and the PPS. The Peasants' Party (Stronmictwo Narodowe) and the Catholic Labour Party (Stronnictwo Pracy) were part of the government, as were 'national figures' such as the Undersecretary for Defence, General Józef Haller, whose legions were infamous for their pogroms against Jews in the Ukraine in 1920 during the Polish–Bolshevik war.[26] A National Council (Rada Narodowa) – an outgrowth of the Polish Sejm – was established alongside this Government, and Ignacy Schwarzbart represented the Jewish minority in it. The main purposes in giving Schwarzbart this appointment were to silence Westerners who criticized the newly formed Polish government for perpetuating the traditional pre-war policy of discriminating against the Jews, and to express the wish to recompose the Polish exile as a democratic, pluralistic framework. Schwarzbart had accrued experience in public activity before the war. A lawyer by training, and a Zionist leader, he was well placed in Jewish and Polish political life; in 1938 he had even been elected as a deputy to the Sejm. By all accounts, and from the perspective of the leaders of the Polish government, he was a worthy candidate to represent the Jewish minority.[27]

Although the Bund was initially suspicious of this government, because of its composition and nature,[28] it could not, as a party that considered itself a fixture in the Polish political constellation, avoid contact with the political entity that represented Polish independence and the Polish state in the West. In March 1940 the Central Committee in Wilno decided to send a six-member delegation to Paris – Mendelsohn, Wasser, Zygielbojm, Szerer, Kurski and a representative of Tsukunft.[29] Kurski and Zygielbojm were already in France, but the others needed special visas. With the German invasion of Western Europe and the downfall of France several months later, this could not be arranged.

In fact, Zygielbojm was the first of these Bundists to establish a practical relationship between the Bund and political organizations in the West and the Polish government-in-exile. In late February 1940 he took part in a meeting of the secretariat of the Socialist International in Belgium and apprised his comrades of developments in Warsaw during the German occupation. At that time, he also strengthened his acquaintance with important members of the International – personalities who had influence in socialist political circles in the West – such as Camille Huysmans of Belgium, Friedrich Adler of Austria and William Gillis of Britain. In a report which he delivered to the members of the International, Zygielbojm stressed the resistance of the Polish and Jewish proletariat during the German siege of Warsaw, the assaults that the occupier had inflicted on members of the PPS and the Bund in Łódź, and the imprisonment of Jewish and Polish socialists by the Soviets in the annexed areas of eastern Poland. In a special section on the fate of the Jews in Poland, Zygielbojm described the mass expulsions of Jews from western Poland, the economic deprivation, the establishment of the first ghettos in Poland and the deportations to labour camps.[30]

Zygielbojm's report to the Socialist International secretariat was also the basis for a memorandum that he submitted to the Polish government-in-exile in April 1940.[31] In the memorandum – unlike the first report, which was informative in nature – Zygielbojm presented several demands on behalf of the Bund Central Committee. He asked the Polish government to express the tenets of its future policy toward the free Poland that would evolve after the war; to support the principle of full equality of rights for all national minorities in Poland; to introduce far-reaching land reforms; to assure cultural autonomy for Jews and other minorities; and to apply a foreign policy based on relations with the free democracies in Europe.[32]

Zygielbojm's quasi-diplomatic political activity in Brussels and Paris during those months is puzzling. At that time, the Bund was not represented in the institutions of the Polish government-in-exile and did not even have an active mission in France, as it had, for example, in New York. This being the case, why did the Polish government-in-exile agree to treat Zygielbojm as the Bund's representative in negotiations of a political nature? It agreed to do this, first, because Zygielbojm represented a party that had much influence among Polish Jews and – more importantly – had stature in the Socialist International and, through its mediation, in important entities such as the British Labour Party. Second, Zygielbojm and the Bund had powerful supporters and friends among Polish politicians in exile who belonged to the PPS. Adam Ciołkosz – a member of the Polish Sejm, one of the leading socialist politicians in exile, and a prominent friend of the Bund – tendered the Minister of Interior, Stanisław Kot, an opinion on Zygielbojm's memorandum to the government-in-exile. Kot ruled that Zygielbojm's memorandum was vastly important to Polish interests and could be exploited to stress the difference between the Bund and other Jewish political agencies in respect to their attitude toward Poland. During those months rumours circulated among members of the government-in-exile and in Polish émigré circles about the Jews' staunch support of the Red Army and the Soviet regime that had been established in the eastern provinces of Poland, and the Jews were subjected to a climate of distrust and hostility because of their ostensible disloyalty to the Polish interest. Ciołkosz, influenced by these reports, regarded the Bund's response and the fact that its activists had also been victims in the round-up of Polish socialists in these territories as evidence that the Bund shared the greater national interest of Poland. The exodus of Bund leaders from Wilno to the United States, where they had great influence over Jewish public opinion, should be encouraged, Ciołkosz said, in the belief that this would further the Polish cause. Accordingly, he also considered it very important to let the Bund be represented on the Polish National Council:

> It is important to give the Bund representatives on the National Council. [The Bund] commands a large enough percentage of

support among Polish Jewry to warrant two members on the Council. The Bund is undoubtedly the largest Jewish party. It is not proper for Schwarzbart to be the Jews' only delegate to the National Council. The matter is very important and crucial and it will echo positively in the United States, where various organizations regard the Bund favourably.[33]

However, Ciołkosz added, the Bund would support the Polish government and use its connections in the United States to influence public opinion only if the Polish government declared its support of the principle of equal rights for all Polish citizens and explicitly opposed the idea of emigration, in any form, as the way to solve the Jewish problem in Poland.

Although the Polish government did not meet Zygielbojm's demands it did not rule out Bund representation on the National Council, and recognized the importance of the support of American Jewish public opinion. However, the conservative members of the government, some of whom were anti-Semitic, did not wish to issue any statement in support of equal rights for the Jews at that time. They were convinced that the Jews were identified with the Soviet Union, which had colluded with Germany to eradicate Polish independence. This conviction – reinforced in particular by information that, as stated, was coming in from Poland at this time concerning Jewish support of the Soviet Union – had become conventional wisdom in government-in-exile circles. Moreover, it was not popular to show support of Jewish rights even in Poland itself, for the same reasons.[34]

Zygielbojm and Kot reached an agreement: the Bund would participate in work of the Ministry of Information and Propaganda provided that the government-in-exile expressed its stance on Jewish emigration clearly. But Sikorski had stated explicitly on 4 September 1940 that the Polish government regarded Jewish emigration to Palestine as an appropriate solution to the Jewish question in Poland and an important way to solve Poland's economic problems.[35] As for appointing a Bund representative to the National Council, again no real progress was made. Although Zygielbojm negotiated with Kot in this matter, and even proposed candidates for the position, the negotiations ran aground because of developments in the war and the German invasion of Western Europe. Zygielbojm's first discussion with Schwarzbart, the Zionist delegate to the National Council, also made no substantive progress. Schwarzbart suggested that the Bund join the activity as part of the Representation of Polish Jews (Reprezentacja

Żydostwa Polskiego), but Zygielbojm ruled this out categorically, maintaining that the Bund did not conduct a policy that was Jewish-national in nature.[36]

During his few months in France, Zygielbojm operated on his own counsel. The Bund had not authorized him to negotiate with the government-in-exile, and in this matter a dispute erupted between the Central Committee in Wilno and the American Representation. Zygielbojm's colleagues in Wilno wanted him to stay in France and wait for the representatives whom they had chosen to negotiate for the Bund's integration into the activity of the National Council. They even designated Emanuel Szerer as the party delegate to the council.[37] Despite the sympathy Zygielbojm commanded among members of the Socialist International and PPS members of the Polish National Council, his comrades in Wilno apparently were not convinced that he was the right person to represent the Bund in the institutions of the Government-in-Exile. Nowogrodzki and his colleagues in the United States demanded that Zygielbojm leave France for the United States at once, in order to take up a position in developing and raising funds for the American Representation. It was the New York activists' belief that a person of Zygielbojm's stature, who had left Poland after the occupation began, could do much to enhance their activity in the United States.[38]

These early months of Bund political activity in France were marked by an internal dispute that erupted between the American Representation and the Central Committee in Wilno. Szerer and Mendelsohn implored Nowogrodzki to refrain from conducting his own policy on behalf of the Bund until the activists from Wilno could arrive. They refused to recognize the Bund Representation as an agency that spoke in the Bund's name and took a stance in a matter as important as activity in the institutions of the Polish government-in-exile.[39] Nowogrodzki accepted his comrades' attitude and limited the Representation's activities to relief and assistance. However, the question of the Bund's non-participation in the Polish National Council continued to preoccupy the party activists in New York, especially after the party solidified its structure in 1941. In March 1941 Nowogrodzki wrote to William Gillis, secretary of the foreign relations committee of the British Labour Party, and asked him to help procure British entrance visas for a Bund mission that would set up a political representative body *vis-à-vis* the Polish government-in-exile.[40]

The activists in New York believed it extremely important to have a Bund delegation that would interact with the Polish institutions in exile, not only to underscore their status as representatives of the Jewish working class in Poland, or because they believed this would enable them to stay in touch with their underground comrades, but because they felt that they would find it difficult to stress issues of major ideological significance unless they had a base in the Polish exiles' political centre. They were especially fearful of undermining of the status of the PPS members in respect of the future of Polish Jewry after the war. Labour Minister Jan Stańczyk of the PPS ruled that, after the war, such Jews as wished to express their national aspirations could do so by emigrating to their national home in Palestine. The Bund considered this stance, which had been accepted in various PPS circles even before the war, a legitimization of Jewish emigration from Poland as a possible solution to the Jewish problem in that country.[41]

When the first Polish National Council in London dissolved in the summer of 1941 and the new council was formed, the Jewish party began to work intensively in London and the United States to secure the appointment of both delegates whom the Polish government had allocated for the Jews on the new National Council.[42] Schwarzbart continued to serve as a council member; as for the second candidate, Agudath Israel, the Bund and the Revisionists pressured Polish political players in London to choose one of their number.[43] The American Representation of the Bund demanded that the party be allocated two slots on the council for Erlich and Alter, who in the meantime had been released from prison in the Soviet Union.[44] Jan Stańczyk explained to the Bundists in New York that it would be impossible to appoint two Bund delegates to the council but that efforts were being made to ensure that the second Jewish delegate would be a Bundist. The Polish deputy prime minister, Stanisław Mikołajczyk, made similar assurances.[45] In August 1941 the Bund representatives in the United States asked the Polish Interior Ministry in London to arrange British entry visas for three of their comrades – Szmuel Zygielbojm, Emanuel Szerer and Emanuel Nowogrodzki – so that these men could interact with the National Council that was being formed.[46] This request came in the aftermath of the Bund's aforementioned decision in March 1941 to post several Bund activists to London and establish a large party delegation there.[47]

When Erlich and Alter were re-arrested in December 1941, it became clear that they would not be able to travel to London, and the Bund activists in New York began to seek an alternative delegate to appoint to the council.[48] The Bund leadership in New York preferred Emanuel Szerer over Zygielbojm, as they had at the time the first

National Council was formed in France, and intended Zygielbojm to be a member of the political delegation that would interact with the council in London. The activists in New York doubted that Zygielbojm had the talent and ability to meet the requirements of the position. Frantz Kurski wrote on this subject to John Mill, the veteran Bundist and a party leader since the years preceding World War I, who was living in Miami at the time:

> Artur is still here ... Unfortunately, he is not the right candidate. He has not got the appropriate schooling and intellectually he is too weak for this job. Our candidate is Szerer, but the parties cannot send the delegates of their choice to the National Council. The Council members are appointed by the Government, and therefore Sikorski and certainly the PPS would find it more convenient to have the Bund representative be the least intelligent man on the Council, which is made up of professors and the like ... Artur is more convenient for them than Szerer. It's a lost cause! There is nothing we can do about it.[49]

One doubts that the Polish politicians had Zygielbojm's limited capabilities in mind when they preferred him over Szerer as the Bund delegate to the council. It stands to reason that they favoured Zygielbojm because he had taken part in the defence of Warsaw at the beginning of the war, formed relations with the Polish underground, and was known and amenable to the American Jewish working class – a collectivity whose sympathies the Polish Government wished to attract.

Even after it became clear that Zygielbojm would represent the Bund on the National Council, the activists in New York tried to stop him from leaving alone for London. In February 1942, the Bund Representation contacted the Polish Consulate in New York, requesting that British entrance visas be urgently arranged for the members of the delegation (Nowogrodzki, Szerer and Wasser), because 'Zygielbojm cannot travel to London alone.'[50] That month, the Representation established a coordinating committee with the Jewish Labour Committee and the *Arbeter Ring* to instruct Zygielbojm in the light of positions adopted by the party in New York.[51] On 3 March 1942 the American Representation and members of the Central Committee held another meeting and resolved that any issue pertaining to the activity of the National Council in London would be debated by the Party Representation in New York. Zygielbojm was ordered to refrain from presenting the Bund's position on any controversial political topic until he consulted with his comrades in New York. The members were afraid that he would fail to navigate the political maze in London and that his position would harm the Bund's relations with officials in the Polish government. Although he realized that they were shackling him, and argued that the members might not be able to solve problems that came up in London, Zygielbojm accepted the view of the majority and did not contravene its decisions.[52] He knew he had been given the appointment in the absence of an alternative candidate, understood that he had little latitude, and may have realized too how strongly his comrades doubted his ability to do the job.

Upon his arrival in London, Zygielbojm explained the guidelines that he would follow in cooperating with the second Jewish delegate to the National Council.[53] In an interview with the Jewish Telegraphic Agency in early April 1942, he said:

> Being a socialist, I am convinced that the problems of Poland and the Polish Jews and the world as whole can be solved only according to the socialist principles about building a new world ...My policy in the council will be based on these principles. So far as the other Jewish member [Schwarzbart] will be prepared to adhere to the same principles we can join in our efforts. But if Dr Schwartzbart's attitude in the council to both general and Jewish questions will be in accordance with Zionist principles and in contradiction to our demands, then there will naturally be a rift between us.[54]

From the very start, Zygielbojm rejected every request from Jewish organizations to establish an all-Jewish entity that would coordinate activities on behalf of Polish Jewry. When the Council for Polish Jewry in London made such an appeal, and when the World Jewish Congress did the same, he said he had nothing in common with them. He refused to accept invitations to attend and speak at meetings unless it was made clear that he would appear as a representative of the Bund and not of Jewish organizations at large.[55]

Zygielbojm's initial contacts with representatives of the Polish government and his PPS colleagues were also marked by friction and misunderstandings. On 3 April 1942, he met for his first talk with the Polish deputy prime minister and Interior Minister, Mikołajczyk. At this session, Zygielbojm presented a string of demands in the name of the Bund: to arrange British entry visas for his colleagues whom he had left behind in New York; to act more vigorously for the release of

Erlich and Alter from the Soviet prison; and to arrange the departure from the USSR of some 50 Bundists among General Anders' forces, which were leaving that country. Zygielbojm informed the Polish minister that his government was not doing enough in these matters.[56] In May 1942 Zygielbojm presented the National Council with a draft resolution that would declare anti-Semitism a crime. This proposal drew fire not only from the Endek delegates but also from several PPS members who accused him of demagogy.[57] The Poles also took a dim view of his relations with Western European socialists. In London, a forum of Second Socialist International activists from occupied European countries met on a non-partisan basis under Camille Huysmans of Belgium and other socialists. Huysmans invited Zygielbojm to participate in the forum, but the latter turned this down, stating that the Bund Representation in New York had not taken a decision on this matter. Contacting his comrades in America, Zygielbojm argued that non-participation in the Socialist International would diminish the Bund's ability to present its case to the leaders of the European socialist movement.[58] The party leaders in New York stuck to their guns, explaining that the Socialist International forum was not a Polish framework and that the Bund should eschew participation in any political entity that did not act in direct connection with events in Poland. The Bund leaders feared that Zygielbojm's activity in political settings that were unpopular among many Polish politicians might infringe on the party's ability to mobilize these politicians to help Bund members in Poland and in the Soviet Union.[59]

At the beginning of his tenure in London, Zygielbojm managed to establish good relations with members of the British Labour Party. (These relations were used mainly for propaganda purposes.) Several Labourites – Arthur Greenwood, Henry-Noel Brailsford and Harold Laski – helped him in his efforts to release Erlich and Alter and took up the matter with the Labour secretariat.[60] Walter Citrine, the British trade union leader (as noted earlier, see Chapter 3), told Zygielbojm that the cases of Erlich and Alter had been raised with Foreign Secretary Anthony Eden, who had refused to intervene lest the Soviets regarded this as interference on the part of the British in their internal affairs.[61] At this time, Zygielbojm also established a party entity that helped raise funds from Bund sympathizers in Great Britain and influenced Jewish public opinion. In late April 1942 a conference of some 500 trade union members who sympathized with and supported the Bund took place in London.[62]

From the very first weeks of his stay in London, however, Zygielbojm complained of severe isolation and difficulties. He accused his comrades in New York of not staying in touch with him, not keeping him abreast of developments in American and not sending him the party publications.[63] 'I find my workload exceedingly heavy and very difficult', he wrote to Frantz Kurski, 'since I have no one with whom to consult and no one to come to my aid ... I would like to have all the "Emanuels" and "Chayims" [Emanuel Nowogrodzki, Emanuel Szerer and Chayim Wasser] here with me but I do not know when that will happen...'[64]

In May 1942 an activist in the Bund underground in Warsaw, Leon Feiner, sent to London the first report with information on mass murders in various parts of Poland. It included details about genocidal actions against Jews in the Lwów area, the murders in Wilno and the massacres in Chełmno, as well as information about the deportations from Lublin that had begun in March 1942. Feiner also retold the events of the gruesome night in Warsaw in April 1942, and estimated at 700,000 the number of Polish Jews whom the Germans had murdered by May. In the absence of real measures to stop the carnage, Feiner stated, there would be no Jews left in Europe by the end of the war. He demanded, in the name of the Bund, that the Polish government take immediate steps to stop the murder and to pressure other countries to threaten Germany with revenge against its citizens in Allied countries if the annihilation campaign against the Jews continued.[65]

The Polish government distrusted the details in Feiner's report. Officials at the Polish Foreign Ministry, including the acting Foreign Minister, Edward Raczyński, considered Feiner's information exaggerated. Since the beginning of the war, the Polish government had sought to downplay the Jews' suffering as a singular phenomenon and to consider the entire Polish people the subjects of a reign of terrorism and danger. Sikorski, in a radio speech to Poland on 9 June 1942, spoke about the Nazis' having killed several tens of thousands of Jews.[66] Mikołajczyk, in a meeting of the National Council in July 1942, described the Jews' agonies as part of the general suffering that the occupier was inflicting on Poland.[67]

These reports, however, became more firmly grounded and copious as time passed, and even the Polish government could not treat them with scepticism and doubt for long. Schwarzbart, the veteran Jewish deputy to the National Council in exile, was the first Jewish political activist in the Free World to receive information in this matter directly from the Polish government.[68] At that time (late June or early July 1942), Zygielbojm also received the material that his movement comrade had sent from Poland.

Zygielbojm found the information in Feiner's report hard to digest.

Not until the middle of July 1942, after he perused additional reports from Polish sources on the murder of Jews in Poland, did he begin to realize that the details Feiner had forwarded from Warsaw were truly indicative of the new and horrific reality that was unfolding there.[69] At approximately that time, he met with Prime Minister Sikorski and presented him with two requests: (1) public confirmation of the reports from Poland in the name of the government and expression of identification with the Jews' suffering; and (2) an appeal from the government to the Polish governments of the United States and Great Britain for action against Germany. Sikorski rejected these demands and informed Zygielbojm that he had long since issued a statement on the Jews' distress in Poland and for the time being had no intention of augmenting it.[70]

In the summer of 1942, after the reports from Poland had arrived, Zygielbojm began to mobilize public support in Britain in protest against the destruction of the Jews. In early July 1942 Polish Foreign Minister Raczyński, Zygielbojm and Schwarzbart called a press conference and provided British journalists with the information from Poland on the destruction of the Jews. Socialist leaders – members of Huysmans' forum and the Labour Party – issued a protest leaflet on the subject.[71] On 2 September 1942 Zygielbojm addressed a conference of Labour leaders from Poland, Czechoslovakia, Britain, Norway, France and Belgium, which had been called at the initiative of members of Labour to protest against German crimes in Poland and Czechoslovakia. In a speech he delivered at this conference, he drew a clear distinction between the German occupier's policies toward the Poles, whom the Germans fated to become 'a slave people that will serve the master race', and the Jews, whom the Nazis intended to obliterate from the face of the earth. Then, describing himself as the representative of these masses on their way to extinction, he urged the Free World to halt the greatest crime in human history.[72]

In the initial period after the reports from Poland arrived, Zygielbojm – like other Jewish officials in their first encounter with reports on the Final Solution – displayed a wide gap between the information he possessed and his ability to fathom its meaning. Zygielbojm's inability to understand and internalize the significance of the wholesale murder campaign and to change, in one stroke, his traditional *modus operandi* was evident in the summer and early autumn of 1942. He continued to consider himself foremost a representative of his party, charged mainly with representing the Bund in various political forums and to British public to the best of his ability. On 14 August 1942, as the National

Council met in special session to mark Polish Soldiers' Day, Sikorski expressed a wish to merge the two Jewish delegates to the National Council into a single mission. Zygielbojm responded angrily, stating in a speech that he represented not all the Jews but the Bund only.[73] In the middle of September 1942, Huysmans obtained a list of Belgium Jews who had fled to southern France and obtained British entrance visas. Zygielbojm refused to meet with him and take possession of the list because the Belgian socialist leader had first handed the list for study to Berl Locker, the Jewish Agency representative in London.[74] In early October 1942 Zygielbojm protested to the National Council members about their choice of Schwarzbart as a member of the council's social affairs committee. When the PPS delegates asked why he did not form a joint Jewish bloc with Schwarzbart, he replied, 'Would you sit in a joint bloc with the Endeks?'[75]

In the summer of 1942 the Bund leadership in New York became even more dubious about the ability of its delegate to the Polish National Council in London to navigate the thicket of political problems on the agenda. As reports about the annihilation of Polish Jewry came in, the Representation in New York decided to establish a six-member reaction committee that would coordinate relations with the American and British press and give the journalists the party's authoritative responses.[76] The members in New York continued to forbid Zygielbojm to take part in Huysmans's forum and to publish an article in the *Forverts* on what was happening in Poland.[77] In August 1942 Zygielbojm attempted to gain membership of one of the most important National Council committees, which dealt in developments in Poland and received reports from the Polish underground. The American Representation forbade him to join the committee. Zygielbojm protested against this in view of the importance of his request, even though he was sure he would be turned away. By applying for membership of this committee, he said, the Bund would stress its being an actor on behalf of the Polish interests and a participant in the underground work in the homeland.[78] He also protested his comrades' injunction against his participation in Huysmans' forum. This, he explained, kept the Bund from expanding its connections and circulating its propaganda among members of the Socialist International.[79] The Representation members, however, continued to instruct Zygielbojm in the light of the decision they had made shortly before he set out for London[80] (i.e., to rely on PPS members in political matters and to second their views).

Apart from this dispute over the party's *modus operandi*, Zygielbojm and his colleagues disagreed on a much more important matter: how to respond to the reports about the annihilation of the Jews. Details about the deportation of Jews with Polish citizenship from the occupied zone of France came to light in the summer of 1942. In July, the Vichy authorities began to round up these Jews and deliver them to the Germans, who in turn deported them to the east.[81] In July and August 1942 Zygielbojm took up this matter with the National Council and insisted that these fugitives be provided with countries of refuge. The Representation in the United States criticized Zygielbojm's demand, arguing that his preoccupation with countries of refuge would divert attention from the fact that these Jews held Polish citizenship. Shloime Mendelsohn gave the Polish Embassy in Washington a memorandum in which the Bund demanded a statement entitling all Jews from Poland who reached a country of refuge to return to Poland after the war.[82] Zygielbojm protested to his colleagues in the United States for constricting his latitude in responding to the deportation of Polish-origin Jews from France. He said that he possessed important information in this matter that had prompted the Polish government to respond.[83]

The American Bund Representation's response to the annihilation reports indicates that the American Bundists did not fathom the significance of the new reality and did not realize that they must confront it by changing their methods of action. In early August 1942 the journal *The Ghetto Speaks*, which the Bund had begun to publish in the United States, carried a report on the annihilation.[84] Several days before the journal appeared, the Bund leadership in New York met with the heads of the JLC to discuss the general protest conference of Jewish organizations at Madison Square Garden in July 1942, in which the leaders of the JLC had taken part. The Bund activists criticized the JLC leaders for having participated in this rally alongside Zionist activists, stating that the organized American Jewish proletariat, led by the JLC, should have organized a protest activity of its own.[85]

During September–November 1942 Zygielbojm began to realize that the events in Poland were different from anything he had known and comprehended when the first reports of the genocide had arrived, and he began to adjust his *modus operandi*. The rescue of Polish Jews from death became his main concern, and his psychological distress mounted. The Bund leadership in New York, by contrast, continued to view developments from its traditional political perspective. As the gap between Zygielbojm and the New York leadership widened, there was a virtual parting of the ways.

Another Bund report by Leon Feiner was dispatched from Warsaw in late August or early September 1942. Forwarded to the Polish government and evidently handed to Zygielbojm in late November, it included details about the mass deportation from Warsaw and information about extermination camps in Poland and deportations from other towns in the *Generalgouvernement*.[86] Zygielbojm had known about the deportation from Warsaw even before he received Feiner's report, having seen a cable from the Polish mission in Istanbul in mid-November 1942. On 18 November he wrote the following to Nowogrodzki in New York:

> I have undertaken not to publicize the matter for now. The Government has given an instruction to publish the matters fully and comprehensively as soon as this becomes possible and the material is completed. I will cable you in another two days, and then you will ask why I wrote this letter. [I did so] because I cannot be silent. I wanted to write to you about my activity in the most recent council meeting, but I cannot concentrate. Anything said and done is superfluous and unimportant compared with what is happening there.[87]

From late 1941 onwards, reports on mass murders of Jews in Poland, Lithuania, Byelorussia and Ukraine continued to arrive and make their way to the Polish government-in-exile. Schwarzbart received such information, in a rough and less than fully reliable form, from November 1941. It took until the autumn of 1942, however, for the matter to come to full awareness and for limited protest actions in the capitals of the Free World to begin. Schwarzbart's despairing frustration with the Allies' failure to act on behalf of the mortally threatened Jews[88] in November 1942 was comparable with the feelings experienced by his colleague on the Polish National Council, Szmuel Zygielbojm.

Feiner's report of late August 1942 did not come into Zygielbojm's possession (at least formally) until late November 1942. Zygielbojm made explicit mention of the letter from Berezowski (Feiner) in a communication to Nowogrodzki on 27 and 28 November 1942, in which he presented a lengthy and detailed account of all information that Feiner had provided.[89] There is no doubt, however, that the grisly details in Feiner's report, including information on the deportations from the Warsaw ghetto, were in his possession before 27 November, when he disclosed them at a meeting of the National Council. His great frustration over his inability to respond at once, now that he was fully aware of the situation, stands out in his letter of 18 November, in which he had to use allusions and leave out details in order to avoid censorship by the Polish government, which was not yet willing to release the information in its entirety.

On 27 November 1942 the National Council held a special meeting at which Mikołajczyk reported details from various reports from Poland about the extermination of the Jews. Zygielbojm wrote to his comrades that he and the Polish minister had got into an argument in which he found himself totally isolated. He demanded that the Polish government should not content itself with statements of protest, and presented three practical demands: a series of measures meant to force the Germans to halt the murders; an entreaty to the Allies to threaten Germany with reprisals against its citizens in the event of non-compliance; and an undertaking to drop leaflets over German cities to apprise the German population of its government's actions and their consequences for this population if the murders continued. These demands, included in Feiner's report in the name of underground activists in Poland,[90] did not win the support of the other delegates to the National Council. On 28 November 1942 Zygielbojm met with Polish Foreign Minister Raczyński, who told him that the proposals had been taken up with the British Government, which had rejected them out of hand.[91]

In December 1942 Zygielbojm circulated hundreds of copies of Feiner's report among British MPs, the Polish National Council, journalists and public figures. To his astonishment, the British government avoided any substantive response, even though the annihilation of the Jews was beginning to have an impact on British public opinion. In one of his meetings with Raczyński during this time, Zygielbojm argued that one could not evade measures of some kind to halt the murders by claiming that rescue was virtually impossible; it was inconceivable to content oneself with statements about the punishment that awaited the murderers after the war. Such conduct, Zygielbojm maintained, made no impression on the murderers because they had nothing to lose if defeated.[92] Zygielbojm was well aware of the British stance on the Great Powers' response to the extermination of Polish Jewry. On 15 December 1942 he sent the British Foreign Office a cable addressed to Prime Minister Churchill. Four days later, the Foreign Office forwarded the cable to the office of the prime minister, along with a request to give Zygielbojm an evasive and non-committal response.[93] Even before he received an official answer from the prime minister's office, however, he wrote to his comrades in New York stating that he now clearly understood Britain's attitude. The government was reluctant to encourage too much public sympathy for the Jewish cause lest it interfere with the British war effort.[94]

These matters made it clear to Zygielbojm that he must collaborate with Ignacy Schwarzbart. The two Jewish delegates to the National Council attempted to address a joint appeal to the American and British governments concerning the annihilation of the Jews, but the Bund leadership in New York forbade its representative to take a political measure in conjunction with the Zionist delegate.[95] Feiner's last report showed Zygielbojm how isolated the Jews were in Poland and how emphatically the Polish underground was denying them its assistance. In a discussion at the National Council on the response of the Polish underground to the extermination of the Jews, all the parties, including the PPS, resisted the idea of launching a Polish uprising for reason of the extermination. Zygielbojm met with Mikołajczyk on 14 December 1942 and made some remarks on this matter. Mikołajczyk, however, told him that the Poles regarded a general uprising, which Soviet radio was urging the Poles to instigate, as a treasonous move at that time. The Poles would eventually be included in the extermination operation, Zygielbojm told the Polish deputy prime minister, adding that the underground should respond to the annihilation of the Polish Jews, who were full citizens of Poland, with an uprising. The Germans must be shown that they cannot obliterate Polish Jewry without a response from the Polish population at large, he maintained. Furthermore, he stated, an all-out uprising would prompt the world to take substantive action against Germany to halt the murders and would make a greater impact than all requests and entreaties. Zygielbojm vacillated about whether or not to present this demand – for a total Polish uprising – in meetings of the National Council, lest he again be isolated among the Polish parties. His comrades in New York advised him against bringing the matter before the National Council and urged him merely to demand that the Jews be given arms to defend themselves.[96]

Zygielbojm's mounting isolation also reflected his distrust of the Polish government and the National Council delegates in regard to their willingness to take serious action against anti-Semitism in Poland. Zygielbojm informed his comrades in New York that he was not being allowed to study reports from the Polish underground to London; he was not even allowed to read the Polish underground press freely. The reason, he was told, was that these documents contained state secrets. However, he believed that the injunction was really meant to blind him to anti-Semitic manifestations that resonated in a small part of the Polish underground press. Feiner, too – Zygielbojm believed – could not write freely because the Polish underground was censoring the information being cabled to London.[97] The very fact that he could not take up the matter with the National Council for lack of unequivocal evidence left him dejected. At the Council meeting on 23 December 1942, he fiercely criticized the Polish government for its response concerning the attitude of the Polish population toward the Jews:

> The tragedy that is under way will reach the consciousness of humankind only after the tempest of the war wanes and the curtain is lifted. Then the shocking tragedy will be revealed to the world. I am speaking of horrific, repulsive matters [and am doing so] in great anguish, with no interest whatsoever in starting a personal struggle. Those who have died have no interests, and even the living have few. These matters pertain to the attitude of the population and the Government toward the tragedy of Polish Jewry ... Do not tell me that I am defaming Poland before the world. The damage is being caused not by those who talk but by those who have perpetrated the actions. The war will end and the tragedy of Polish Jewry will beset the conscience of humankind for many generations to come. Unfortunately, the tragedy will be associated with the attitude of some of the Polish population toward the situation. I leave it to you to find the correct response.[98]

This peroration upset Mikołajczyk, who told Zygielbojm that if he did not call off his 'settling of scores' against the Polish Government in the National Council, he would personally release information about unpatriotic behaviour by Jews in Poland.[99]

At this time, Zygielbojm met with the Polish underground courier Jan Karski, who had reached London. Before leaving Warsaw, Karski had met with Feiner and a representative of the ŻKN and had even toured the ghetto. Feiner asked Karski to communicate Polish Jewry's desperate protest to the Free World and to report its accusation of their representatives outside of Poland for not having done enough to rescue such Jews as remained alive in Poland. If Polish Jewry could not be saved, Feiner demanded (according to Karski) that they too should forfeit their lives as a manifestation of their protest and to shock the leaders of the Great Powers into taking real action. Karski's description of Zygielbojm's response to the remarks, as reported to him – a response that supports the hypothesis that Zygielbojm's inability to take any action against the mass murder was causing him severe distress.[100]

Slowly Zygielbojm realized that he could not meet the expectations of Feiner and his associates in Poland. His personal distress deepened because he knew that every day of inaction ended with another wave

of extermination. Zygielbojm disengaged himself from all party activity
at this time. He was despondent about his inability to stem the measures
in Poland, disillusioned with the Polish government's attitude and
response to anti-Semitic manifestations in Poland, and disappointed
with the action guidelines that his comrades in New York had sent him.
The Bundists in New York had asked him to carry out various party-
related tasks, e.g., to arrange British entry visas for Bund leaders who
had left the Soviet Union and American visas for members who wished
to join their families there. He treated these requests indifferently and
told his associates in New York that he could not request the discharge
of comrades in the Polish army because they were Bundists.[101] Zygielbojm
considered himself Polish Jewry's representative and spokesman *vis-à-
vis* the Free World. As his sense of personal responsibility toward the
Jews mounted, so too did his dejection and despair. He explained his
ordeal to his comrades in New York:

> All of this [the murders that began in the spring of 1942] took
> place over four months. How many [Jews] remain alive today, and
> where are they? Our protest actions are of no practical significance.
> We began to operate after the first report about the murders in
> eastern Poland that began in the spring arrived in July ... At that
> very time, mass murders were raging in Warsaw and throughout
> central Poland ... We did not succeed, I did not succeed, in doing
> anything in the aftermath of the publicity, anything that would
> save even one person, even one Jewish child, from the terrible death.
> How can I carry on with routine daily work, take part in sessions,
> in questions [in the Council, and], attend meetings, when it is so
> clear ... Today, all of them ... every child is referring his prayers
> and grievances [to me]. [I] am the representative of them all.[102]

The Bund members in New York sensed Zygielbojm's distress and
realized that he could no longer discharge his function in the National
Council. He himself wrote to them in early January 1943 and entreated
them to replace him on the Council.[103] When Sikorski visited New York
in January 1943 the members of the Representation tried again to
arrange British entrance visas for Emanuel Nowogrodzki and Chayim
Wasser. Nowogrodzki was slated to take over from Zygielbojm because
Emanuel Szerer refused to head for London in view of disagreements
with his comrades in concerning the Bund's posture toward the Polish
government in that city. Nowogrodzki refused to take a strongly critical
stance against the Polish government. Szerer, by contrast, argued that

this government should be asked to urge the population in Poland to help the Jews as best it could. However, this attempt to obtain British visas for members of the Bund Representation, like previous attempts, did not fare well.[104]

In early March 1943 Zygielbojm obtained a cable from Orzech and Feiner, in Warsaw, containing the desperate appeal of the underground to save such Jews as remained in the ghetto after the January 1943 *Aktion*. Zygielbojm met with Polish Foreign Minister Raczyński, who agreed to forward the plea of the two Bund members in Warsaw to Pope Pius XII, as they requested. To encourage broader public reverberations, Zygielbojm asked his comrades in New York to allow him this time to coordinate the protest actions with Schwarzbart:

> Such an appeal would make a greater impact on world opinion, which knows nothing about our disagreements with Schwarzbart, than one expressed in the name of the Jewish workers' mission. If you forbid me to do this, I will not do it, of course, but it will weigh heavily on my conscience. It is much more important to attempt [to rescue] than to make plans for the future, if we have a future at all. I believe everyone feels this way.[105]

These were Zygielbojm's last days. The dispute with Schwarzbart and the Jewish organizations, which he loathed and from which he had dissociated himself, were no longer meaningful to him. His last attempts to take some small action on behalf of Polish Jewry had no partisan or personal aspects whatsoever. His comrades in New York squabbled with each other about whether or not to appeal to the Pope jointly with Schwarzbart and gave Zygielbojm no explicit guidelines in this matter.[106] Several members of the Representation said that even at that grim hour, as the Jews were being annihilated, the movement must maintain its singularity and follow its traditional ideational path. Nowogrodzki stated explicitly that the Bund should adhere to its traditional and historical attitudes even amidst the ordeal that had overtaken the Jews in Poland.[107]

Zygielbojm evidently decided to take his own life in late March or early April 1943. Despite this, he carried on with the matters in hand as though nothing had changed.[108] Slowly he parted from his closest colleagues, the group of members who had remained in Warsaw. On 4 April 1943 he attempted to explain in a message to Poland that he had exhausted all efforts to mobilize world opinion on behalf of the murdered Jews of Poland – with no appreciable results:

Your outcry at the end of the last cable [that of February 1943], in which you held me accountable to history, was officially relayed by myself from the National Council podium to the entire world. I am now issuing a new, direct appeal, in your names, to the Government and the public in the Allied countries. You can see from everything I wrote to you that we met your demand to mobilize the world immediately after your first report.[109]

When reports about the ghetto's valorous resistance arrived in April 1943, Zygielbojm apparently made his suicide decision irrevocable. Itzchak Deutscher, his friend in London, was the last person to see him alive. On the night of 11 May 1943 he was summoned by telephone to Zygielbojm's apartment. Zygielbojm sounded discouraged and broken, Deutscher related. He refused to tell Deutscher what he wished to discuss with him, but asked him to come urgently. Their last talk dealt with Zygielbojm's decision to launch a hunger strike outside the British Prime Minister's home – an action that he had ruled out several months previously. Deutscher told him that this was pointless, since the British police would drive him away and the incident would be censored. Instead, he suggested that Zygielbojm resign from the Council in protest against the Polish underground's failure to arm the Jews in self-defence. Zygielbojm refused – lest his resignation be harmful to the remaining Bund members in Poland – and continued to affirm the need to make some sort of a demonstration near the home of the British Prime Minister.[110]

By the time he met with Deutscher, several hours before his suicide, Zygielbojm had already made the decision to end his life. That day, he wrote to the chairman of the National Council, Professor Stanisław Grabski, asking him to appoint Emanuel Szerer to replace him on the Council. In another letter, left behind for Polish President Władysław Raczkiewicz and Prime Minister Sikorski, he wrote:

> The responsibility for the crime of the murder of whole Jewish nationality in Poland rests first of all on those who are carrying it out, but indirectly it falls also upon the whole of humanity, on the peoples of the Allies, and on their governments, who to this day have not taken any real steps to halt this crime.[111]

He wrote the following farewell letter to his brother in Johannesburg:

> A night in April 1943. I walk the streets of London with two men. Thinking about the Warsaw ghetto – why am I far from there?

Why am I not with them in their last struggle? Why am I not fighting with them for the ramparts and the ruins of the ghetto?... I am especially troubled by the fact that I was there, together, with all of them. What right have I to survive? Did I not share their fate? I have been deprived the relief that might be instilled by the illusion that my work was somehow important in rescuing someone from the brutal gallows of extinction.[112]

He expressed his last hope to his comrades in New York: 'I hope that upon my death I will achieve what I failed to achieve in my life – real action to rescue at least a few of the 300,000 Jews who have survived, out of slightly more than three million who had been there before.'[113]

At this point it seems appropriate to discuss briefly the background of the man who was negotiating on behalf of the Bund at the National Council, and who carried such a heavy burden of responsibility at such a crucial and dreadful time for European Jewry. Szmuel Zygielbojm was born in February 1895 in Borowica, a small village in the Chełm area, near Lublin. He attended *cheder* but at the age of 11 had to begin working to help support his impoverished family (there were 11 of them). He first discovered the Bund and its activities in 1907, when he went to Warsaw in search of work. From then on, his life and the Jewish labour movement in Poland were intertwined. In 1920 he was chosen as secretary of the Jewish metalworkers' union in Warsaw; from 1924 on, he was a member of the Bund Central Committee.[114]

Zygielbojm was symbolic of a group of Bund activists who came to prominence in the movement during the interwar years. Unlike well-schooled senior leaders who were products of the Russian Bund (Erlich, Alter, Kossovski and Portnoy), Zygielbojm ascended to the Bund leadership from the ranks of the Polish-Jewish working class. He considered himself a close associate and a member of this collectivity in which he lived. He lacked formal education and his only pre-war experience in public activity outside Jewish settings was membership in the Bund delegations to town councils in Warsaw (1927) and Łódź (1938). Like other members of the Bund who experienced their political and ideological development between the wars in the light of tensions and rivalries among Jewish parties, Zygielbojm viewed the Bund ideology as the only possible way to solve the Jewish problem in Poland. He was known for his ideological allegiance and his resistance to any deviation, especially in regard to political relations with the Zionists.

The war forced him to perform duties for which he had never been prepared. As the only member of the Central Committee who remained in Poland, he became the underground leader of the Bund during his brief stay in Warsaw – in the first few months of the occupation – before he left for the West. After he reached the United States, he became a much sought-after speaker for the Jewish labour movement in Poland. For these reasons, he was also given a highly complex and difficult political function: as a member of the National Council in exile in London.

Zygielbojm committed suicide on the morning of 12 May 1943. A loyal and devoted activist in the Jewish labour movement in Poland, he had been handed an impossible mission by the force of circumstances. The need to bear the workload of a member of the National Council in London, to deal in Party affairs, and to navigate the labyrinth of internal Polish political problems as reports on the annihilation of the Jews were coming, was beyond his capacity. In his efforts to shoulder the burden, however, Zygielbojm did develop some degree of political acumen. Having begun as the representative of the Bund, he became the representative of all Polish Jewry. He undoubtedly managed to attract much public attention in London to the fate of Polish Jewry, especially among important members of the British Labour Party and members of the Socialist International. Schwarzbart, too, who had conducted innumerable arguments with him, ruled appreciatively that Zygielbojm had contributed vastly to the formation of sympathetic public opinion for the Jewish cause.[115] Zygielbojm did not hesitate to confront the Polish government – usually alone – and to accuse it of evading the problem of anti-Semitism and the attitude of the Polish population toward the Jews, as the massacres proceeded. His severe isolation also stemmed from his feeling that his comrades in New York did not support him sufficiently and did not share his acute distress in view of the extermination. We may also understand his anxiety over the fate of his dear ones – his wife Mania and his son – who perished during the uprising in early May 1943. Zygielbojm was exceptional among Jewish activists from Poland who operated in exile during the war in the guilt he felt for not having been with those who perished. All these factors, and the hope that he could achieve in death what he had not managed to accomplish in life – to create a way to help the Jews in Poland – drove him to suicide.

A POLISH-JEWISH DIPLOMAT: EMANUEL SZERER

The day after Zygielbojm's suicide in London, the American Representation of the Bund cabled Mikołajczyk and asked him to consider Lucjan

Blit as the Bund's liaison in London until Zygielbojm's replacement could arrive. Blit was one of the Bund activists who had reached London after having left the Soviet Union with the Polish army at the beginning of 1943. Leon Oller had left with him, and the two of them began to work at Zygielbojm's side during the last few weeks of the latter's life. The Representation empowered Blit to coordinate the work of the Bund in London and to liaise with the underground in Warsaw.[116] Although Blit was the senior representative *vis-à-vis* the Polish political system, the guidelines given him and Leon Oller by the party leaders in New York left these officials in London utterly powerless to make political decisions except in consultation with the Representation in New York.[117]

Zygielbojm's suicide left the Bund representatives in London overwhelmed and confused; the American Representation made efforts to bolster their morale so they could carry on with the work. In this matter, Chayim Wasser wrote the following to Oller:

> Your activity and mine ... is being hindered by the annihilation of our people in Europe, especially in occupied Poland by the Nazis. Who knows how many of our kin are among those murdered? [Then came] the murder of Erlich and Alter, and now – Artur's tragic death. It is too much, even for us ... We are orphans; orphanhood reigns everywhere ... Nevertheless, we have to overcome this sense of despair. Despair leads to passiveness and to the kind of action that Artur took. I am not about to judge whether Artur did the right thing or not.[118]

Blit and Oller found it difficult to collaborate and occasionally disagreed on how to present the Bund's stance. The two were at odds even in explaining Zygielbojm's suicide. Oller, in an article submitted to the PPS London journal, *Robotnik*, stressed that Zygielbojm had taken his life in protest against the murder of the Jews and the world's indifference. Blit responded by submitting his own article to the PPS journal, in which he took exception to Zygielbojm's action, tracing it to his sense of loss after the death of his wife and son in the Warsaw ghetto, and dismissing it as a way of prompting international officials to act on behalf of the Jews.[119]

On 4 July 1943 Prime Minister Sikorski died in a mysterious accident while flying from Gibraltar to London. His death sent the Polish government and the National Council into shock. Sikorski was a soldier-statesman who had earned much prestige and sympathy in

Poland. He was welcome among the leaders of the British government, and had become a confidante of Churchill. The new government that was set up under Mikołajczyk, who lacked Sikorski's international prestige and sympathy, lost its lustre and international political stature in the summer of 1943. These developments, along with disputes among the Polish factions in exile, made Blit believe that the Polish political institutions in London were losing their practical importance. Among the leading Bund activists in exile, only Blit began to give thought to the post-war period and Poland's future situation. Thus, he pledged full effort to strengthening relations with Feiner and the underground in Poland, and to reinforcing relief efforts for the Jewish survivors. Blit found ways to forward relief money to Poland with the assistance of socialist friends in Sweden. In January 1944 he reached Stockholm and arranged additional conduits for money from Stockholm to Feiner in Warsaw.[120] As for the Bund's tasks and its activity in the National Council, he wrote the following to his colleagues in New York:

> We must prepare for the situation in Poland after the war. When the war ends, we will be in dire condition. The impression of the glorious past still lives in our hearts … The whole tragedy should be assessed soberly … The question of emigration [of Jews from Poland] slipped off the agenda in 1939. We have no interest in the results of the 1938 elections but rather those of 1944 … The National Council is a stupid matter (Szerer does not know this, since he is still in New York…). We have no interests here … We cannot wield political clout here and we will not be heeded here as we were in our rallies in Poland … One may die over Treblinka, one may commit suicide, but one may not live … We are 'getting old', as are all of the political movements here, and this fact deserves some thought.[121]

In November 1943 Emanuel Szerer reached London and became the Bund's new delegate to the National Council. Personal problems and rivalries for prestige, coupled with disputes in matters of principle, drained the Bund delegation of its influence, in contrast to the respect it had commanded during Zygielbojm's tenure. Szerer insisted on being the only official representative of the Bund, demanded the right to see his colleagues' correspondence in party affairs and appointed himself as the Bund delegate to all international public forums to which the Bund was invited.[122] The delegation in London stopped holding coordination meetings and discussions of issues on the agenda; practically speaking, Blit and Oller lost all interest in its work. Relations among members of the delegation slid into total chaos in October–November 1944, just as crucial political questions were coming on the agenda. A new situation was evolving in Poland: the Polish National Committee of Liberation, the PKWN (Polski Komitet Wyzwolenia Narodowego), was consolidating itself in Lublin after that town was liberated in the summer of 1944, and the Soviets recognized it as the new government. In October 1944 Blit informed Emanuel Szerer and the Bundists in New York that he was retiring from the delegation's work in London. In a reasoned, detailed letter, he explained to his colleagues that he saw no point in continuing to work at the mission in London after Szerer had monopolized all the powers.[123] These internal problems and their effect – virtual paralysis of the delegation's work – perturbed the Bund activists in New York. Nowogrodzki and his comrades attempted to persuade their three colleagues in London to transcend their personal rivalries and prestige struggles and find a way to work together.[124] However, they backed Szerer, the senior Bund representative in London, and gave him broader powers than they had given Zygielbojm.

Szerer's working methods in London were totally different from Zygielbojm's. Szerer had been one of the young Bund leaders in the interwar period. A doctor of law who was immeasurably more fluent in Polish than in Yiddish, Szerer was a suitable candidate for the political assignment in London. His attachment to Jewish affairs was weaker than that of Zygielbojm, who had always been immersed in Polish Jewry and Jewish realities. Szerer viewed his role in the National Council through the prism of a Polish-Jewish statesman and sought to participate in the largest possible number of Polish forums in London and to attain full coordination with his counterparts in the PPS. In November 1943 Szerer demanded that Stanisław Grabski, chairman of the National Council, put his name forward to five Council committees: budget, law and justice, social affairs and economics, security and foreign affairs.[125] The PPS activists in London gave Szerer a very warm welcome and introduced him to the forum of party activists in London as 'the representative of our sister party'.[126] Several months after he reached London, he cooperated with PPS members on the National Council in establishing a coordinating committee comprised of the Bund and the Polish socialists.[127]

In his first few months of activity Szerer tried to put pressure on the Polish government to be more active on behalf of the Jews. After he met with Prime Minister Mikołajczyk on 26 November 1943, he demanded that Mikołajczyk establish a Polish government delegation that would appear before representatives of the three powers at war with Germany and demand action for Polish Jewry. He also demanded the formation of an international body that would rescue the Jewish remnant in Poland. In December 1943 Szerer and several PPS delegates to the National Council passed a series of resolutions protesting against the continued annihilation of Jews in Poland and urging the Polish government and the Allies to rescue such Jews as remained alive.[128] At that time, Szerer apparently still believed that some kind of international action on behalf of Polish Jewry could be taken. He got on better with Schwarzbart than did Zygielbojm at the beginning of the latter's tenure in London. The two officials appeared together in conferences of Jewish organizations in Britain and expressed shared views on various current problems in early 1944.[129]

However, Szerer evidently realized at this time that the powers would not take drastic action in the last phases of the war to rescue the surviving Jews in Poland, and began to give more thought to the condition of Polish Jewry after the war. In January 1944 he informed the Polish Interior Minister, Stańczyk, about resolutions that one of the National Council committees had adopted at his initiative. Szerer's letter described the two decisions in detail: an assurance that the Jewish population in Poland would be allowed to rehabilitate its national and cultural life after the war, and a promise to apply Jewish cultural autonomy. For this purpose, planning of appropriate projects would begin. In early 1944 Szerer presented these matters for debate to the National Council, in the joint forums in which he participated along with socialist activists from other European countries, and to members of the Labour Party.[130]

In January 1944 anti-Semitism among the Polish forces that were stationed in Britain became a topic for debate in the National Council and in British public opinion. Sixty-eight Jews serving in the Polish army requested discharge from the Polish forces so they could enlist with the British as volunteers. After negotiations between the British and Polish Ministries of Defence, the British agreed to annex the soldiers to a unit of the British army. About a month later, another 140 Jewish soldiers asked to leave the Polish army. They too were admitted to the British ranks, but the British government announced that they would be the last. On 13 March 1944 the Polish Defence Minister, Marian Kukiel, announced that any soldier missing from his unit would be considered a deserter and punished as such. Nevertheless, 23 additional Jewish soldiers deserted several days later. The last-mentioned desertion caused the issue to make waves. It was taken up for debate in the British parliament and embarrassed both the British and the Polish governments. The Jewish soldiers reported that they had left their units not out of unwillingness to take part in the war but because both enlisted men and officers in the Polish army had fomented a seriously anti-Semitic climate there.[131]

The desertion affair embarrassed Szerer and his colleagues in New York. Although the American Representation had severely criticized the phenomenon of anti-Semitism in the Polish army, these Bund members could not support the desertion of Jewish soldiers because desertion was a criminal offence and an affront to a treasured principle: equal participation of Jews, like other Polish citizens, in the war effort. Moreover, Szerer was concerned that Jews who would be turned away by the British forces after their desertion would join the Jewish Brigade units in Palestine at this time.[132] The affair lost its currency in November 1944 after the Polish units army joined the Allies in invading France, after the Polish uprising in Warsaw, and since Germany's downfall became imminent.

However, despite Szerer's aspirations to integrate activity on behalf of Polish Jewry into a broader framework of Polish political activity, his main achievements in the last years of the war actually focused on aid and forwarding of relief funds to the surviving Jews in Poland. American Jewish organizations began to provide *Żegota* (the Council for Aid to Jews in Poland, created by Polish underground activists in September 1942) with money for its operations. The funds were delivered through underground conduits from the Polish Government to the *Delegatura*, its representative on Polish soil, and thence to Adolph Berman and Leon Feiner, the two Jewish representatives in Zegota. They handed the relief funds that came into their possession to concealed Jews and Party associates, or used them for needs of the Jewish underground in the ghettos and the camps. Some of the money was used to pay for the current activity of *Żegota*.[133]

From late 1942 the JLC transferred large amounts of money to the Bund representatives in Poland for the Jews' relief and aid needs. That year, the JLC forwarded $19,000 to Zygielbojm for remittance to Warsaw, but this was only some of the money that Zygielbojm sent to Feiner in Warsaw. In a cable he sent to Warsaw on 6 May 1943, shortly before he committed suicide, Zygielbojm informed Feiner that from September 1942 to May 1943 he had sent $58,000 to the Bund underground in Warsaw by means of the Polish government, but Feiner had received only $33,000. By the end of 1943 the JLC had raised $81,000 and relayed that sum to London for transfer to Feiner, the Bund representative on the *Żegota* council.[134] In 1944 (January–November), the Bund representatives in London, Szerer and Blit, sent another $83,000 that the Jewish JLC had given the Polish Consulate in New York for remittance to Warsaw.[135] Reports from Feiner to Szerer confirm the arrival of smaller sums than these. Feiner affirmed the receipt of $38,000 by October 1943 (i.e., an additional $5,000 that the *Delegatura* had given him between May and October 1943) and $72,000 between February and November 1944.[136] These figures support the conjecture that much of the money sent by Jewish organizations in the West to the two Jewish representatives on the *Żegota* council did not reach its destination. Feiner was well aware that Polish officials were helping themselves to funds that had been earmarked for rescue and relief for surviving Jews in labour camps in Poland and frequently complained about this to representatives in the *Delegatura*. Feiner claimed that these funds were needed to rescue Jewish children, to aid Jewish slave labourers in a series of camps and to pay for operations of the ŻOB. Vehemently demanding the money that Schwarzbart and Szerer had sent from London, he argued that any delay in turning over the funds endangered the lives of the thousands of Jews who desperately needed help.[137]

In November 1943 the Polish Consulate in New York presented Pat and the heads of the JLC with a demand: that the money destined for Bund representatives in London be transferred to them by a Central Committee of the Polish government that would receive and apportion all relief funds from the Jewish organizations. The Polish Consulate argued that the direct transfer of funds from political agencies exposed the Polish government to pressure and placed it in an uncomfortable position. The JLC and the Bund activists in New York rejected the Consulate's demand outright, suspecting that the Polish government wished thereby to appropriate the relief money for itself.[138] Feiner ran into severe financial hardship; in May 1944, he informed Szerer by cable that he had been 'left penniless' and that a transfer of additional relief funds must be arranged at once.[139]

In April 1944, by which time almost no Jewish centres remained in Poland, the Polish Government in London responded to Szerer's and Schwarzbart's persuasive efforts by establishing the Council for the Rescue of the Jewish Population in Poland (Rada do Spraw Ratowania Ludności Żydowskiej w Polsce), headed by Adam Ciołkosz. The decision to establish this council was prompted, in part, by the political considerations of the government-in-exile. The War Refugee Board had been established in the United States in January 1944, and the

Polish government-in-exile realized that it dared not lag behind the relief efforts of the American president just when his attitude toward the future of Poland after the war had become crucially important.[140] The Council was headed by political activists from the Polish parties in exile in London in concert with Jewish associate members, including Emanuel Szerer as the Bund representative. From August 1944 on, the Polish Ministry of Labour and Social Affairs and the JLC forwarded relief money to Bund member Jerzy Gliksman, who had left Anders' army in Palestine and settled in Tel Aviv. Gliksman used these funds to create an extensive operation in which parcels were sent from Palestine to Jewish refugees in the USSR and Romania.[141]

The Council for the Rescue of the Jewish Population in Poland accomplished little of substance in relation to the large sums of money that Jewish organizations and others gave it.[142] In the main, it discussed the future of the Jewish population in liberated Poland, planned future rehabilitation actions and appealed to international players to help Polish-Jewish refugees who had reached various countries.[143] Blit realized that the Polish government was actually perpetrating a fraud, and ridiculed Szerer for having agreed to cooperate with it in an organization that was doing nothing for the Jewish refugees.[144] In the middle of February 1945 a Council delegation, with the participation of Emanuel Szerer, visited liberated France and Belgium to study the needs of Polish-Jewish refugees there. This outing, too – chiefly a media event – was preceded by five months of arguments and delays until the Polish government authorized it to set out. Upon its return, the delegation recommended that the Polish government immediately redirect all funds of the Council to assistance for Jews in liberated camps, whose poor health placed them in mortal danger even after the liberation.[145]

Emanuel Szerer began to serve as a member of the National Council in London after the Jewish cause had substantially slipped off the public agenda in the West. The protest actions that had erupted upon the arrival of reports on the extermination in the spring and summer of 1942 waned considerably; the public's attention was captured by the offensive against Germany and the effort to win the war as quickly as possible.

The London delegation consolidated itself during Szerer's tenure. Despite their personal rivalries, Szerer and the two activists, Lucjan Blit and Leon Oller, established a well-run liaison office *vis-à-vis* European socialist parties and public figures, and even issued intermittent party publications. Zygielbojm, in contrast, had operated in London alone and unaided, waging the struggle for the Jewish cause almost unassisted. Nevertheless, he had managed to call the attention of the British public to the tragedy of Polish Jewry, to a greater extent than Szerer, Blit and Oller managed to do. Even in the spring and summer of 1944, as the Jews of Hungary were being transported to Auschwitz, Szerer was unable to stir as great a tempest in the National Council or in British public opinion as Zygielbojm had evoked in the summer and autumn of 1942. Szerer, in contrast, carefully maintained orderly and sound relations with the Polish government and members of the PPS, in the belief that quasi-diplomatic action and participation in committees, conferences and public events would enable him to accomplish more.

Although they were often reminded of the limitations and the realities that they faced, membership in the National Council was an important component in the Bund's wartime activity. By establishing a delegation in London – an important junction of political activity in Europe during the war, the place to which information on developments in Poland flowed and from which money and instructions were sent to the under-ground organizations – the Bund was able to participate in this activity to some extent. The Bund Representation in New York and its emissaries in London managed to make proper use of the channels of communi-cation that had become available to them in London and New York and exploited them to move money and relief to Poland, the Soviet Union, Palestine and party members in Shanghai. However, the Bund's activity in the National Council in London also revealed its weakness as a purported source of influence over the Polish government on the Jewish issue. The National Council, not a democratically elected body, was actually a tool that General Sikorski and other politicians manipu-lated in pursuit of their political goals. The Bund, which had never sent a delegate to the parliament of independent interwar Poland, was awarded one delegate in the Council mainly because the Polish politicians in exile believed this might help them make headway in American Jewish public opinion. However, the Bund representatives in London failed to persuade the Polish government to take substantive action on behalf of the Jews in Poland, i.e., to condemn anti-Semitic manifestations in Poland unequivocally, to urge the Polish population clearly and artic-ulately to help the Jews, to instruct the Polish underground to assist the ghetto rebels by providing weapons, or to be more generous in allocating aid to the Jews as the war wound down. In so far as the Polish government acted in the Jewish cause, it did so for reasons of cold political calculus; in this sense, the Bund suffered a stinging defeat.

Realities challenged the Bund deputies to the National Council as they did in occupied Poland. The Jews' isolation during the war and their inability to find true allies in the midst of the tragedy that befell Polish Jewry were shared by the Bundists in the Polish exile institutions and the party's activists in Warsaw. The partnership of fate in which the Bund believed – an alliance between the Jewish and the Polish peoples against the common enemy – did not pass the test of reality. Zygielbojm and, to some extent, Lucjan Blit understood this fact more astutely than Emanuel Szerer did.

NOTES

1. Nowogrodzki to Mendelsohn, 15 November 1939, BA, MG-1/17.
2. Report on the results of the fundraising campaign in Boston area, BA, MG-1/50.
3. Nowogrodzki to Mendelsohn (see note 1).
4. Nowogrodzki's November 1939 circular, which announced the formation of the American Representation of the Bund in Poland, BA, ME-18/38.
5. Nowogrodzki to Miller, 2 December 1939, BA, M-12/8-A.
6. Nowogrodzki to Erlich and Alter, 8 November 1941, BA, M-7/20.
7. Nowogrodzki and Dubinsky to Labour secretariat in London, 2 October 1939, BA, MG-1/44.
8. Kurski to Nowogrodzki, 2 November and 5 December1939, BA, M-7/12.
9. Nowogrodzki to Mendelsohn (see note 1).
10. Pat to Nyomark, 6 February 1940, BA, MG-2/47.
11. Nowogrodzki to Zygielbojm, 13 November 1940, BA, MG-2/32; Sonya Nowogrodzki to Emanuel Nowogrodzki, 16 January 1941, BA, ME-16/80; Hertz (ed.), *In di Yorn*, p. 15.
12. Portnoy, Wasser and Mendelsohn to secretariat of the JLC, 5 February 1940, BA, MG-1/36.
13. Goldstein, *Finf Yor*, p. 412.
14. Minutes of meeting of the American Representation of the Bund, 25 September 1940, BA, ME-18/31.
15. Report of the Bund Relief Committee for the period between 1 December 1940 and 1 December 1941, BA, ME-1/61.
16. Report of expenditures of the American Representation of the Bund for the period between 1 October 1940 and 1 December 1941, BA, ME-18/35; minutes of meeting of the American Representation of the Bund, 3 February 1942, BA, ME-18/35. The confirmations that came from Warsaw to the American mission in February 1942 pertained to the receipt of 50,000 złoty. This sum approximates the moneys gathered by the party mission in 1941 and forwarded to Poland.
17. Sonya Nowogrodzki to Emanuel Nowogrodzki, 1 May 1941, BA, ME-18/60.
18. Minutes of meeting of the American Representation of the Bund, 11 February 1941, BA, ME-18/33.
19. Rotenberg, *Fun Varshe*, pp. 318–19; minutes of meeting of the American Representation of the Bund, 18 March 1941, BA, ME-18/33; Nowogrodzki to Erlich and Alter, 8 November 1941, BA, M-7/20; minutes of meeting of the American Representation of the Bund, 9 October 1941, BA, ME-18/32, D. H. Kranzler, *Japanese, Nazis and Jews: The Jewish Refugee Community in Shanghai 1938–1945* (New York: Yeshiva University Press, 1976), p. 347.

20. Minutes of meeting of the JLC board *et al.*, 16 January 1942, BA, JLC/15.
21. Ibid.
22. Ibid.
23. Financial statement of the American Representation of the Bund, 1 January 1943, BA, ME-18/39.
24. List of Bund members in the USSR, to whom relief money from the JLC had been sent, November 1941–May 1942, BA, ME-18/14-B.2.
25. Nowogrodzki to Polish Consulate in New York, 2 May 1942, BA, MG-1/40.
26. E. Duraczyński, *Rząd Polski na uchodźstwie 1939–1945* (Warsaw: Książka i Wiedza, 1993), pp. 41–2; Coutouvidis and Reynolds, *Poland 1939-1947*, pp. 26–7.
27. D. Stola, *Nadzieja i zagłada* (Warsaw: Oficyna Naukowa, 1995), pp. 29–34.
28. Zygielbojm to Nowogrodzki, 1 June 1940, BA, MG-2/5.
29. Mendelsohn to Nowogrodzki, 17 March 1940, BA, MG-1/36.
30. Ar. Zi, 'Bericht an die Socjalistische Arbeiter-International: Die Lage in Polen', BA, MG-1/50.
31. The American Representation of the Bund in New York to Polish government-in-exile, April 1940, YVA, M-2/269.
32. Memorandum from Zygielbojm to Kot, 18 April 1940, YVA, 025/222.
33. Ciołkosz to Kot, 25 April 1940, YVA, 025/222.
34. 'Stosunek Ukraińców i Żydów do Polaków', Report from Polish General Gustav Paszkiewicz to the government-in-exile, 15 May 1940, YVA, 025/220; D. Engel, *In the Shadow of Auschwitz: The Polish Government-in-Exile and the Jews 1939–1942* (Chapel Hill, NC, and London: University of North Carolina Press, 1987), pp. 55–69.
35. Zygielbojm to Nowogrodzki, 1 June 1940, BA, MG-2/26; Engel, *In the Shadows of Auschwitz*, pp. 75–6.
36. Schwarzbart to Tartakower, 22 October 1940, YVA, M-2/530.
37. Mendelsohn to Nowogrodzki, 17 March 1940, BA, MG-1/36.
38. Nowogrodzki to Mendelsohn and Szerer, 24 and 26 September 1940, BA, MG-1/36.
39. Mendelsohn to Nowogrodzki (see note 37).
40. Nowogrodzki to Gilles, 26 March 1941, BA, MG-1/63.
41. P. Schwartz, 'Vegn Ayner a Rede', *Unser Tsayt*, 7 (1941), pp. 18–20.
42. Engel, *In the Shadow of Auschwitz*, p. 122.
43. Schwarzbart, *Diary*, YVA, M-2/766.
44. Nowogrodzki to Stańczyk, 5 September 1941, BA, ME-18/34.
45. Stańczyk and Mikołajczyk to Nowogrodzki, 11 September 1941, BA, ME-18/34.
46. Letter from the secretary of the Polish Interior Ministry, to the Polish Foreign Ministry, 19 August 1941, YVA, 055/5.
47. Minutes of meeting of the American Representation of the Bund, 18 March 1941, BA, ME-16/32.
48. Nowogrodzki to Strakacz, the Polish consul in New York, 19 February 1942, YVA, 025/279.
49. Kurski to Mill, 10 March 1942, BA, ME-40/80.
50. Minutes of meeting of the American Representation of the Bund, 10 February 1942, BA, ME-18/35.
51. Ibid.
52. Minutes of meeting of the American Representation of the Bund and the Central Committee, 2 March 1942, BA, ME-18/35.
53. Blatman, 'On a Mission against all Odds', p. 167.
54. JTA bulletin, 7 April 1942, YVA, M-2/453; Zygielbojm's personal notebook, 2 April 1942, BA, M-16/151.
55. Zygielbojm's personal notebook, 5 April 1942, BA, M-16/151.
56. Ibid.

57. Zygielbojm to Kurski, 3 May 1942, BA, MG-2/5. The subject of Zygielbojm's relations with members of the PPS resurfaced in a meeting of the Bund mission in New York on 14 April 1942. See minutes of meeting, BA, ME-18/37; and Schwarzbart, *Diary*, 21 May 1942, YVA M-2/767.
58. Zygielbojm to Nowogrodzki, 17 April 1942, BA, MG-2/5.
59. Minutes of meeting of the American Representation of the Bund, 6 August 1942, BA, MG-18/37.
60. Zygielbojm to Nowogrodzki, 29 May 1942, BA, MG-2/5.
61. Zygielbojm to Nowogrodzki, 8 May 1942, BA, MG-2/5.
62. YVA, M–2/534, M-2/601.
63. Zygielbojm to Nowogrodzki, 29 May 1942, BA, MG-2/5.
64. Zygielbojm to Kurski, 3 May 1942, BA, MG-2/5.
65. For details of Feiner's report, see Hertz (ed.), *In di Yorn*, pp. 20–23.
66. Engel, *In the Shadow of Auschwitz*, pp. 176–80.
67. Zygielbojm to Nowogrodzki, 13 July 1942, BA, MG-2/5.
68. Stola, *Nadzieja i zagłada*, p. 153.
69. Zygielbojm to Nowogrodzki, 13 July 1942, BA, MG-2/5.
70. Zygielbojm to Nowogrodzki, 3 July 1942, BA, MG-2/5; Engel, *In the Shadow of Auschwitz*, p. 180.
71. Zygielbojm to Nowogrodzki, 3 and 13 May 1942, BA, MG-2/5.
72. 'German Atrocities in Poland and Czechoslavakia – Labour's Protest', BA, M-16/151-C.
73. Zygielbojm to Nowogrodzki, 31 August 1942, BA, MG-2/5.
74. Schwarzbart, *Diary*, YVA, M-2/768.
75. Ibid., YVA, M-2/769.
76. Minutes of meeting of the American Representation of the Bund, 2 June 1942, BA, ME-18/35.
77. Minutes of meeting of the Bund American mission Presidium, 6 August 1942, BA, ME-18/37.
78. Zygielbojm to Nowogrodzki, 31 August 1942, BA, MG-2/5.
79. Ibid.
80. Minutes of meeting of the American Representation of the Bund and the Central Committee, 2 March 1942, BA, ME-18/35.
81. D. Engel, 'The Polish Government-in-Exile and the Deportations of Polish Jews from France in 1942', *Yad Vashem Studies*, 15 (1983), pp. 101–2.
82. Minutes of meeting of the American Representation of the Bund, 22 September 1942, BA, ME-18/37.
83. Zygielbojm to Nowogrodzki, 6 January 1943, BA, MG-2/5.
84. *The Ghetto Speaks*, 2 (1 August 1942).
85. Minutes of meeting of the American Representation of the Bund and heads of the JLC, 4 August 1942, BA, ME-18/37.
86. Details of this report are presented in Hertz (ed.), *In di Yorn*, pp. 24–37.
87. Zygielbojm to Nowogrodzki, 18 November 1942, BA, MG-2/5.
88. Stola, *Nadzieja i zagłada*, pp. 157ff.
89. Zygielbojm to Nowogrodzki, 27 and 28 November, 1942, BA, MG-2/5.
90. Hertz (ed.), *In di Yorn*, pp. 36–7.
91. Zygielbojm to Nowogrodzki, 28 November 1942, BA, MG-2/5.
92. Zygielbojm to American Representation of the Bund, 11 December 1942, BA, MG-2/26.
93. Memorandum from Foreign Office to prime minister's office, 11 December 1942, PRO, FO/371/31097.
94. Zygielbojm to American Representation of the Bund, 11 December 1942, BA, MG-2/26.

95. Zygielbojm to American Representation of the Bund, 17 December 1942, BA, MG-2/26.
96. Minutes of meeting of the American Representation of the Bund Presidium, 16 February 1943, BA, ME-18/39.
97. Zygielbojm to American Representation of the Bund, 17 December 1942, BA, MG-2/26. Remarks at a meeting of the National Council on 23 December 1942, Schwarzbart, *Diary*, YVA, M-2/770.
98. Zygielbojm to American Representation of the Bund, 24 December 1942, BA, MG-2/26.
99. Ibid.
100. J. Karski, *The Story of a Secret State* (Boston, MA: Houghton Mifflin, 1944), pp. 264–8.
101. Zygielbojm to Nowogrodzki, 14 February 1943, BA, MG-2/5.
102. Zygielbojm to Nowogrodzki, 1 January 1943, ibid.
103. Zygielbojm to Nowogrodzki, 4 January 1943, ibid.
104. Nowogrodzki to Zygielbojm, 17 February 1943, ibid.; minutes of meeting of the American Representation of the Bund, 11 May 1943, BA, ME-18/39.
105. Cable from Zygielbojm to Nowogrodzki, 11 March 1943, BA, MG-2/5.
106. Minutes of meeting of the American Representation of the Bund, 16 March 1943, BA, ME-18/35.
107. Nowogrodzki to Zygielbojm, 4 May 1943, BA, M-16/151.
108. Zygielbojm to Iwenska, 1 February 1943, BA, M-16/151; Zygielbojm to Nowogrodzki, 7 April 1943, BA, MG-2/26; letter from Raczyński, 16 February 1966, YVA, 055/5.
109. The message was published in the Bund underground newspaper *Biuletyn W.B.* on 11 April 1944.
110. R. Ainsztein, 'New Light on Szmul Zygielbojm's Suicide', *Yad Vashem Bulletin*, 15 (August 1964), pp. 8–12.
111. Arad *et al.* (eds), *Documents on the Holocaust*, p. 326.
112. F. Zygielbojm, *Der Koyakh tsu Shtorbn* (Tel Aviv: Peretz Farlag, 1976), p. 280; A.S. Stein, *Haver Artur, Demuyot uFerakim miHayei haBund* (Tel Aviv: M. Newman, 1963), p. 297.
113. Hertz (ed.), *Zygielbojm Bukh*, p. 366.
114. The biographical details on Zygielbojm are culled from Y.S. Hertz, 'Szmuel Mordechai Zygielbojm (Khaver Artur)', ibid., pp. 11ff.
115. Schwarzbart to Tartakower, 25 August 1943, YVA, M-2/534.
116. Minutes of meeting of the American Representation of the Bund Presidium, 13 May 1943, BA, ME-18/39.
117. Minutes of meeting of the American Representation of the Bund Presidium, 24 May 1943, BA, ME-18/39.
118. Wasser to Oller, 30 June 1943, BA, ME-17/171.
119. Oller to Wasser, 4 January 1944, ibid.
120. Blit to Nowogrodzki, 12 January 1944, BA, MG-2/45.
121. Blit to Nowogrodzki, 19 July 1943, ibid.
122. Minutes of meeting of the delegation in London, 27 March 1944, BA, ME-42/20; Blit to American Representation of the Bund, 20 October 1944, BA, MG-2/45.
123. Blit to American Representation, 20 October 1944, ibid.
124. Nowogrodzki to Blit, 22 December 1943, and Nowogrodzki to Oller, 14 February 1944, BA, ME-17/172.
125. Szerer to Grabski, 30 November 1943, BA, MG-2/23.
126. Szerer to Nowogrodzki, 10 November 1943, ibid.
127. Minutes of meeting of American Representation of the Bund, 8 March 1943, BA, ME-18/42.

128. Memorandum by Szerer, forwarded to Mikołajczyk, 26 November 1943, BA, MG-2/23; *The Ghetto Speaks*, 20 (1 February 1944).
129. Schwarzbart, *Diary*, YVA, M-2/774.
130. Szerer to Stańczyk, 15 January 1944, BA, MG-2/23; phrasing of the draft resolution that Szerer presented to the National Council on 17 February 1944, BA, ME-42/3.
131. Engel, *Facing a Holocaust*, pp. 108ff.
132. Szerer to Wasser, 14 October 1944, BA, MG-2/23.
133. T. Prekerowa, *Konspiracyjna Rada Pomocy Żydom w Warszawie 1942–1945* (Warsaw: Państwowy Instytut Wydawniczy, 1982) p. 98; I. Gutman and S. Krakowski, *Unequal Victims: Poles and Jews During World War II* (New York: Holocaust Library, 1986), pp. 266–7; Engel, *Facing a Holocaust*, p. 282, note 82.
134. Feiner to Jan Stanisław Jankowski, the delegate in Poland, 28 May 1943, AAN, KC PZPR, 202/xv-2 file 4; copy of the report on relief funds that the JLC forwarded to the economic envoy at the Polish Consulate in New York: Pat to Szerer, 3 April 1944, BA, ME-42/23.
135. Pat to Szerer, 7 June 1944, BA, ME-42/23; Pat to Hyman (JDC), 21 July 1944, BA, JLC/15; Szerer to Pat, 23 December 1944, BA, ME-42/23.
136. Berezowski (L. Feiner) to Szerer, 23 November 1943, 13 April 1944 and 2 December 1944, BA, ME-42/3.
137. Feiner to Bieńkowski, 24 February 1944, and to Jankowski, 8 March 1944, AAN, KC PZPR, 202/xv-2 file 4.
138. Nowogrodzki to Szerer, 23 November 1943, BA, MG-2/23.
139. Berezowski (Feiner) to Szerer, 10 May 1944, BA, ME-42/3.
140. Engel, *Facing a Holocaust*, pp. 150-5; Szerer to Nowogrodzki, 21 March 1944, BA, M-7/19, and to Berezowski (Feiner), 30 May 1944, BA, ME-42/3.
141. Gliksman to Polish Ministry of Labour and Social Affairs, 9 February and 9 April 1945, BA, ME-14/B-2; report of relief actions, sent by Gliksman to the JLC, undated (evidently August 1945), BA, MG-9/155.
142. In 1944 various Jewish organizations, mainly in the United States, gave this council $1.7 million: Engel, *Facing a Holocaust*, p. 155.
143. Minutes of discussions in the Council for Matters Relating to the Rescue of the Jewish Population in Poland, YVA, M-14.
144. Blit to American Representation of the Bund, 21 March 1945, BA, ME-17/172.
145. Report of delegation on its trip to France and Belgium, 24 May 1945, BA, M-7/42.

6

Efforts to Regroup and Revitalize

TOWARDS A NEW POLAND?

On 31 December 1943 the Homeland National Council – the KRN (Krajowa Rada Narodowa), the first organization of communist underground members and their associates in Poland held its first conference. The KRN challenged the legitimacy of the Polish government-in-exile and rejected its assumed status as representative of the Polish people. The Red Army crossed the old Polish–Soviet frontier in early January 1944, and on 22 January Moscow announced the formation of the PKWN. This committee was made up of Polish communists who had spent the war in the Soviet Union and activists organized under the umbrella of the Union of Polish Patriots, the ZPP. The PKWN activists reached Lublin after the liberation of that town and settled there on 23 July 1944. For all practical purposes, the PKWN became the new provisional government of Poland and was recognized as such by the Soviet Union in October 1944. Several Jewish public figures reached Lublin in July 1944 and established the first post-Holocaust Jewish committee about a month later. They included Mendel Kosovar, Reuven Ben-Shem, Emile Sommerstein (a member of the Polish Sejm before the war and a prominent Zionist leader from Galicia who had been incarcerated in the USSR during the war), Yonas Turkow and a Bundist, Dr Shlomo Hirszenhorn, who was chosen to chair the committee. Sommerstein, the most conspicuous Jewish public figure in this group, was the Jewish representative to the PKWN.[1]

The Red Army's entry into Poland and the coalescence of pro-Soviet political forces to form a Polish government after the liberation plunged the National Council in London into a political crisis that ended with the resignation of Prime Minister Mikołajczyk in November 1944. Mikołajczyk, whose purpose was to take part in the new regime, negotiated at length with the Kremlin authorities and, together with Churchill, met with Stalin for talks in August 1944. He welcomed the possibility of Soviet–Polish cooperation, agreed to integrate the Armia Krajowa (AK) into the Polish army that had fought alongside the

Soviets in the east, and – under pressure from Churchill – virtually ceded the eastern territories (western Ukraine and western Byelorussia) to the Soviet Union in return for territorial compensation in the west at the expense of Germany. By accepting the Kremlin's uncompromising demands, Mikołajczyk lost the support of the Polish parties in London – including PPS members who brooked no compromise on the eastern frontier issue and rejected any Soviet influence on the regime in Poland – and was forced to resign. In late 1944, out of office, he began to build a centre of influence in liberated Poland as the leader of the Polskie Stronnictwo Ludowe (PSL).[2]

In late January 1944 the Bund delegation in London resolved to make no overt statements about the attitude of the Bund toward Polish–Soviet relations. Nevertheless, in response to the new political situation the Bund mission in New York released an official statement on these relations in early February 1944. In this statement, the Bund congratulated the Red Army on its entry into Poland and deemed this to be the first step toward the liberation of Poland from the fascist yoke.[3]

Although the statement was cautious – avoiding unequivocal support of the Soviet Union and taking no stance on territorial issues – its release precipitated a crisis in relations between the Bund and the Polish exiles in London. In March 1944 Lucjan Blit explained to his comrades in America that the climate in Poland was severely anti-Soviet and that the AK, with support of the government, was planning an uncompromising military struggle against the Red Army and the USSR's lackeys. Ciołkosz and his comrades, too, stated Blit, were loath to accept any compromise in the matter of the eastern Polish territories.[4] Back in January 1944, the PPS secretariat in London had written a letter of protest to the leader of the British Labour Party, Clement Atlee, concerning the Soviet annexation of Polish territories. Among other remarks, the secretariat explained that the Polish socialists rejected any compromise with the Soviet state in the matter of the eastern Polish territories and that Poland's territorial integrity, within its pre-war borders, must be maintained to thwart Soviet expansionist ambitions and to ensure stability in post-war Europe.[5]

The Polish hostility and suspicion toward the Jews again reared its head in the West at this time. A wave of anti-Semitic publications, prompted by the new political situation, appeared in New York and London. In May 1944 even the newspaper *Dziennik Polski*, the official organ of the Polish government-in-exile in London, published a bluntly anti-Semitic article accusing Jewish communists in Poland of having murdered Polish patriots in territories that the Soviets had controlled until the German invasion in the summer of 1941. Blit and his comrades tried to deflect these false charges by means of apologetics. In a letter to the editor of *Dziennik Polski*, Blit claimed to have been in these territories in early 1940 and stated that 'The myth about Jewish communists who brutally executed Poles is utterly divorced from the truth, just as all the stories about Poles who collaborated with the Hitlerist murderers are groundless.'[6] In New York, the pro-government Polish exile journal *Wiadomości Polskie* depicted the Bund's position in favour of understanding and compromise with the Soviet Union as contrary to the Polish constitution and a 'crime against the Polish people'.[7]

At that time, the Bund activists in London and New York disagreed about the policy to adopt in response to the new political situation in the summer of 1944. Leon Oller argued that the Bund should continue to participate in the Polish government-in-exile. The Polish government, he said, was still the entity that represented Polish interests and received the support of the Polish people. Oller believed that a schism with the PPS members in London should be avoided, considering this nexus crucial for the Bund if it wished to resume its activity among Polish Jews after the liberation of Poland. If the Bund adopted a pro-Soviet attitude, he warned, Poland would be engulfed in anti-Semitism. He and his comrades, he said, had to contend with anti-Jewish leanings among the Polish exiles in London; the Poles had even begun to depict the Warsaw ghetto uprising as part of the Polish struggle against the Nazi occupier, without noting that it had been perpetrated by Jews.[8]

During those months, the American mission had a better grasp of the new situation in Poland than did the London delegation. Nowogrodzki explained to Oller that the Bund, not having forgotten the murder of Erlich and Alter, had no illusions about the nature of the Soviet regime. However, the formation of a solid anti-communist front with the PPS and other players in the National Council would not solve the problem of anti-Semitism in Poland:

> The comrades in New York think the government-in-exile no longer represents all Poles, that is [does not represent], Polish Jewry. It does not do everything within its power to fight the problem of anti-Semitism. Neither does the PPS. When does it deal with anti-Semitism? When a problem of Jewish soldiers in the Polish Army comes up. Then it comes alive and spares no effort to hush the matter up.[9]

In a letter to Szerer, Chayim Wasser added in this context that the Bund should not be the Jewish political entity that preaches an anti-Soviet line. Jews will return to Poland after the war, he said, and the Bund should give thought to the future that they would face in an independent Poland. The returning Jews would not speak as the Polish exiles did, Wasser stated.[10]

The Bund veteran Frantz Kurski understood that the internal disputes among members of the Polish government concerning the attitude toward the Soviet Union had nothing to do with the future of Poland's rump Jewish community. In an anguished tone, he explained to his colleague, the movement veteran John Mill, 'There are no more Jews in Poland. There is no more Poland ... We do not know what the Soviets will make out of Poland, a small Poland in which there are almost no Bundists ...' He indicated that some individuals in the United States advocated the view that Bundists in Poland ought to work with 'the Zionists and with all Polish Jews', while others suggested that they work with the PKWN in Lublin. It was a disservice of reality, he said to view the Bund's partnership in the Central Committee of Jews in Poland (Centralny Komitet Żydów w Polsce: CKŻP) and in educational institutions, cultural organizations and vocational rehabilitation agencies from a pragmatic perspective only.[11]

The political and military events in the summer of 1944 left no doubt about who would soon determine the nature of governance in Poland and dictate the manner of Poland's rehabilitation. On 1 August 1944, a day after Mikołaczyk came to the Kremlin for talks with the Soviet leadership, the population of Warsaw rose against the Germans. For the next 60 days, the AK, the Armia Ludowa (AL) and other underground organizations engaged the Wehrmacht in a bloody war that claimed some 150,000–200,000 Polish lives and reduced most of Warsaw to rubble. When the Polish uprising broke out, it was joined by the few surviving members of the ŻOB, who had gone into hiding in and near Warsaw after the liquidation of the ghetto.[12]

On 8 or 9 September 1944, four Bund activists who had reached liberated Lublin – Grisza Jaszunski (who had come from Lithuania), Michał Szuldenfrei and Leo Finkelstein (who had come from the Soviet Union) and Shlomo Hirszenhorn – met for the first time and began to organize the first post-war Bund conference in Poland. After the Polish uprising was quelled, additional members reached Lublin from Warsaw. Leon Feiner, Salo Fiszgrund and Bernard Goldstein came in January 1945. It was clear to all members that Poland would be included in the Soviet sphere of patronage, and this fact had been of decisive importance in their resolutions. On 8 February 1945, the newly established Bund committee in Lublin issued a statement of support for the KRN, backed by all members apart from Goldstein.[13] Leon Feiner, who did not take part in this activity for reasons of poor health, was hospitalized in Lublin with a severe blood disease and died on 22 February 1945.[14]

The group of Bund members that gathered in Lublin published a plan including a series of resolutions that created both a theoretical and a practical basis for the resumption of Bund work in Poland. The plan included the following clauses, inter alia:

(1) During the Hitlerist occupation, the Jewish people was visited with a tragedy that no other people in history had suffered – the murder of millions by the Hitlerist fascists. The annihilation claimed the lives of masses of members of the Jewish working class and greatly diminished the influence of the Bund ...

(2) The committee expresses its gratitude and appreciation to the Soviet Union for its contribution in obliterating German fascism and German, Italian and Japanese imperialism, and for its contribution toward the creation of a socialist and democratic society in post-liberation Poland.

(3) The Hitlerist barbarians and their anti-Semitic supporters in Polish society are spreading emigration propaganda that, in current terms, is a manifestation of anti-Semitism; they are supported by reactionary Jewish elements, thus obstructing progress toward the democratization and rehabilitation of Poland ...

(4) The committee expresses its appreciation to the Soviet Union, the Red Army and the Polish Army for their contribution to and assistance in the building of a democratic society based on the PKWN manifesto.

(5) The Bund considers itself part of the Polish socialist movement, including in its traditional struggle against fascism and reactionism, and an associate of the PPR in the common effort to revitalize Polish Jewry.[15]

This programme clearly aligned the Bund with the pro-Soviet forces and the backers of the new regime in Poland. In January 1945 Szuldenfrei delivered a speech to the KRN, the united political council of the Polish communists and pro-Soviet circles, headed by Władysław Gomułka. Szuldenfrei noted in his speech that the Jewish working class in Poland considered itself part of the newly formed camp and endorsed this camp's positions on how to solve the problem of Poland's frontiers, ordain Polish–German relations after the liberation and establish Poland's new regime.[16]

On 24 November 1944 the Polish government-in-exile was dissolved again with the resignation of Mikołajczyk as its prime minister. The new government, a politically inconsequential agency in the last few months of the war, was formed by a member of the PPS, Tomasz Arciszewski. This government rested on a bizarre alliance between the PPS and the Endeks, sponsored by three PPS activists in London (among others): Adam Ciołkosz, Jan Stańczyk and Jan Szczyrek. The glue that united these two long-time rival parties was their uncompromising opposition to the concessions that Mikołajczyk and his colleagues in the PSL were willing to make to the Soviet Union to retain at least some of their influence in reconstituted Poland. In early 1945 Ciołkosz initiated the formation of the new government-in-exile, actually an anti-communist front composed of all anti-Soviet Polish political entities in exile. Ciołkosz even accused Mikołajczyk, as well as the members of the PPS left flank in Poland, of complicity in the continuing loss of Polish independence.[17]

In late 1944 members of the London delegation of the Bund re-examined their relations with the exiled Polish government and National Council. Szerer ruled that under the new situation – that prevailing after the Polish uprising – the Polish government no longer represented the Polish people. The Bund, he asserted, should support both the PPS and the KRN in Lublin.[18] Oller, though not favouring an overt anti-Soviet approach, opposed public support of the KRN because the Soviets had not assisted the Polish uprising. Oller did not understand the new conditions in Poland and the Jewish survivors' immediate need of protection and support from the new political forces that were about to assume the reins of power.[19] However, the Bund activists in the West were left with few choices. In January 1945, in response to the PPS–Endek alliance in Arciszewski's government, the Bund broke its political ties with the Polish exile for good.

In March 1945, three Bund leaders in Poland – Salo Fiszgrund, Shlomo Hirszenhorn and Grisza Jaszunski – were accepted as members in the KRN.[20] On 1 May 1945 Szerer delivered his last radio broadcast to Polish Jews from London. He expressed the Bund's hope that a free and socially just regime would be established in Poland, and noted the Jews' sense of partnership in fate with their homeland and their wish to rebuild in Poland the lives that the occupier had destroyed. Additional remarks that Szerer wished to broadcast were censored by the Polish Ministry of Information in London, but are reproduced here:

> It is not from gratitude but from our socialist and democratic aspirations that we have always aspired to neighbourly relations between Poland and the Soviet Union. We have always wished to regard the Soviet Union as a participant in the great United Nations family, born during the years of war and continuing in the post-war era. May it lead Poland, like the rest of the world, to final victory over violence and to a social order of equality, freedom and justice, both in international relations and in all domains in the lives of countries and nations.[21]

The new political situation, coupled with the hope that a socialist regime would eventually come into being in Poland, prompted the Bundists in Poland and their colleagues in the United States and Britain to place their trust in the new Polish regime and sever the close relations that they had established with the PPS exiles during the war. Pragmatism, a characteristic of the movement at all times, proved itself this time, too. The Bund leaders in the West – Nowogrodzki, Szerer, Mendelsohn and Kurski – realized that the horrific extermination of Jews during the war had obliterated the Bund in Poland as an independent and influential political party. It is true that the party had neither forgotten nor forgiven the Soviets for the persecution they had inflicted on its members and the murder of numerous Bund activists on Soviet soil, foremost Erlich and Alter. However, unlike the Polish socialists in exile, the Bund did not regard the Soviet Union as Poland's enemy, and always believed that bridges of understanding should be built with the Soviets. In view of the situation in Poland, the Bund repeatedly stressed this position. Furthermore, the still-embryonic new regime was not suspected of anti-Semitism and encouraged Jews to hope that they could integrate into the Polish state as equally empowered citizens.

STARTING OVER AGAIN

The first Jewish survivors who appeared in the liberated areas had outlasted the occupation on Polish soil. Some had found hideouts in towns and villages with the help of assumed identities and 'Aryan' papers; others had stayed in bunkers, in forests or with Poles who had admitted them to their homes, concealed them and met their needs. The exact number of Jews who survived in Poland in these ways is unknown. In the liberated areas of eastern Poland, some 8,000 Jews were registered in the Jewish relief committees in 1944, 3,000 of them in Lublin, 1,500 in Białystok and 2,000 in provincial towns in the district. Most had survived in hiding; a smaller number were survivors of camps.[22]

The survivors emerged from their hiding places with no idea of what they would do the next day. Many were convinced that they were the last Jews on earth; others thought hardly any Jews remained in Poland or anywhere else in Europe. Estranged and disoriented after their years in hiding, eyewitnesses to the murder of their people and bereft of family and community, they were overtaken by apathy, despair and depression, not to mention poor physical condition and health. Some were disabled or ill; others suffered from severe malnutrition. They were driven as if by an inner fire to hunt for relatives, determine whether anyone dear to them had survived, and to find other Jews with whom they could share their distress.[23]

By the summer and autumn of 1944 Jews were migrating along the ruined roads of Poland, in the liberated areas, and even in places on the front where they came under fire. Their destinations were their former places of residence – the homes from which they had been expelled or had fled – and their purpose was two-fold: to find out whether anyone in their families had survived and to determine what, if anything, could be salvaged of the property they had left behind. A small group of survivors – sometimes two or three Jews – gathered in almost every town in the areas liberated between the summer of 1944 and the end of the war. The homing impulse was so strong that Jews often entered liberated towns with the Red Army, even before the guns fell silent. Almost all of these survivors had gone into hiding in a nearby forest after the deportation of the local Jews or had found shelter with Polish peasants in the vicinity.[24]

The re-institutionalization of life by survivors in their pre-war places of residence gathered momentum with the return of Jews who had survived the concentration camps from Germany after the surrender in May 1945. The exact number of these survivors, too, is not known, but one may state that they accounted for a large proportion of survivors until the repatriation from the Soviet Union began in early 1946. In Łódź, for example, 944 survivors from concentration camps were recorded in January 1945, and in March of that year 695 of the 2,179 survivors living in this town had returned from the camps. Between May and December 1945, 18,188 Jews released from camps were registered in Łódź, out of 38,471 Jews in the town. Obviously most of them had returned from Germany to Poland after May 1945, since in April there were only 4,778 camp survivors in Łódź. Almost all of them came from camps on Polish soil, having survived Auschwitz, the Łódź ghetto, or labour camps in the vicinity of Częstochowa.[25]

The advent of the first survivors in the summer of 1944 resulted almost immediately in the formation of Jewish entities to meet their initial day-to-day needs. It was obvious that the pre–war division of political forces had become meaningless. A Central Committee of the Jews in Poland (CKŻP) was founded in Warsaw in February 1945 and recognized in April of that year by the Polish government as the representative body of Polish Jews. That committee, which undertook to rehabilitate the lives of Jews in Poland, included representatives of most Jewish parties except for the Revisionists and the Orthodox. Emile Sommerstein, the veteran Zionist leader from eastern Galicia, and the person of the greatest public stature among Jewish public figures in post–war Poland, was appointed to its chair. Shlomo Hirszenhorn, a Bund representative, served as his deputy and as a member of the Presidium. Three additional members of the committee plenum were representatives of the Bund: Salo Fiszgrund, Michał Szuldenfrei and Grisza Jaszunski. By May 1945 local committees of the CKŻP were operating in eight Polish towns, and additional local committees were established later on as waves of repatriates arrived and resettled in Silesia and the annexed western territories.[26]

Apart from the participation of Bundists in this umbrella organization of Polish Jewry, survivors and supporters of the movement began to organize everywhere to establish Bund branches and institutions without planning and facilitation from the activist group in Warsaw. In Łódź, some 300 Bund members and sympathizers convened in October 1945 to mark the 48th anniversary of the founding of the movement.[27] In Warsaw, where there were some 13,000 Jews at the end of 1945,[28] several members established a club at 44 Targowa Street, in the Praga quarter, where the Bund Central Committee subsequently housed itself. About a hundred people participated in a conference of members at this club in October 1945, and 60 members attended a gathering in Tarnów that month. Tsukunft also began to re–establish its institutions at this time. Members of Tsukunft gathered in Łódź in July 1945, and approximately 50 of them participated in a conference of young Bundists in that town on 21 October 1945. In the winter of 1946, Tsukunft started its first camp for youth in Łódź, in which 30 young people took part.[29] Members of the movement began to organize in smaller localities, too. In Przemyśl, 11 Bundist survivors got together in August 1945 and opened an orphanage that took in 50 Jewish children.[30] In the summer and autumn of 1945 Bund members held meetings in Piotrków–Trybunalski, Częstochowa, Katowice and Kraków. In June 1945, shortly before the first Bund conference in Łódź, the records in party branches showed 280 members.[31] About half a year later, Salo Fiszgrund, secretary of the Central Committee in Warsaw, sent a report to the American Representation of the Bund containing the following membership figures: a total of 482 members in party branches in January 1946 – 175 in Łódź, 87 in Tarnów, 53 in Częstochowa, 42 in Warsaw, 41 in Kraków, 22 in Piotrków–Trybunalski, 17 in Lublin, 16 in Reichbach, 13 in Białystok, nine in Włocławek and seven in Międzyrzec–Podlaski.[32]

On 16–17 June 1945 the Bund held its first national conference in post–war Poland; its 44 delegates, from seven Polish cities, elected a new Central Committee of the Bund. Salo Fiszgrund was chosen a secretary, and the other members were Shlomo Hirszenhorn, Michał Szuldenfrei, Ignacy Falk, Grisza Jaszunski, Leib Podlawski and Liber Brener.[33] The conference adopted a series of resolutions concerning the struggle against anti–Semitism and anti-Semites who were assailing Jews across Poland; expressed full support for the Polish government and the social and economic reforms that it was planning; and voiced its opposition to the Polish government-in-exile in London, which, in the view of the committee members, represented the reactionary and anti-Semitic forces in Polish society that were spearheading the campaign of incitement against the Jews. As for the Bund's status in Poland and its attitude toward the Bund missions in the West, Szuldenfrei pronounced as follows:

> The comrades [members of the Bund] in London and the United States objected to our political path in Poland and associated themselves with the government in London. They even have a representative there.

> … We have long been in touch with the comrades in the Diaspora. These comrades opposed the PKWN and spoke out against it … These comrades do not speak for the Bund in Poland. Only the comrades in Poland can speak on behalf of the Bund. Our stance in Poland is the realistic and warranted stance …[34]

Szuldenfrei spoke vehemently against his colleagues in the West, even though the Bund representatives in Britain and the United States had already withdrawn much of their support of and identification with the Polish exiles by that time. These disputes were an outgrowth of Poland's complicated post–war political reality. In the first few months of 1945 the PPR waged a crude propaganda campaign against the right flank of the PPS, which belonged to the WRN. In May 1945, however, the PPR's policy toward the Polish socialists turned around. The PPR stopped attempting to split the party and erode it from within and began to favour unity in the Polish Socialist Party and the formation of a multipartisan government in Poland, based on the left–wing parties and the Peasants. Władysław Gomułka, who drafted this policy – which was adopted by the PPR Central Committee, understood that one could not ordain a socialist regime in Poland without full cooperation from the PPS and other parties for two reasons: the need to contend with the strength of the Polish Right and its armed units, and the strenuous effort needed to revitalize Poland's devastated economic infrastructure. In the new policy, which received backing from the Kremlin, the PPR intended to expand the basis of governance and create a National Unity Government composed of the Left and the peasants.[35]

In the first months after the liberation, Szuldenfrei and his comrades understood that the future of the Jewish community in Poland depended on victory by the government in the bloody struggle that had erupted between itself and various fascist, anti-Semitic and anti–communist underground circles. Therefore, the Bundist members gave the KRN and the new government of Poland, headed by the socialist Edward Osóbka–Morawski, their total support. They sought to dispel any doubts among the partners in the government – especially among PPS leaders in Poland – about their fealty to the new regime and their avoidance of ideological identification with exile PPS circles in London. On 7 June 1946 Szuldenfrei stated in a speech at a KRN conference that Polish Jews placed their trust in the Polish government, which would know how to fight anti-Semitic manifestations in the country and disable the fascist organizations.[36]

In his remarks at the Bund conference in Łódź and to the KRN, Szuldenfrei attempted to explain that the Bund had no relations whatsoever with the emigrationist circles in London that supported the anti–government organizations. The Bundists in New York accepted the demand of the Bund in Poland to be recognized as an autonomous political organization,[37] but despite its firm stance on Bund independence in Poland, Salo Fiszgrund explained to Nowogrodzki in September 1945 that the comrades in Poland did not wish to sever relations with the Bundists in the West.[38]

FROM REPATRIATION TO KIELCE: TO STAY OR TO GO?

Initial agreements concerning the repatriation of Polish citizens from the Soviet Union were signed in September 1944. The ZPP worked out accords with three Soviet Socialist Republics (SSRs) – the Ukraine, Byelorussia and Lithuania – in which the return of members of these nationalities from Poland to the three SSRs was also approved. In July 1945 the governments of Poland and the Soviet Union concluded an agreement for the repatriation of Polish citizens, including Jews, who had spent the war in the USSR. To implement the agreements, a Polish–Soviet committee was established in Moscow to oversee the Poles' departure and special committees were set up to supervise the returnees' integration.

Between 8 February and late July 1946, 136,550 Jews returned from the Soviet Union to Poland under bilateral repatriation agreements. More than 50 per cent of them gravitated to the Jewish centres in Lower Silesia.[39] Large Jewish communities took shape there, e.g., in Wrocław, where 13,000 repatriates settled, and in Reichbach (10,000), Wałbrzych (7,500) and Bielawa (5,000).[40] These communities joined Szczecin and Łódź as the most important centres of Polish Jewry in the summer of 1946, when its total strength came to some 240,000.[41]

The initial impression is that the picture of the refugee–survivors of 1945 repeated itself. The tens of thousands of Jews returning from the USSR – some 50 per cent of whom came from the Asian republics or Siberia,[42] where they had been exiled or fled during the war – resembled in their economic distress the Jews who had congregated in Poland in 1945. Jewish public figures, members of the Jewish committees and emissaries from Palestine were shocked by the appearance of returnees on the first trains that pulled into Polish cities in February 1946. The children and teenagers, many of whom for several years lacking a family and school setting that would care for them, left an especially grim impression.[43]

A few Bund members survived in the Soviet Union at the end of the war. According to data in the possession of the American Representation of the Bund in the summer of 1942, some 1,500 Bund members and associates, including their relatives, remained in the USSR after Anders' army left that country along with civilian evacuees.[44] The party in Poland undertook to deal with their repatriation. Józef Cyrankiewicz, a PPS leader and one of the heads of state at this time, contacted the Polish embassy in Moscow and asked, on behalf of the Bund, to arrange the repatriation of the Jewish refugees who belonged to the movement.

In 1945, after Fiszgrund asked the PPS secretariat to give thought to the matter, Józef Cyrankiewicz made a special enquiry with the Polish–Soviet repatriation committee on behalf of the Bund members. In 1947 the office of the Polish prime minister also intervened in the matter by instructing the Polish Embassy in Moscow, in a memorandum, to arrange the departure of Bund members who wished to return to Poland.[45]

For well–known Bundists, especially those who had participated in underground work in Poland and Lithuania, the repatriation evoked questions and fears. Yosef Musnik, a Bund activist in the Wilno ghetto, was about to leave for Poland in 1945 with another six comrades. Before he left, the NKVD in Wilno summoned him for an interrogation in which he was asked about Bund activists from Poland who had gone to the United States at the beginning of the war and about the nature of his and his comrades' relations with them. After the investigation, he was released – in his opinion, because of his background as a partisan. Once he returned to Poland, he was stunned by the realities in which his comrades in Warsaw were operating. Musnik adduced from the situation that the Bund had no chance of operating freely in Poland and decided to leave Poland, despite Grisza Jaszunski's remonstrations.[46] Ya'akov Tselemenski and Bernard Goldstein made the same decision in the summer of 1945.[47]

In June 1946 the Bund Central Committee in Poland estimated the number of Bundists among the repatriates from the Soviet Union at about a thousand, all of whom had been members of the party before the war.[48] In early 1947 Szymon Zachariasz, the most prominent PPR member in the CKŻP, gave Roman Zambrowski, a leading figure in the PPR, a report on the condition of the Jewish parties in Poland and their activity in the committees. Zachariasz estimated the number of Bundists in Poland at 1,500, mostly long–time party members and a few young people who had enlisted in the Bund institutions in 1946.[49]

Seventy–two representatives of party branches in Poland took part in a Bund conference in Wrocław in February 1947. The newspaper *Folkstsaytung* released statistics on the participants' age and occupations:

Participants in the Wrocław congress			
Distribution by age		Distribution by occupation	
60+	1	Civil servants	15
51–60	14	Tailors	13
41–50	24	Liberal professions	7
31–40	25	Metal-workers	5

cont.

cont.

Under 30	8	Textile-workers	5
		Teachers	5
		Party activists	5
		Shoemakers	4
		Construction-workers	3
		Journalists	2
		Other	8

The newspaper also reported figures on the duration of the representatives' membership in the Bund. Forty-six delegates had been party members for more than 20 years; 26 had joined more recently. Only four delegates had been members for fewer than ten years. Among the 72 participants, nine had previously belonged to some other political organization, foremost the Communist Party and the PPS.[50] Although it is difficult to draw inferences from these figures about all Bund members in Poland at that time, the data give an indication of the movement's make-up. Most members who participated in Bund work after the war had been members since the interwar period. They were a young group, mostly in their thirties and forties, and they became active in the party mainly because of their former affiliation with it. The members of this group, who had been in their twenties before the war, had belonged to the young people's organizations of the Bund, had been educated in Tsukunft youth groups and had maintained their emotional and ideological attachment to the Bund even while they were in the Soviet Union. It was this group that re-established the infrastructure for party activity in Poland after the war.

In occupational terms, Bund members were no different from other Polish Jews after the war. At this time, Polish Jews went over from the predominant traditional pre-war Jewish occupations, such as petty crafts, trade and peddling, to the civil service, the liberal professions and state-owned industries, from which they had been almost totally excluded during the interwar period.[51] Forty-four (61 per cent) of the 72 participants in the Wrocław conference worked in these fields, and 20 were civil servants or paid political functionaries.

After the war, Bund members held various conflicting views about the movement's future in Poland. According to Zachariasz's report, several groups with different ideological standpoints operated within the Bund. One of these groups, headed by Central Committee member Ignacy Falk and composed mainly of young veteran party members who had participated in Jewish fighting organizations or partisan groups, reached the conclusion that Bundists should leave Poland because Polish Jewry had no future.[52] Avraham Zilberstein, the secretary of Tsukunft in Warsaw, wrote on this matter in May 1946 to Bund member Avraham Litewka in New York:

> The situation in Poland is difficult both politically and econom- ically. I must tell you that 90 per cent of our comrades country- wide are in favour of emigration. Most of the members want to emigrate to America and join the comrades who are already there ... You in America do not understand the situation very well. You speak about rehabilitating Jews who are returning from the camps to Poland and rebuilding their lives in Poland ... It is very hard for people here to continue living atop their relatives' graves ... The Jewish masses will emigrate from here to any place they can reach ... We Bundists have no 'Jewish masses' here, and there is no Jewish labour movement whatsoever. When you ask how the Jewish community is getting along here, I answer: they are doing their best to leave; it is an unstable community, unstable indeed ...[53]

Another group, headed by Fiszgrund, believed that the Bund could carry on in Poland as an independent Jewish proletarian framework by cooperating with the broad-based government that was ruling that country. A third group, led by Szuldenfrei and Jaszunski, came to the conclusion in early 1947 that the Bund could not carry on for long as a separate Jewish entity. Szuldenfrei believed it should join the PPS as a separate section; Jaszunski preferred that the Bund members join the PPR – an approach that carried little support among the Bundists.[54]

After the German occupation was lifted, Poland plunged into a bloody struggle between the government and an array of underground anti-communist circles, headed by the AK and fascist and anti-Semitic organizations. These armed groups regarded the Jews as a social factor that supported the hated pro-Soviet regime; by attacking the Jews who had returned to Poland they sought to undermine the status and stability of the new government. The conflict that raged in Poland in the first two years after the liberation – a civil war, in effect – exposed the Jews to severe violence, incessant assaults, plunder and dispossession, and, worst of all, lethal attacks. In addition to the schemes of right-wing underground groups, a spree of anti-Jewish violence spread among the Polish population, which displayed much hostility to the collectivity of survivors who wished to return to their homes. The regime, just getting organized, was unable to impose its authority on the violent gangs that operated in various parts of the country and could not provide the Jews with security and protection. Most Poles identified the Jews with the Communist regime that had imposed itself on a population that, in greater part, considered it illegitimate. The Jews, in contrast, could not but support the regime and seek its protection because the estrangement of most of Polish society and its refusal to help them after their years of terror under Nazi occupation had rendered them helpless.[55] According to official and unofficial Polish sources, at least 350 Jews were murdered in Poland between November 1944 and December 1945.[56]

The armed groups' bloody struggle against the regime claimed victims other than Jews. Between August 1944 and December 1945, thousands of government bureaucrats and supporters were murdered and wounded in Poland.[57] However, unlike the violent attacks on the regime and its accomplices, which were political in nature, the anti-Jewish violence was fomented by an anti-Semitic incitement campaign orchestrated by anti-communist players. Many Jews in Poland sympathized with the new regime, which promised them an opportunity to become equally entitled citizens in Poland and opposed anti-Semitism and anti-Jewish discrimination. The anti-Semitic propaganda that marked the Jews as pillars of the new regime unleashed eruptions of hate and violence. The Poles exploited the anti-Jewish climate and the government's inability to protect the Jews to murder Jews in order to dispossess them of money, property and homes. The anti-Semitic wave reached a climax on 4 July 1946 in Kielce – where more than 40 Jews were murdered in a savage pogrom by a Polish mob against a residence where survivors and a group of young Jews had settled to wait for immigration permits to Palestine.[58]

These eruptions were one of the factors that prompted a mass exodus of Jews from Poland. In the summer of 1945 tens of thousands of Jews began to leave the country in a huge migration movement. By September of that year, 111,537 Jews had left, most of them in the *Berichah* (flight) movement (created by Zionist activists in order to organize clandestine emigration of Jews from Poland) and others on their own. The great exodus resumed after the Kielce massacre: 19,000 Jews left Poland in July 1946, 35,346 in August and 12,379 in September. By early 1947, more than half of the Jews who had resided in Poland after the war had left, and the number of those remaining was estimated at 90,000.[59]

The Bund leadership construed the countrywide spree of anti-Jewish attacks as part of the pitched battle between fascist and reactionary elements and the new regime. The party leadership placed its trust in the government's will to quash the violence, and urged its members and the greater Jewish community to support parties that totally opposed attacks on Jews. These attacks and their result – the exodus from Poland – were at the top of the agenda in party discussions in 1946. After the Kielce pogrom, the Central Committee of the Bund published a resolution calling for an emergency session of the National Council of the Bund on 6–7 July 1946. The resolution included the following points:

(1) The pogrom was perpetrated by fascist elements and had clear anti-Jewish attributes. Its purpose was to bring about the departure of the entire Jewish community from city of Kielce and the Kielce District.

(2) The murderous fascist players themselves belong to the local militia and members of the Polish army also took part in [the pogrom] ...

(3) The [Bund] Council urgently calls on the progressive forces in the country, those who are struggling against anti-Semitism, headed by the PPR and the PPS – the two great forces of the working public – to become the spearheads of action against anti-Semitism. The Council urges and demands of the institutions of state to act to halt and eradicate anti-Semitism and arrest its disseminators and carriers. May Poland's name never again be associated with the disgrace of the annihilation of the Jews, as it was during the Hitlerlist occupation ... in the new and democratic Poland.[60]

The Bund leadership made prodigious efforts to persuade party members and Jews at large that a frantic flight from Poland was not needed, especially since the emigrés had not been promised another country of refuge. The Bund did not rule out emigration from Poland as such, but depicted panicky departure as a surrender to the Zionist propaganda that (it claimed) exploited the temporary distress and the political situation in Poland to preach emigration among the Jews. At the party conference held in Wrocław in February 1947, the Jews were urged not to fall prey to the rising tide of Zionist emigration propaganda that exploited the fanning of anti-Semitic tendencies in Poland to persuade the Jews to leave the country. Instead of engaging in a timorous and purposeless escape, the Bund stated, Polish Jewry should cooperate with the new government and the anti-fascist parties, since its fate depended on that of their country of residence.[61]

The exodus of Jews from Poland, and *a fortiori*, that of party leaders and sympathizers, was the toughest issue on the agenda of the Bund leadership. The leadership invested limitless efforts in persuading the branch members that, even after the pogrom in Kielce, there was no reason to flee Poland in panic. A circular from the Central Committee to the branches in early 1947 stated, 'There is no reason for fear and panic. Life in Poland is settling down. The anti-Semitic forces are being halted, everyone can stay and continue to work. This is our mission – to warn the Jewish community about this Zionist action [encouraging Jews to emigrate from Poland].'[62] However, the Bund activists, like the communist members of the CKŻP, worked themselves into frustration in their futile efforts to counter the powerful emigrationist wishes of the Zionist activists in the *Berichah* movement.[63]

To what extent did ordinary Bund supporters share the party leadership's attitude? To what extent were rank-and-file members influenced by the Bund leaders' conviction that Jewish existence had a future in Poland, that the struggle to remain in Poland was worth waging, and that the government should be trusted to restrain the spree of murder and assault?

Apart from the Jewish communists, only the Bund on the Jewish political scene gave the government total support. Its leaders – Szuldenfrei, Fiszgrund and Jaszunski – participated in political activity in Poland and believed that their future was there. From the ideological standpoint, they moved steadily towards the PPR and, under certain conditions, were willing to transform the Bund into a Jewish section of the PPS or even to merge with the PPR.

Jakob Pat toured Poland on behalf of the JLC in February 1946. In an article published after his return from Poland, Pat estimated the likelihood that the Bund would continue operating in Poland as an independent Jewish socialist party:

> The attitude of the Bund has its origins in a lengthy tradition of Jewish life, in the existence of a large collectivity, in the Jewish working class that once existed in Poland ... Bundists living in Poland think the Bund really has nothing to do in Poland. There is no Jewish working class, there is no Jewish people in Poland, and accordingly, there can be no Bund. There can be Jewish socialists in the Polish Socialist Party. The Bund's only remaining missions in Poland are to fight Polish anti-Semitism, to organize

the settings of Jewish life in Poland, to establish cooperatives, and to take care of the young people – but does any of this add up to a hope for the building of a Jewish working class in Poland?[64]

After the pogrom in Kielce, the JLC received some 300 requests from Bund members wishing to emigrate from Poland. Accordingly, the JLC established a special board – composed of Alexander Erlich (son of Henryk Erlich), Emanuel Pat (brother of Jacob Pat) and Shloime Mendelsohn – to handle departure arrangements. Pat and his colleagues believed that every Bund member who wished to leave should be assisted. The Central Committee of the Bund in Poland demanded that the JLC coordinate with it in arranging the departure of prospective emigrant members. The Bund leadership also demanded that party members submit their departure requests to the Central Committee and not directly to the JLC.[65]

Pat, who met with a group of Bundists in Częstochowa while visiting Poland, brought home his impressions of their attitude toward remaining in Poland. One member of the group, Moshe Lederman, described the decision to stay in Poland as stemming from lack of choice. There is nowhere to go, Lederman stated; one must carry on even though the eyes of relatives and friends whom the Nazis had murdered were reflected everywhere and Jewish life in Poland did not stand a chance.[66] Thus, as Polish Jewry was striving to leave Poland – for reasons including but not limited to the murders and the violence – the Bund leaders continued to voice their habitual slogans about the Jewish future in Poland.[67] However, as stated, there was a gap between the views of the party leaders and those of rank-and-file members who had returned from the Soviet Union, the forests and the hideouts. It is doubtful that the group of professional, interested functionaries that led the Bund during those years truly represented the party's trend of thought. Most members wished to rebuild their shattered lives and find a place where they could make a new start. Their affiliation with Poland was weakening and many of them sensed clearly – even before the last exodus of Bund members from Poland in 1948–49 – that they could not continue living there.

1947–49: STABILIZATION?

The rehabilitation of Jewish life in Poland was an exceptional social and economic phenomenon in the post-war Jewish experience. Within two or three years, the remnants of Polish Jewry established systems of education, culture and religion, community life and economic institutions on an extraordinary scale, over the ruins of their former homes, amidst a complicated political reality and under continual pressure from anti-Semitic factors. Polish Jews, most of whom were repatriates from the Soviet Union, were given access to a new area of settlement in western Poland that evolved into the new centre of post-war Polish Jewry. The ancient Jewish centres in eastern and central Poland, destroyed during the occupation, did not attract Jewish populations after the war; apart from Łódź and Warsaw, post-war Jewish life took shape in the areas annexed from Germany – Silesia, Poznań and eastern Prussia. In these regions, which were also Poland's new economic centres, the Jews received new economic opportunities in industrial and agricultural domains that had been barred to them before the war.[68]

The branches that the Bund established in post-war Poland reflected the new settlement array. At the beginning of the post-war era, as indicated in a report from Fiszgrund to the Bund mission in New York in January 1946,[69] only 16 of 482 card-carrying Bund members at that time settled in the new areas in western Poland. Most of the other members, survivors of the camps or the forests, who returned to their former towns of residence, came from Łódź, Warsaw, Kraków, Tarnów and Częstochowa. In 1947, after waves of repatriates settled in western Poland and the Jewish community there jelled, important Jewish centres took shape in various western towns and the focus of party activity moved there. In early 1948 the Central Committee in Warsaw sent the Bund mission in New York a list of all registered Bund members in Poland at the end of 1947. Of 1,400 members who were registered with Bund branches during those months, according to the report, only 500 or so were living in traditional Jewish places of settlement. About 350 were in Łódź, where the economic infrastructure had survived the war unscathed and, therefore, attracted many Jews. Lublin and Białystok, by contrast, which had had Jewish populations in excess of 30,000 before the war and had been important centres for the Bund and the Jewish trade unions, were eclipsed in the Jews' economic and residential redeployment. In 1945 several Bund-member survivors returned to Piotrków-Trybunalski, where the Bund had been very influential before the war, but over the next two years this town emptied of Bund activists. In contrast, the party's largest branches in Poland were those in Wrocław (120 members), Wałbrzych (100 members) and Legnica (115 members).[70]

Until 1947, when Jewish life in Poland stabilized and the community and economic frameworks in the western areas began to solidify, Bund

activity in the peripheral towns was provisional, the size of the membership fluctuated and newly established branches vanished within several
months as members left Poland or relocated to the western areas. In
1947, for example, Bund members established branches in Nowy-Sącz,
Międzyrzec and Sosnowiec, but terminated this activity several months
later when they left the area.[71] In the centre in Warsaw, too, the number
of card-carrying members fluctuated. In the middle of 1946, 75 members
were registered with the party branch in the Polish capital; their
numbers declined to 69 in early 1947 and climbed back to 75 by the
end of the year.[72] In Tarnów, which became an important centre of
Jewish settlement after the war, the Bund membership fluctuated from
46 in September 1945 to 85 in November of that year and 125 in June
1946. The major exodus of Jews from Poland in the second half of 1946
reduced the registered membership in Tarnów to 76 in June 1947 and
60 later that year. In early 1948, when Jewish life in Poland stabilized,
the membership in Tarnów climbed to 92.[73]

The cooperative movement and the cooperative Jewish association
Solidarność were very important factors in the post-war economic revi-
talization of Polish Jewry. The cooperative movement enabled Jewish
artisans to practise their traditional vocations in a productive setting
that was consistent with the intentions and economic goals of the new
Polish regime. In 1946, 106 Jewish cooperatives in Poland employed
2,387 workers. Their numbers climbed to 160 in 1947, 203 in 1948 and
220 in 1949, in which year the cooperatives employed about 9,000
Jewish artisans in needlework, textiles, metals, construction and other
trades. The output of the Jewish cooperatives was worth $10,000,000
in 1948 and $28,000,000 in 1949.[74] The Bund, which found these coop-
erative settings consistent with its worldview, ran about 20 cooperatives
in 1947 in various locations in Poland. The most important of them
were in Legnica, where there were two cooperatives for needlework and
shoemaking; in Szczecin, which had shoemaking and building cooperatives, and Tarnów, where the Bund ran a needlework cooperative with
about 120 members.[75] The cooperatives, established and supported by
the JDC, were not built along party lines and had no party affiliation.
Reports from Bund members indicate frequent friction between Bund
members and other members of cooperatives in various locations because
the Bundists wished to maintain a closed (Bundist) shop. In Legnica,
for example, Bund members of the construction cooperative demanded
that only party members be allowed to work there, a demand that the
party leadership rejected because it breached the terms that the JDC
had set down for support of the cooperative.[76]

In 1945 the JDC began to make large financial investments in Poland to meet the Jewish community's economic and cultural rehabilitation needs. In its four years of activity in Poland after the war (1945–48), the 'Joint' invested about $18,000,000 in Poland.[77] About 70 per cent of the money was forwarded to the Central Jewish Committee and the TOZ health-care organization; the rest was apportioned among public and political entities to finance special needs. Examples are the *Kehilla* organization, which met the Jewish communities' religious needs; training farms of the Zionist pioneering movements; and, indirectly, the *Berichah*.

In March 1947 the *Folkstsaytung* published a list of the Bund's relief, education and cultural institutions across Poland. The list included 13 food kitchens, three orphanages, 14 public libraries and six night schools for teenagers and adults.[78] Detailed financial statements for the period between October 1946 to October 1947, sent by the Central Committee to the JDC office in Warsaw, point to the scope and cost of activity in various respects. According to these statements, the party supported approximately 90 needy members between October 1946 and March 1947, at 280,000 złoty per month. In the summer of 1947 the number of supported members declined to around 70, and the cost of their relief was 180,000 złoty.

The Bund's public kitchens provided about 1,800 meals per day on average during this time, and three orphanages which it maintained housed 170 children. Bund-sponsored shelters for the elderly housed about a hundred clients, and the party's convalescent homes had 160 beds. The Bund also reserved some of the JDC money for responses to anti-Semitic articles and publications, its institutions' administrative needs and the expenses of the Central Committee. In all, the party spent some 3,000,000 złoty per month (about $10,000) on current requirements.[79]

In addition to the JDC allocations, the Bund received some money from the JLC. In 1946, the JLC sent $89,000 to Poland for allocation among the Bund, Left Po'aley Tsiyon and HaShomer haTsa'ir, plus $20,000 for the Central Jewish Committee to fund the Jewish press in Poland.[80] After returning from Poland in early 1946, Jacob Pat decided to forward more money to the united representation of Polish Jews and to reduce direct assistance to political organizations. Ignacy Falk, a member of the Bund Central Committee and the director of the party's administrative division, complained to Pat that this policy diverted JLC money, collected from members of the American Jewish working class, to non-proletarian organizations. In response, Pat explained:

The main matter of concern to the JLC is helping Polish Jews …
In terms of political principle, the JLC has not changed its attitude
toward the CKŻP and this subject is not at the top of our agenda
… Are we not talking about cooperatives, schools, clubs, activities
for children, and the like? Why not send them assistance for these
activities of theirs?[81]

In 1945–46, Tsukunft also resumed its activity in Poland. The main
participants in its post-war leadership – Luba Bielicka-Blum, Lilka
Glaser-Jaszunski, Marek Edelman, Bono Winer and others – had taken
part in Bund underground activity during the occupation. The first
post-war meeting was held on 25 December 1945, during which it was
decided to ask all party committees in Poland to help to establish
branches of Tsukunft wherever members of the movement had settled.[82]
Tsukunft held its first post-war national conference in June 1946, and
its journal, *Yugent Verker,* made its debut in October of that year. As in
the pre-war era, Tsukunft devoted most of its efforts to organizing
recreation camps and activities for young people, evening clubs, sports
groups and libraries. About 500 children and teenagers participated in
the movement's summer camps in July–August 1946.[83]

The Tsukunft activists did not take part in the party's political activity;
instead, they devoted most of their attention to educational activity under
the movement's own auspices. None of the movement leaders belonged
to the post-war Central Committee of the Bund, and the Tsukunft
leadership elected to place its headquarters in Łódź, where many young
Jews had gathered, and not in Warsaw. Tsukunft activists in the new
areas of Jewish settlement – Upper Silesia or Szczecin – often complained
to the Bund Central Committee that the leaders of the Bund in these
areas were not giving educational work enough attention. The Bund's
orphanages occasionally suffered from budget shortfalls, and the party
leadership in Warsaw, itself financially beleaguered, rejected the demands
of the young staff of these institutions to provide additional funding.[84]

The young people who joined Tsukunft after the war were influenced
by the Polonization trend that was making broad inroads among Jewish
children and youth in post-war Poland. These young people, unlike
the cadre of leading activists, had not been raised on the Yiddishists'
educational tradition; their decision to join the movement was prompted
not necessarily by ideological awareness but by the wish to belong to
a youth organization that provided social programmes, sports activities
and the like. A similar calculus inspired children and teenagers to join
the cells of Zionist pioneering youth movements.[85]

In early 1947 the Tsukunft journal *Yugent Verker* carried a debate about the cultural assimilation tendencies of young Jews in Poland. One of the writers assailed the trend that had infiltrated the movement to conduct its cultural and social activity in Polish. It was unthinkable to conduct public activity of Tsukunft in Polish, he asserted. The Yiddish tradition must be maintained; Polish may be spoken only in activities associated with general frameworks of the Polish state.[86] Another Tsukunft member wrote that young Jews in Poland were assimilating not for ideological reasons but as a result of the war and the suffering that Jews and Poles had shared as inhabitants of Nazi-occupied Poland. The Bund's Yiddish tradition, although a heritage of historical importance, had no practical significance in the daily lives of Jews in Poland: 'Yiddishism is not our ideal, but by means of Yiddish we safeguard our contribution to the struggle for the liberation of the human race, the liberation of all peoples, the liberation of the Jewish people ...'[87]

More than anything else, this controversy symbolized the new path that the Bund was following after the war. Internal processes that had begun during the Nazi occupation – relations between veteran leadership and young members, the question of participation in pan-Jewish settings, and the attitude toward the Polish state – found expression during the Bund's few years of autonomous political activity in post-war Poland.

The Bund in post-war Poland was a small movement that had lost most of its members and supporters. Its leaders at this time were not its veteran pre-war functionaries; none of them belonged to the Central Committee of the Bund. Most of the new activists came from the Soviet Union and were out of touch with the changing trends of thought among rank-and-file members. They were closer in mind to Jewish activists who participated in pro-Soviet Polish organizations and found their way to the ZPP and, afterwards, to the PPR. This group preferred, for ideological reasons or pragmatic calculations, to interact with Polish parties – especially the PPS – than to be full partners in the Jewish organizations that operated in Poland. They took part in the Central Jewish Committee for practical reasons and were closer to the PPR representatives on that Committee than to delegates from Zionist parties and movements.

The new regime in Poland gave the Bund an opportunity to take part in building the new Poland – a possibility that had been denied to the Bund before the war, despite its size and influence in Jewish society in the 1930s. The Bund leaders believed it possible to establish a multi-party socialist regime in Poland, based on a partnership between the

Peasant Party and labour parties, in which there would be a place for a Jewish socialist party that would fulfil its traditional doctrine concerning the Jewish–Polish proletarian partnership, build a Jewish education system, and maintain the particularistic cultural tradition of Polish Jewry.

Convinced that such an opportunity would come about, the Bund tackled the grim questions of post-war Jewish existence in Poland, especially the phenomenon of Polish anti-Semitism, with its murderous manifestations, and the Jews' wishes to emigrate. The government depicted the assaults against Jews as part of the struggle of right-wing underground groups against the pro-Soviet government and spared no effort to stamp out these groups' activity. However, the Jews who had returned to Poland found it no simple matter to rebuild their lives over their families' graves and their destroyed communities. Many members of the Bund, especially young members who had spent the occupation in Poland and witnessed the terror of the devastation from close quarters, were leaving Poland along with the masses of Jews, in defiance of the leadership which counselled against hasty departure and opposed any encouragement of emigration from Poland. The main desire of young Jews who remained in Poland was to work with Jewish youth in order to sustain the tradition of their activity during the occupation; they distanced themselves from political involvement at the country-wide level.

After the war, little remained of the grand autonomous economic, social and cultural framework that the Bund had established among Polish Jews. The Bund maintained several autonomous social and economic entities, but they were the exceptions that proved the rule. Most Bund members at the party branches took part in general Jewish activity, worked in jointly run Jewish cooperatives, and considered themselves in no way distinct from the rest of the Jewish community. Even their decision to stay in Poland after the stabilization of Jewish life in 1947 was prompted not by ideology but by personal considerations: the fear of leaving without a formal exit visa; reluctance to languish purposelessly as refugees in camps in Germany or Austria; the economic opportunities available to Jews in the new areas of settlement in western Poland; and the hope that the anti-Semitic tide was forever stemmed. As participants in the Jewish community that had decided to stay in Poland, Bund members and sympathizers sought to integrate into Polish entities and exercise the opportunities now accessible to them as fully-fledged Polish citizens. The confluence of these factors also deprived Yiddish and its culture of the unique importance they had commanded until 1939 in the minds of rank-and-file Bund members.

NOTES

1. K. Kersten, *The Establishment of Communist Rule in Poland 1943–1948* (Berkeley, CA/Oxford: University of California Press, 1991), pp. 37–8; Coutouvidis and Reynolds, *Poland 1939–1947*, pp. 99–101,107–8; H. Shlomi, 'Reshit Hit'argenut Yehudei Polin beShil'ei Milhemet ha'Olam haSheniyah', *Gal-Ed*, 2 (1975), pp. 290–92, 296, 301–3; J. Adelson, 'W Polsce zwanej ludową', in J. Tomaszewski (ed.), *Najnowsze dzieje Żydów w Polsce* (Warsaw: Wydawnictwo Naukowe PWN, 1993), pp. 425–6.
2. Duraczyński, *Rząd Polski*, pp. 381–97, 411–18.
3. Minutes of meeting of London delegation of the Bund, 28 January 1944, BA, ME-42/20; *The Ghetto Speaks*, 21 (5 February 1944).
4. Blit to Nowogrodzki, 16 March 1944, BA, ME-17/73-A.
5. Memorandum from PPS Secretariat in London to Atlee, 10 January 1944, YVA 025/280.
6. See article in *Dziennik Polski* and Blit's response to the editor on 8 May 1944, BA, ME-17/73-C.
7. *The Ghetto Speaks*, 24 (15 April 1944).
8. Oller to Wasser, 23 May1944, BA, ME-17/172.
9. Nowogrodzki to Oller, 27 June 1944, BA, ME-17/172.
10. Wasser to Szerer, 21 August 1944, BA, ME-17/172.
11. Kurski to Mill, 2 September 1944, BA, ME-40/80.
12. The Polish uprising, its background, progression and results, is the subject of a wide literature. For example, see W. Bartoszewski, *Dni walczącej stolicy* (Warsaw: Wydawnictwa ALFA, 1989); J. M. Ciechanowski, *Powstanie warszawskie* (Warsaw: Państwowy Instytut Wydawniczy, 1989); Zuckerman, *A Surplus of Memory*, pp. 520ff.
13. Blit to American Representation of the Bund (details on talk with Jaszunski in London), 26 August 1945, BA, ME-17/172; Goldstein to American Committee of the Bund, 10 October 1945, BA, MG-1/91-A.
14. Hertz (ed.), *Doyres Bundistn*, Vol. 2, p. 87.
15. *Biuletyn fun 'Bund'*, Warsaw, April 1945.
16. Ibid.
17. A. Ciołkosz, 'Polska jest wieczna', *Robotnik*, 13 (1–14 July 1945).
18. Szerer to Feiner, 21 November 1944, BA, ME-42/3.
19. Oller to Wasser, 8 December 1944, BA, ME-17/172.
20. Letter from Bund Central Committee in Poland to KRN Presidium, 26 March 1945, AAN, KC PZPPR, 30/IV-7.
21. Typescript of Szerer's radio speech, 1 May 1945, BA, ME-42/4.
22. Adelson, 'W Polsce zwanej ludową', p. 387; Y. Gutman, *HaYehudim beFolin Aharei Milhemet ha'Olam haSheniyah* (Jerusalem: Zalman Shazar, 1985), p. 19.
23. See memoirs of Marek Bitter, a Jewish Communist activist, on the first few months in Lublin after liberation: *Dos Naye Lebn*, 34 (25 September 1946).
24. See, for example, *Reysha (Rzeszów) Sefer Zikaron* (Tel Aviv: Rzeszów societies in Israel and United States, 1967), p. 367; *Olkusz, Sefer Zikaron liKehilat Olkusz* (Tel Aviv: Olkusz Association in Israel, 1972), p. 230; *Eth ezkera, Sefer Kehilat Tzoyzmir (Sandomierz)* (Tel Aviv: Association of Tzoyzmir Jews and Moreshet, 1993), p. 439.
25. D. Engel, *Beyn Shihrur liBerichah* (Tel Aviv: Am Oved, 1996), p. 39; L. Dobroszycki, *Survivors of the Holocaust in Poland: A Portrait Based on Jewish Community Records 1944–1947* (Armonk, NY, and London: M. E. Sharpe, 1994), p. 13.
26. H. Shlomi, 'Pe'ilut Yehudei Polin lema'an Hidush Hayei haYehudim baMedina, Yanuar 1945–Yuni 1945', *Gal-Ed*, 10 (1987), pp. 214–16.
27. *Biuletyn fun 'Bund'*, 3 (Warsaw), October 1945.

28. Dobroszycki, *Survivors of the Holocaust*, p. 81.
29. *Biuletyn fun 'Bund'*, 3 (Warsaw), October 1945; *Biuletyn fun 'Tsukunft'* (Brussels), December 1947, BA, MG-9/287.
30. Reinharts (Przemyśl) to American Committee of the Bund, 1 August 1945, BA, MG-2/494.
31. From report on discussions at the first post-war conference of the Bund in Poland, 17–18 June 1945, BA, MG-2/494.
32. Fiszgrund to American Committee of the Bund, 24 January 1946, BA, M-7/10.
33. *Biuletyn fun 'Bund'*, 2 (Warsaw), July 1945.
34. Ibid.
35. Kersten, *The Establishment of Communist Rule*, pp. 46–7 ; Coutouvidis and Reynolds, *Poland 1939–1947*, pp. 187–99.
36. Record of Szuldenfrei's speech to the KRN, 10 May 1945, BA, MG-1/91-A.
37. Minutes of meeting of American Committee of the Bund, 28 May 1945, BA, ME-18/43.
38. Minutes of meeting of Presidium of American Committee of the Bund, 29 September 1945, BA, ME-18/43.
39. Adelson, 'W Polsce zawnej ludową', p. 399.
40. Dobroszycki, *Survivors of the Holocaust*, p. 24.
41. *Tetikayts-Barikht fun Tsentral-Komitet fun de Yidn in Poyln fun 1 Yanuar 1946 biz dem 30 Yuni 1946* (Warsaw, 1947), p. 21.
42. Dobroszycki, *Survivors of the Holocaust*, p. 23.
43. For example, report of a HaShomer haTsa'ir emissary, I. Barzilai, to the leadership of his movement in Palestine, 22 March 1946, HHA, Giv'at Haviva, 1–2, 56 (1b).
44. According to the relief lists forwarded to Bund members in the Soviet Union by the Jewish Labour Committee, BA, ME-18/14-B-2.
45. Cyrenkiewicz to Polish Embassy in Moscow, 2 November 1945, AAN, KC PZPR, 30/IV-7; Chrempiński, an official at the bureau of the Polish prime minister, to the legal adviser at the Polish Embassy in Moscow, 20 May 1947, AAN, KC PZPR, 30/IV-6, file 2.
46. Musnik to Nowogrodzki, 17 August 1945, BA, M-7/20.
47. Tselemenski to Nowogrodzki, 10 September 1945, BA, M-7/20.
48. Szuldenfrei and Fiszgrund to Bund delegation in Paris, 4 June 1946, AAN, KC PZPR, 30/IV-3, file 11.
49. Charakterystyka działalności poszczególnych partii i organizacji wchodzących w skład Komitetów Żydowskich, AAN, KC PZPR, 295/VII–149, p. 19.
50. *Folkstsaytung*, 4 (13), April 1947.
51. Gutman, *HaYehudim beFolin*, pp. 61–2.
52. Charakterystyka działalności (see note 49), p. 19.
53. Zilberstein to Litewka, 19 May 1946, BA, MG/9-1-A.
54. Charakterystyka działalności, (see note 49), p. 19.
55. In this matter, see K. Kersten, *Polacy-Żydzi-Komunizm. Anatomia półprawd 1939–68*, (Warsaw: Niezależna Oficyna Wydawnicza, 1992), pp. 76–88.
56. See D. Engel, 'Patterns of Anti-Jewish Violence in Poland 1944–1946', *Yad Vashem Studies*, 26 (1998), pp. 43–85.
57. Coutouvidis and Reynolds, *Poland 1939–1947*, pp. 216, 241.
58. Concerning the Kielce pogrom and its results, see B. Szaynok, *Pogrom Żydów w Kielcach 4 lipca 1946* (Wrocław: Wydawnictwo Bellona, 1992); Gutman, *HaYehudim beFolin*, pp. 34–41.
59. Y. Bauer, *Flight and Rescue: Berichah* (New York: Random House, 1970) pp. 119, 211–12; Dobroszycki, *Survivors of the Holocaust*, pp. 86–90; Engel, *Beyn Shihrur LiBerichah*, pp. 150–51.

60. Resolution of National Council of the Bund in Poland after the pogrom in Kielce, 6–7 July 1946, BA, MG-2/479.
61. *Folkstsaytung*, 2 (11), March 1947.
62. Circular from Bund Central Committee, 3 (47), March 1947, BA, MG-2/246.
63. See Engel, *Beyn Shibrur liBerichah*, pp. 117ff.
64. J. Pat, 'Bundistn und Bund in Poyln', *Unser Tsayt*, 5 (1946), pp. 15–16.
65. Pat to American Representation of the Bund (undated – evidently September or October 1946), BA, MG-18/51; Nowogrodzki and Pat to Central Committee of the Bund in Poland, 10 December 1946, BA, MG-2/482; minutes of meeting of American Representation of the Bund, 16 December 1946, BA, ME-18/46.
66. J. Pat, *Ash un Fayre*, (New York: Cyco Bicher-Farlag, 1946), p. 133.
67. *Folkstsaytung*, 6 (August 1946).
68. See B. Szaynok, 'Ludność Żydowska na Dolnym Śląsku 1945–1950', PhD dissertation, University of Wrocław, 1993, pp. 175ff; Adelson, 'W Polsce zwanej ludową', pp. 417ff.
69. Fiszgrund to American Representation of the Bund, 24 January 1946, BA, M-7/10.
70. Central Committee of the Bund in Warsaw to American Representation of the Bund (undated, evidently early 1948), BA, MG-2/491.
71. Bund Committee in Kraków to Central Committee in Warsaw, 12 May 1947, AAN, KC PZPR, 30/IV-2, file 2; list of Bund members in Sosnowiec, sent to the Central Committee in Warsaw, 7 October 1947, AAN, KC PZPR, 30/IV-2, file 5; Bund Committee in Międzyrzec to Central Committee in Warsaw, 11 April 1946, AAN, KC PZPR, 30/VI-2, file 3.
72. List of Bund members of Warsaw, September 1946, and report on activities at the branch for January–June 1947, submitted to the Central Committee, AAN, KC PZPR, 30/IV-2, file 7; Fiszgrund to American Representation of the Bund, 24 January 1946, BA, M-7/10.
73. Reports from Blayvays (Tarnów) to Central Committee in Warsaw, 28 November 1945, 9 October 1946, 21 March 1947, 21 January 1948, AAN, KC PZPR, 30/IV-2, file 6.
74. Gutman, *HaYehudim beFolin*, pp. 64–5; Y. Bauer, *Out of the Ashes: The Impact of American Jews on Post-Holocaust European Jewry* (Oxford: Pergamon Press, 1989), p. 163.
75. *Folkstsaytung*, 2 (11), March 1947; Falk to Bund Committee in Legnica, 25 November 1947, AAN, KC PZPR, 30/IV-4, file 2; Trade Committee of the Bund to Secretariat of the Frayheit shoemaking cooperative in Szczecin, 6 December 1947, AAN, KC PZPR, 30/IV-4, file 2; report on Bund activity in Tarnów, sent to the Central Committee, 21 January 1948, AAN, KC PZPR, 30/IV-2, file 6.
76. Falk and Feldman, for the Bund Trade Committee, to the secretariat of the construction cooperative *Budowa*, 6 December 1947, AAN, KC PZPR, 30/IV-4, file 2.
77. Bauer, *Out of the Ashes*, p. xviii; the dollar exchange rate was about 100 złoty in 1945 and 300 in 1946.
78. *Folkstsaytung*, 2(11), March 1947; report on party activity in the first six months of 1947, sent to the Bund in New York, BA, MG-2/482. The report lists all locations where soup kitchens, orphanages and vocational training courses operated.
79. Financial statements submitted by the Bund to the JDC office in Warsaw, October 1946–October 1947, AAN, KC PZPR, 30/IV-9, 30/IV–10.
80. Central Committee of the Bund to Pat and Tabaczynski, September 1946, BA, MG-2/485.
81. Pat to Falk, 22 December 1946, BA, MG-2/485.
82. Circular from Tsukunft organizing committee to Bund committees in Poland, 1 January 1946, BA, MG-9/256; *Biuletyn fun Y.B. Tsukunft*, December 1947, BA, MG-9/287.

83. Circular from Tsukunft Central Committee, no. 5, June 1946, BA, MG-9/256.
84. Tsukunft Central Committee in Łódź to Bund Central Committee, 8 November 1947, AAN, KC PZPR, 30/IV-23, file 1; Fiszgrund to Bund committee in Szczecin, 3 February 1948, and Falk to Bund committee in Legnica, 10 September 1948, AAN, KC PZPR, 30/IV-5, file 1.
85. See minutes of discussions among members of the HaShomer haTsa'ir main leadership in Poland, 15 January and 10 April 1947, HHA, 1–2, 64 (3).
86. *Yugent Verker*, 1 (2), February 1947.
87. *Yugent Verker*, 2 (3), March 1947.

7

Facing a Changing Reality

WORLD BUND VS. POLISH BUND: HEADING FOR SCHISM

At the end of the war, Bund members in the United States vacillated about whether to return to Poland and take up a role in the efforts to revitalize the movement and Jewish life in that country. In July 1945 Lucjan Blit, who remained in London, reported to the Representation in New York that he and members of the PPS in Poland had looked into the advisability of a return to Poland by members who had gone to the West during the war. Associates in the PPS urged these members to stay in the United States, it being their assumption that Soviet agents and associates in Poland would not allow Bund activists to operate freely and might even imprison them upon their return to Poland.[1] The American Representation did not discuss the question of returning to Poland and left the decision to each member individually. By June 1946, when it became clear that no Bundists in America intended to return to Poland, the mission debated the priorities of the movement and the role it should play in Bund activity in Poland. Emanuel Szerer said:

> ... Although we remain in America, we must not be neglectful about assisting Poland, the 'old home', our movement there. Still, we are living here, here is the center of world Jewry in terms of size, and it is our duty to help create a general socialist movement in America. There are many Bundists in the United States, several hundred, and they must retain their singularity ...[2]

The American Representation, which had done much to assist the Bund in Poland during the German occupation, lost its practical importance as a political centre and a source of aid after the war. As a political player, it was powerless and devoid of influence since the Central Committee in Poland had replaced it as the mouthpiece and representative of the Bund *vis-à-vis* Polish state institutions. Moreover, the Bund activists in America were suspect in the eyes of the new regime in Poland because of their wartime relations with PPS exile circles that strongly opposed Poland's pro-Soviet regime and attacked the PPS leadership in Poland fiercely for its collaboration with the PPR.[3] Even as an important source of relief and assistance, the mission lost much of its role because Jacob Pat and the JLC had adopted a different policy in these matters.

In February–March 1946 the three leaders of the Bund in Poland – Michał Szuldenfrei, Grisza Jaszunski and Salo Fiszgrund – visited the United States as a delegation from the Bund in Poland to the first post-war national conference of the JLC.[4] Their visit made it clear, both to the Bund leadership in Poland and to the members in New York, that the Bund's self-assumed role during the war as the voice of Polish Jewry had come to an end and that the Bund could no longer be regarded as a single political entity. Benjamin Tabaczynski attempted to arrange meetings for the three activists from Poland with officials of the US State Department, to give them an opportunity to present the Bund's views concerning the new regime in Poland and describe the regime's attitude toward the Jews. The State Department agreed to let them meet with a low-ranking official of the Eastern Europe Department, and even that for goodwill purposes. They explained to Tabaczynski that nothing about the regime in Poland or issues of relief and financial aid should be brought up at the meeting. The Bund members would be allowed only to present a general report on the situation of Polish Jewry.[5]

After the war, relations between the Bund in Poland and the American Representation were administered by the JLC. In view of the situation in Poland, the mission, as an American political organization, was unable to participate in relief and assistance operations in Poland. Bund members in Poland also seemed to realize that direct relations between the party in Poland and the American Representation might embroil the former in difficulties with the authorities. In talks between Bund leaders in Poland and members of the mission and the JLC it was agreed that Chayim Wasser, a member of the Bund Central Committee before the war, would visit Poland, help revitalize the party, and serve as a liaison between the Bund in Poland and the Bund in America. In August 1946 the Central Committee in Warsaw asked the Polish Consulate in New York to give Wasser an entry visa to Poland, explaining that Wasser wished to return to that country.[6] When the application met with difficulties, the JLC extended its patronage to Wasser's mission. In November 1946 Wasser was given an entrance visa to Poland as a representative of the JLC. His duties, as described to the Polish Consulate, were to prepare reports and surveys on assistance and relief operations

for vocational projects that belonged to programmes for the produc-
tivization of Polish Jews.[7]

As the JLC took over American Representation's powers of political
representation with respect to activity in Poland, it also coordinated all
relief and assistance operations. After his visit to Poland in early 1946,
Pat understood that the Polish government would not permit any relief
that it construed as assistance for political activity or political entities.
However, it would encourage financial investments in Jewish vocational,
educational and cultural settings. Accordingly, Pat categorically ruled out
relief for any purpose other than vocational and cultural rehabilitation
in Poland. Deeming rehabilitation a necessity of the highest order, he sent
no money directly to the American Representation for direct support
of the party in Poland.[8] Fiszgrund and Szuldenfrei contacted their
comrades in New York several times and asked them to step up their
financial relief, claiming that the money forwarded by JLC did not
suffice to assist Bund members who had returned from the Soviet Union.[9]
In December 1947 Nowogrodzki explained the Representation's problem
to a member of the Bund Committee in Łódź: 'The reason we are short
on dollars is that, to this day, we have not received even one dollar from
the JLC. No more need be said. We are acting on our own ... and are
trying to raise whatever we can among the Bundists, but they are few.'[10]

The new situation transformed the nature of the Representation's
activity. Instead of the political framework that the Representation had
been, it now became mainly an ideational and cultural organization that
placed activity among members of the American Jewish working class
at the top of its agenda. Nowogrodzki listed the Bund's future roles in
the United States: organizational activity among Jewish workers in the
spirit of the principles of socialism; action against assimilation and reinforcement of Jewish cultural consciousness; collaboration with American
socialist players to form a common front against anti-Semitic manifestations; creation of a modern Yiddish-language Jewish cultural system;
counteracting Zionist propaganda among American Jews; creating a
Yiddish-language Jewish education system and placing Yiddish books
in all Jewish libraries; establishing a Jewish university that would use
Yiddish as its language of instruction; Jewish community activity; and
organizing Jewish communities as representative agencies of American
Jewry.[11] This view of the post-war political and social reality among
Western Jewry – a reality that left no room for an autonomous Jewish
socialist party – and the wish to sustain the Bund's particularistic cultural
heritage in Eastern Europe, precipitated a sweeping upheaval in the
structure and organization of the Bund outside of Poland.

In late 1945 the main activists at the American Representation –
Szerer, Nowogrodzki and Mendelsohn – decided to establish a world
coordinating committee of Bund organizations and Jewish socialist organizations of similar mind, and to convene representatives of these
organizations for a joint conference. There had never been such an
organization in the history of the Bund, a movement that rejected any
trend of thought that regarded Jews' existential problems as shared by
all Jews worldwide. The proponents of the idea argued that, in view of
the condition of the Jewish people after the war, the Bund must adjust
itself to the new needs of world Jewry. A clutch of circumstances – the
establishment of Displaced Persons (DP) camps in Europe, the struggle
for the creation of a Jewish state in Palestine, the uncertain future of
Polish Jewry, and doubts about the survival of Jewish culture in Eastern
Europe and the Polish émigré communities in the West in view of
rampant assimilation trends among members of the young generation
– prompted the leaders of the American Representation to conclude
that the Bund's historical heritage would be preserved more successfully
within the framework of a worldwide ideational movement that coordinated its *modus operandi* and defined its goals jointly. A programmatic
document submitted to the participants in the First World Conference
of the Bund, held in Brussels in May 1947, stated:

> The fact that throughout its history the Jewish people struggled
> against the so-called exile for its right to exist as a nation, a struggle
> in which it was the ally of those fighting for a social democratic
> order – is the essence of the existence of the Bund movement and
> the Bund's historical role among the Jews. It is obvious that the
> Bund as it existed between the two world wars no longer exists
> today, from the historical standpoint … In most places in the
> world except for North America and Palestine, the Jews are an
> insignificant percentage of the population and cannot be a polit-
> ical factor of consequence. An independent party with Bundist
> principles cannot be influential among the Jewish public …The
> Bund's … propaganda … should now emphasize the struggle for
> Jewish economic and cultural interests and the right to national
> existence.[12]

The idea of establishing a world umbrella organization for the Bund
ignited a piercing debate among the members of the American Representation, one that was not easily resolved. The senior activists in the
mission favoured the creation of a world organization of Bundist

groups and were joined by members in Western European countries, such as Raphael Riba and Alexander Mintz in France, David Gorfinkel in Belgium and Professor Pessah Liebman Hersch in Switzerland. Szerer, Mendelsohn and Nowogrodzki, who had been involved in political activity since the pre-war era in Poland and had spearheaded the Bund's political activity in the United States and London in 1941–45, were aware of the movement's decline and its organizational and ideological inability to compete with the Zionist movement in the DP camps in Europe and among American and Western European Jews. They hoped that by uniting all forces of socialist Jewish groups that ruled out the Zionist nostrum as the *only* answer to the problem of post-war Jewish existence, they could avert, if only partially, the danger of the Bund's disappearance. They undoubtedly realized that even if the Bund in Poland somehow managed to stay independent, it could not address the cultural and educational problems of Western Jewry and, in all probability, could not offer a solution amenable to Polish Jewry, whose ultimate numbers in Poland were not at all clear in 1946.

The opponents of the umbrella idea noted that it was contrary to the Bund's historical heritage, which had always ruled out the formation of world Jewish settings because of the basic principle that guided the Bund throughout its half-century of existence – the Jewish problem was not a worldwide one but rather one that existed in non-democratic regimes that deprived their Jews of civil and cultural rights. According to the traditional Bund ideology, the Jewish problem would be solved immediately upon the establishment of a socialist and democratic regime that would assure the rights of all citizens irrespective of nationality and race. In December 1945 six of the 13 members of the American Representation submitted a memorandum to the Representation plenum in which they explained their opposition to the establishment of a world coordinating committee on historical, ideological and practical grounds. The establishment of a world committee of the Bund, they said, was both ideologically and practically illegitimate. It would place the party in Poland in a difficult situation by forcing it to sever its ties, problematic to begin with, with Bund members in the West – since the Polish regime would forbid them to belong to such a committee.[13]

The Bundists in Poland deemed themselves to be members of a Jewish political entity that participated in Poland's socialist coalition. Concurrently, however, they wished to maintain relations with their movement outside of Poland, in countries that were increasingly opposed to the encroaching Sovietization of Poland. The opponents of the idea of a 'world Bund' believed, correctly, that Bund members in Poland

would eventually find it difficult to belong to a worldwide Bund insti-
tution that depicted itself as an international Jewish social democratic
movement but which could continue maintaining cultural or social
relations with local Bund groups in the West.

The formation of a world coordinating committee also had opponents
in JLC circles, especially Jacob Pat. Pat, who had steadily distanced
himself from Bund leaders even during the war and whose main concerns
were pragmatic and topical, considered a world committee a meaningless and grotesque entity that would attempt to inject content into
the political activity of a movement that, practically speaking, did not
exist:

> This world conference [of the Bund] is influenced by the fact that
> since all the [other] political organizations (Po'aley Tsiyon,
> Mizrachi, the Orthodox) have created their own world conferences,
> so should the members of the Bund. However, the Bund is differ-
> ent. The Bund offers no territorial solution to the Jewish problem
> ... The Bund speaks about the people, not about a state ... The
> essence of Bundism – is the emphasis of the socialist solution to
> the Jewish problem. 'Socialism leads me to my inner "Yiddishkeit"'
> – Vladimir Medem once said ... A world Bund is a dream and an
> illusion. Since there are no different 'Bunds' in the world, there
> is no world Bund and therefore no need for a conference of Bund
> organizations ... Let us not make ourselves look funny. [14]

Despite this dispute, the senior activists in the American mission
and the members in Western Europe resolved to establish the world
committee. Eight Bund activists – Szuldenfrei, Fiszgrund and Jaszunski
from Poland, Riba and Mintz from France, Hersch from Switzerland,
Berl Ciechanowski from Belgium and Nowogrodzki from the United
States – met in Brussels in January 1947 to prepare the agenda of the
First World Conference of the Bund.[15]

This meeting showed how differently Bundists in the West and
their colleagues in Poland viewed the new framework and its functions.
The issues in dispute pertained to the attitude of the Bund toward the
Socialist International, the German Socialist Party, and the nature of the
coordinating committee as a world organization. Szuldenfrei reported
that the Bund in Poland could not identify with the Socialist International because of the International's anti-Soviet positions and support
of the German SPD. The members even disagreed about the name of
the coordinating committee. Jaszunski stated that 'World Coordinating

Committee' denoted an ideologically uniform organization, something with which the Bund in Poland would find it hard to identify. He and his comrades from Poland proposed the following: 'Inter-Country Coordinating Committee of Bundist and Related Jewish Socialist Organizations' (Tsvishn-Lender Koordinar-Komitet fun Bundishe un Kroyvishe Yidishe Sotsyalistishe Organizatsyes). The Bund members in the West vehemently opposed this proposal, which, practically speaking, drained the committee of its ideational contents and envisaged it as a technical framework and nothing more, and proposed an alternative that was ultimately accepted: the 'World Coordinating Committee of the Bund and Related Jewish Socialist Organizations' (Velt Koordinar-Komitet fun Bund un Kroyvishe Yidishe Sotsyalistishe Organizatsyes).[16]

A ten-member mission of the Bund in Poland took part in the First World Conference of the Bund, held in Brussels in May 1947. Also in attendance were five members of the American Representation, five representatives of Bund organizations in America, five representatives from France, three from Belgium, two from Great Britain, Mexico and Argentina, and one apiece from Bund groups or Jewish socialist organizations in Romania, Italy, Sweden, Switzerland, Canada, Brazil, Uruguay, Palestine, Shanghai, Australia and South Africa.[17]

Despite the size and significance of the mission from Poland, its members were unable to tip the scales on issues that they disputed with the Bund in the West. The conference resolved that the Bund would participate in the Socialist International, ruled that the coordinating committee would be a global framework for the activity of Bund organizations worldwide, and rejected Szuldenfrei's demand to condemn the 'young American imperialism'.[18]

After Szuldenfrei surveyed the Bund's activity in Poland and its efforts to cooperate with the 'progressive forces', as he termed them, in rehabilitating Jewish life in that country, a debate developed in which the members from Western Europe expressed puzzlement about the very existence of an autonomous party in Poland. Alexander Mintz of France argued that the participants should marshal the courage to state that Polish Jewry no longer existed, since even such Jews as remained in Poland wished to leave it. It was but an illusion, he said, to consider the relationship between the Bund in Poland with the PPS a basis on which Jewish life could be rehabilitated, since the Polish socialists were, in effect, satellites of the PPR and the Communist regime. Delegates from Poland, too, such as Zdisław Muszkat, adopted a different tone from that of the movement leaders in Poland. Muszkat stated that if the Bund had to choose between activity dictated to it by the Communist regime and liquidation, it should prefer to liquidate itself in Poland – anything but to violate the principles of political freedom.[19]

The conference's statements of support for the Bund in Poland and its efforts to revitalize Jewish life there could not conceal the widening rift between the Bund leaders in Poland and their counterparts in the West. In June 1947, several weeks after the conference in Brussels, Jaszunski stated in the *Folkstsaytung* that one could no longer speak of the Bund as one party.[20]

Nowogrodzki summarized the functions of the World Coordinating Committee in a document stipulating that the committee would engage in unifying and coordinating the political activity of Bund organizations in matters on the agenda, would organize the movement's cultural and social assistance activity, would coordinate the war on anti-Semitism and the response to anti-Jewish incidents worldwide, would open Bund branches and chapters around the world and in the new Jewish communities that had come into being, would publish its own newspaper in Yiddish and English and, foremost, would serve as the movement's sole voice in its relations with political players in the West – a very far-reaching decision.[21]

After the elections in Poland in 1947, the ascendancy of the PPR and its partners and the deactivation of opposition players in Poland made it clear to the Bund leaders in Poland that they could not continue to maintain unrestricted political relations with an organization of pronounced social democratic orientation, whose members uninhibitedly criticized Soviet foreign policy. The problems that arose between the World Coordinating Committee and the Bund in Poland had nothing to do with proposed solutions to the existential problems of the Jewish people. It is true that the party's attitude toward Zionism, the struggle for Jewish statehood, and support for emigration of Jews from Poland was taken up, but the problem that caused the Bund to split was the different political realities in which Bund organizations in the West and the Bund in Poland operated. The former operated autonomously, within free and democratic frameworks that allowed them to be active without restriction in Jewish education, culture and politics. The Bund in Poland had to fit into a non-democratic political structure that dictated rigid ground rules. Jaszunski, who spoke about revising the ideology of the Bund in Poland, actually returned the party to the historic debate that Erlich and Alter had resolved in the 1930s. Back then, a majority within the Bund ruled out the Soviet way of fulfilling socialist rule, and the revision of which Jaszunski spoke was actually a retreat and an abandonment of the social democratic path that the Bund had adopted.

The Bund leaders in Poland preferred to describe the World Conference to Polish government officials as an entity that would coordinate activity in matters such as anti-Semitism, the Zionist question, and the issue of Jewish culture, that were of shared concern to various Bund organizations.[22] The political conditions in Poland and the state of the Jewish community there left no further room for hope that a new Polish-Jewish working class would arise and, phoenix-like, re-establish the Jewish labour movement that the Bund had helped to build and maintain in pre-war Poland. Polish Jewry, 90,000 strong at the end of 1947, had distanced itself from the Bundist ideology. The few Jews in Poland who espoused socialist principles and were willing to take part in political activity, including the Bund leadership itself, steadily moved toward the PPR and eventually merged with it – since, ideology aside, they concluded that the future of socialist fulfilment in Poland was linked to Polish communism and its powerful ally to the east.

The Bund organizations in the West faced totally different problems. The processes of democratization and political pluralism, which gathered momentum in Western Europe and the United States after the war, coupled with criticism of the consolidation of Stalinist totalitarianism in Eastern Europe, moved the Bund in the West even closer to European social democracy. The inevitable result was a rift between the movement in the West and the party in Poland. When the 'Westerners' realized how pointless and impossible it was to maintain a Jewish socialist party, they began to engage in cultural, social and educational activity that emphasized preserving the Eastern European Jewish tradition and culture in their own communities. They expressed their upholding of this tradition by providing Yiddishist Jewish education, nurturing the Yiddish-language press and literature, and waging war in public opinion against anti-Semitic manifestations – which in any case were not numerous and blatant in Western society after the trauma of the Jewish Holocaust during the war.

The wish to establish an entity for these spheres of activity in the form of a world coordinating committee reflected the changes that had taken place in the perceptions of Bund members in the West. However, it inevitably led to a dispute with the party in Poland, whose members had to endure unabated pressure from the Jewish activists in the PPR. The Polish Bundists' emphasis on Jews' remaining in Poland, on the one hand, and the American Bund leaders' disillusionment about the prospects of maintaining Jewish life in communist Eastern Europe, on the other hand, created a schism between the Polish Bund and the Bundist groups in the West – a schism reflected not only in international issues or on the question of Poland's new regime-information but also on existential Jewish problems.

DISPLACED PERSONS

The problem of Jewish refugees in the DP camps, established in late 1945 and thereafter in Germany, Austria and Italy, was one of the most intricate and daunting in the post-war political reality. A few of these hundreds of thousands of refugees were survivors of camps liberated in Germany; most, however, were Eastern European Jews who had left Poland, Romania and the Soviet Union and congregated in the American and British occupation zones. They presented a painful and distressing humanitarian problem that did not lend itself to any immediate solution. Britain's refusal to allow the DPs to emigrate freely to Palestine, and the refusal of the United States and other immigration countries to admit Jewish refugees who wished to go there, prompted the Zionist movement and Jewish organizations in the West to embark on a pitched political and propaganda struggle among Western governments and at the UN to change the British policy and solve the DP problem mainly in Palestine. In September 1945 there were 53,322 Jewish refugees in DP camps in Germany, Austria and Italy, among some 1,500,000 refugees of various nationalities who had not returned to their places of residence. In early 1947, after the mass escape from Poland in 1946, the population of Jewish refugees – according to JDC and UNRRA (United Nations Relief and Rehabilitation Agency) statistics – climbed to 232,000.[23]

In early 1947, according to figures gathered by the American Representation of the Bund, which coordinated care and assistance for Bund members in the camps, there were 949 Bund members and relatives in DP camps in Germany, about 300 in camps in Austria, and 36 in various locations outside the camps.[24] About 80 per cent of Bundists in the camps were repatriates who had returned to Poland and left that country in 1946, mainly after the pogrom in Kielce.[25]

In 1947 the American Representation prepared a $119,600 relief budget for members, using an allocation in that sum from the JLC. In this budget, $16,500 was earmarked for the absorption of about 400 members and relatives in the United States, Belgium, France and Norway, $20,000 for the establishment of ten cooperatives for some 200 members in the camps, $53,100 for personal relief and $30,000 for medical assistance and for women and children.[26]

This Zionist movement and the leadership of the Yishuv (the Jewish community in Palestine) considered it best and most appropriate to absorb the DPs in Palestine. Their approach was supported by the conclusions of the Anglo-American Committee of Inquiry on the Jewish refugee problem (the Morrison–Grady Committee), which recommended the absorption of 100,000 DPs in Palestine. Bund spokespeople, in contrast, claimed that Jews in the camps were being induced to settle in Palestine by pressure-wielding Zionist activists. In August 1947 the Bund journal in New York alleged that 'various Zionist groups are terrorizing opponents of Zionism in the camps, especially Bundists … The Bundists are discriminated against in work, obtaining relief, etc.'[27]

In June 1947 an emissary of the JLC, Benjamin Tabaczynski, visited the camps in Germany. Upon his return to New York, he informed the American Representation that a debate was underway in the camps between proponents of resettlement in Palestine and the Bund members, and that emissaries from the Yishuv and the Zionist movement were indeed conducting a campaign of persuasion among the refugees to opt for Palestine. Tabaczynski did not speak about a campaign of pressure and stated, as Bund members in the camps also wrote, that Zionism had attracted considerable grass-roots support because of the annihilation wrought by the Nazi occupation and the post-war anti-Semitism in Poland.[28] However, the Bund leaders in the United States were unwilling to admit that such trends of thought existed. Instead, they persisted in accusing the Zionists of terrorizing and pressuring their opponents, and demanded that the Jews in the DP camps be allowed to choose their country of immigration freely. Emanuel Szerer, in a special booklet that he published about the Jewish problem after the war, elaborated on this solution:

> To determine the real needs of the Jews in the DP camps, and to make it possible to refer them to various countries, a plebiscite should be held at once. The main question to ask them should be the following: Where do you wish to resettle? Every person should be allowed to answer with the names of different countries on the basis of first, second and third preference …[29]

The Bund in Poland and the activists in the United States had different perspectives on the problem of the Jews in the DP camps. The delegates from Poland to the conference in Brussels supported the resolutions that the conference adopted concerning the DPs, which denounced what the authors of the resolutions called the climate of terror and pressure that the Zionist activists had created in the camps.[30] However, they also wished to encourage the refugees in the camps, many of whom were distressed and despairing for lack of an immediate solution to their problem, to return to Poland. In the belief that Jewish life in Poland could be reconstituted, and in opposition to the stance of their comrades in the West who preferred to resettle the refugees in the United States and other Western countries, the heads of the Central Committee in Poland wrote the following to Ya'akov Pav, who had organized a group of Bundists from Poland in DP camps in Austria:

> The purpose of the Zionist activity is to sow panic and fear among the refugees in order to pressure the British authorities to allow the 200,000 refugees in the camps to enter Palestine ... Our position is clear. Our party is doing everything it can to keep Polish Jewry on its soil. This effort by the Bund is making our opponents hateful and jealous ... Members have been living in Sweden for quite some time; some of them wish to return to Poland. The Central Committee in America has been writing to them, telling them to stay there a little longer ... We, for our part, urge you to return and help us with our work. Let us finish our historical task – the preservation of Polish Jewry ...[31]

The question of the DPs' future was connected with the political struggle for Jewish statehood and the clandestine immigration to Palestine. In the eyes of the Bund members in the United States, Palestine was not a solution to the Jewish problem. Szerer stated that even if the Jewish population of Palestine grew immeasurably, it would remain a minority among world Jewry and the large majority would continue to rehabilitate its lives in their countries of residence.[32] As for the Jewish–Arab conflict, which was escalating as the UN prepared to resolve to partition Palestine and establish two states, Jewish and Arab (as it indeed resolved in November 1947), the Bund ruled that only a settlement that would assure the national and cultural rights of both peoples, within a bi-national state in Palestine under the patronage of the Great Powers and the UN, would terminate the conflict.[33]

Bund spokespersons in the West ruled out clandestine immigration to Palestine and the Yishuv leaders' policy of encouraging a general exodus of Jews from Europe. They stated that this policy endangered Jewish immigrants to Palestine, exposed them to violent confrontations with the British authorities, and was creating a new Jewish refugee problem, as the clandestine immigrants were being interned in quarantine camps in Palestine or Cyprus. This policy was of no benefit to the Yishuv, they argued, since it exacerbated the confrontation with the Arabs and made a consensual solution to the Palestine problem less likely.[34]

Unlike their colleagues in the West, Bund members in Poland did not hesitate to speak firmly against British policy in Palestine. In February 1946 the Bund mission to the CKŻP issued a condemnation of Britain's White Paper policy and stated that Jews who wished to establish a national home in Palestine should be allowed to do so without interference. However, they added, every Jew who wished to migrate to some other country and unite with his or her relatives, or to stay in Poland and rebuild his or her life there, should be allowed to carry out this wish, too.[35]

A JEWISH STATE

The Bund activists in the United States, the most extreme of all groups of Bund members in the world in their attitude toward the Yishuv's national aspirations, found themselves mired in a severe confrontation not only with the Bund members in Poland but also with the activists of the JLC in the United States. The dispute that erupted between the Bund and this large Jewish labour organization had ideological significance, even though it centred on priorities in allocating the JLC's relief funds. In early 1947 the JLC resolved to begin a large relief project for the Yishuv, budgeted at $250,000, including $100,000 to finance the needs of DP camp refugees who wished to emigrate to Palestine. The JLC even decided to begin organizational work in Palestine and to establish chapters of the *Arbeter Ring* there for members of the Jewish working class.[36] In January 1947 leading members of the JLC and the American Representation of the Bund Presidium held a joint meeting where the JLC leaders apprised the Bundists of the work they were planning to do in Palestine. Kurski informed the JLC leaders that the Bund opposed their policy not because it objected to social relief for Jews in Palestine but because it construed the scope of the relief, especially for immigration purposes, as support on the part of the JLC for the goals of Zionism.[37]

In February 1947, at a national conference of the JLC in Atlantic City, speakers for the Bund in the United States publicized their view on the JLC's work in Palestine. The Bund had nothing against the Yishuv, they said, but under no circumstances should solutions to the problem of Jews in DP camps in Europe be interwoven with solutions to political issues such as the future of the Yishuv. The Bund speakers came out fiercely against the resolutions of the JLC, which, by implication – they said – expressed support for the political goals of Zionism.[38]

The Bund responded unevenly to the Yishuv's proclamation of independence. The party in Poland, loyal to the accepted line among communist countries in Eastern Europe at that time, supported the fledgling Jewish state, while Bund activists in the West expressed criticism of and even opposition to the formation of an independent Jewish state. The Bund in Poland expressed the following view after the declaration of statehood:

> We, together with the Jewish community in Poland and all Jewish communities in the world, wish to send the Jewish workers and the Jewish public in Palestine our warm congratulations ... We hope that the new Jewish State will be built on progressive principles and will find a way to cooperate with the Arab workers ... in the common struggle against imperialism, chauvinism, and reaction, and for internationalist fraternity, peace and socialism.[39]

Poland recognized the Jewish state and official Polish spokespersons sided with the Yishuv in its bloody struggle with the neighbouring Arab countries. The Polish government placed no limits on the support that Jews in Poland could express for the State of Israel and did not forbid fundraising operations and financial assistance activities on behalf of Israel and the purchase of arms in its defence.[40] The Bund in Poland, about to complete its integration into the PPR during these months, did not come out against Polish Jewry's support and sympathy for the State of Israel. Although in its statement on the subject one can sense its reservations about the Zionist movement and its goals, it expressed its support of the Yishuv, which it portrayed as a collective with proletarian elements that was struggling against reactionary forces backed by British imperialism.

Bund speakers in the West, in contrast, bluntly opposed the establishment of a Jewish state. After 15 May 1948 the American Representation stated:

> Fifteenth May 1948, is undoubtedly an important day in Jewish history. As the British Government decided to withdraw its forces, a Jewish state was proclaimed in Tel Aviv ... The Jewish population

in the United States and around the world received the report concerning the birth of the Jewish state with joy and sympathy ... 'Nation mania' has swept the Jewish street. The declaration of war by the Arab world and the invasion [of Israel] by neighboring Arab countries did not disrupt the happiness that gripped the Jewish street. We must admit that we have no part in the happiness that gripped the Jewish street. We are not caught up in the general national passion ... We believe Jewish statehood is a danger to the 600,000 Jews in Palestine. ... They will not be able to withstand 30,000,000 Arabs and the national fanaticism that is sweeping the Arab masses ...[41]

On 1–8 October 1948 the Second World Conference of the Bund was held in New York without the Bund members from Poland. Sixty delegates from 18 countries – Western Europe, the United States, Canada, South America, South Africa and Australia participated. Its agenda included the question of how to relate to the new historical reality: the establishment of a Jewish state in Palestine and the eradication of the Bund in Eastern Europe. The discussions at the conference hardly touched upon the issue of the Bund in Poland, since the Bund in Poland had been liquidated. The main attention turned toward the establishment of the State of Israel and to various political problems related to the socialist movement in the West, and issues in Jewish culture and education in the delegates' communities. A majority of delegates favoured a draft resolution ruling out Jewish statehood because the war with the Arab world endangered the existence of the Yishuv. The resolution stated that a Jewish state would not solve the Jewish problem in the world, since 90 per cent of world Jewry would continue to reside outside Palestine.[42]

The prevailing trends in the post-war movement in the West solidified at the Second World Conference of the Bund. The Bund ceased to exist as an autonomous party after its members in Poland were forcibly inducted into the Polish United Workers' Party (Polska Zjednoczona Partia Robotnicza: PZPR). All that remained were several groups that had a weak organizational common denominator of being composed of Jewish socialists of Eastern European origin who supported Yiddishist education and attempted to maintain their movement's heritage in the midst of a dramatic turnabout in modern Jewish history. All that remained of the great political movement of the Jewish proletariat was a group of activists in America who did not know how to digest the watershed that had occurred in Jewish history with the establishment of the

Jewish state, and a party in Poland that steadily lost its ranks as the Stalinist drive led to the descent of an Iron Curtain on all of Eastern Europe.

NOTES

1. Blit to American Representation of the Bund, 23 July1945, BA, ME-17/72.
2. Minutes of meeting of American Representation of the Bund, 22 June 1946, BA, ME-18/46.
3. Report on the activity Bund members in the United States and their wartime relations with political forces in Poland. The report was submitted by PPR members of the Central Jewish Committee to the party secretariat, October 1945, AŻIH, RR/121/109.
4. *Folkstsaytung*, 1 (February 1946).
5. US State Department to Tabaczynski, 1 March 1946, BA, MG-2/477-A.
6. Fiszgrund and Szuldenfrei to Polish Consulate in New York, 7 August 1946, AAN, KC PZPR, 30/IV-6, file 1.
7. Minutes of meeting of American Representation of the Bund, 8 October 1946, BA, ME-18/46; Nowogrodzki to Central Committee of the Bund in Poland, 30 October 1946, BA, MG-2/482; Pat to Wasser, 5 May 1947, BA, ME-17/171.
8. Pat to Fogel, 7 October 1946, BA, MG-2/485.
9. Fiszgrund and Szuldenfrei to Wasser, 10 September and 31 October 1947, AAN, KC PZPR, 30/IV-4, file 2.
10. Nowogrodzki to Hampel, 5 November 1947, BA, MG-2/485.
11. Memorandum by Nowogrodzki on the role of the Bund in the United States (n.d.), BA, MG-9/286.
12. 'Unser veg in der nayer tekufa', statement of principles written in March 1947 by the American Representation of the Bund in advance of the First World Conference of the Bund in Brussels, BA, MG-2/9.
13. Statement by opponents of the establishment of a world committee, presented at meeting of American Representation of the Bund, 4 December 1945, BA, MG-2/9.
14. J. Pat, 'A bisl apikorses vegn velt-tsuzamenfar fun "Bund"', *Unser Tsayt*, 12 (1946), pp. 15–16, 18.
15. Minutes of meeting of preparatory meeting for World Conference of the Bund, 7–9 January 1947, BA, ME-18/64.
16. Ibid.
17. List of participants in the First World Conference of the Bund, May 1947, BA, MG-2/6.
18. From speech by Szuldenfrei at the First World Conference of the Bund, Brussels, 5 May 1947, *Folkstsaytung*, 7 (16), 1 June 1947; minutes of discussion following Szuldenfrei's speech, BA, MG-2/8.
19. Minutes of discussion following Szuldenfrei's speech at the First Conference of Bund Organizations, Brussels, ibid.
20. G. Jaszunski, 'Nokh der Briseler konferents', *Folkstsaytung*, 7 (16), 1 June 1947.
21. Powers of the World Coordinating Committee, as phrased by Nowogrodzki, BA, MG-9/353.
22. M. Szuldenfrei, 'Vos zogt tsu der Bund in Poylen?' *Folkstsaytung*, 7 (16), 1 June 1947.
23. For data on the number of Jews in the DP camps, see Bauer, *Out of the Ashes*, pp. 45, 203–4.

24. Relief plan for Bund members in DP camps in 1947, BA, MG-1/80; minutes of meeting of Presidium of American Representation of the Bund, 4 February 1947, BA, MG-1/80; report from Tsukunft mission from Poland that visited camps in Germany, to American Representation of the Bund, 11 November 1946, BA, MG-2/286.
25. As reported by a group of Bund members in DP camps in Germany to the American Representation of the Bund, 6 February 1947, BA, MG-1/80.
26. Relief plan for Bund members in DP camps for 1947, BA, MG-1/80; minutes of meeting of American Representation of the Bund, 4 February 1947, BA, MG-1/80.
27. 'Tsiyoynistisher terror in di lagern', *Biuletyn fun Bund*, August 1947, BA, ME-42/59.
28. Gumkowicz to American Representation of the Bund, 29 August 1945, BA, M-7/20; minutes of meeting of American Representation of the Bund, 1 June 1946, BA, ME-18/46 and 6 February 1947, BA, MG-1/80.
29. E. Szerer, *Jewish Future* (London, 1947), p. 6.
30. Resolutions of the first Bund conference in Brussels, May 1947, BA, MG-2/7; *Folkstsaytung*, 8 (17), 15 June 1947.
31. Bund Central Committee in Warsaw to Pav, 17 April 1947, AAN, KC PZPR, 30/IV-3, file 5.
32. Szerer, *Jewish Future*, pp. 10–11.
33. *Folkstsaytung*, 18-19 (27–8), December 1947; Szerer, ibid.
34. Szerer, *Jewish Future*, pp. 9–10.
35. *Folkstsaytung*, 1 (February 1946).
36. Minutes of meeting of Presidium of American Representation of the Bund with Pat and Tabaczynski, 6 January 1947, BA, MG-1/80, and minutes of meeting of American Representation of the Bund, 23 January 1947, BA, MG-1/80.
37. Minutes of joint meeting of JLC Executive and the American Representation of the Bund Presidium, 13 January 1947, BA, MG-1/80.
38. Statement of Bund delegation to JLC national conference, Atlantic City, 2 February 1947, BA, MG-1/80.
39. *Folkstsaytung*, 12-13 (40-41), 1 June 1948.
40. Hundreds of volunteers enrolled at the Zionist parties' mobilization stations in March–August 1948, after the war erupted in Palestine. Reports of the Central Committee of Po'aley Tsiyon in Poland, AŻIH, 333/33 (K 1-140).
41. 'A melukhe iz geboyrn gevern', BA, ME-18/57.
42. Second World Conference of the 'Bund', *The Jewish Labour Bund Bulletin*, 1 (11), November 1948.

8

The Curtain Falls

After the Polish general elections in January 1947, the Communist takeover of the country's political system gathered momentum. Stanisław Mikołajczyk, prime minister in the government-in-exile in London in 1944 who had returned to Poland at the end of the war in the hope of fitting into the new political constellation and becoming a leading force in the state leadership, realized that he could not lead the PSL as an opposition movement to the Communist regime. He left Poland on 23 October 1947 with the assistance of the British and American ambassadors.[1] In May–June 1947, the process that would end with the forced integration of the PPS into the PZPR began. The left flank of the PPS, led by Stefan Matuszewski and Józef Cyrenkiewicz, conducted secret talks with the PPR leadership to merge the two parties and began to publish a separate newspaper. In June 1947 the PPS Secretariat stated that the party favoured the integration of all left-wing forces in Poland and urged PPS members in Poland to enter into a dialogue with the heads of the PPR chapters in order to merge the parties. In the aftermath of the East–West crisis that erupted in early 1948 surrounding the issue of Germany and the Marshall Plan, the Polish Communists placed the PPS under even greater pressure to merge. In March 1948 Cyrenkiewicz announced the beginning of official merger negotiations between the PPS and the PPR. The head of the PPS Edward Osóbka-Morawski (who since 1944 had been orchestrating the cooperation with the Communists and had even served as prime minister of Poland but opposed the merger), was ousted from the movement leadership. The United Polish Workers' Party (the PZPR) was founded in December 1948. The ascendancy of the Stalinist flank of the PPR, headed by Bolesław Bierut, left the moderate socialist forces in the PPS, those that favoured democracy and interparty dialogue, with no means of influencing the united party's policies. The PPS, the last independent political player of influence in Poland, was assimilated into the PZPR, which was headed by the most extreme pro-Soviet players in the PPR.[2]

In late 1947 and early 1948, the Bund leaders held several discussions in view of the political process under way in Poland. On 28 January

Fiszgrund sent a letter to Chayim Wasser, who had returned to New York from his mission to Poland, and reported that the Central Committee was discussing the future of the party and asked him not to return to Poland again.[3] On 14 March 1948 the Bund Central Committee called a national conference of activists, with the participation of members from 24 Bund branches, cooperatives and chapters across Poland. This conference, in which the party leadership revealed its views about the need to secede from the World Coordinating Committee of Bund Organizations, marked the first step toward the end of Bund autonomy in Poland.[4] The rationale for disengaging from the World Committee was the set of resolutions that the committee had adopted in its meeting in Brussels in January 1948 concerning the Bund's membership of the Socialist International and the establishment of an autonomous division within it, and the committee's support of the membership in the International of the German Social-Democratic Party. In *Folkstsaytung* on 1 April 1948, the Polish Bund made the following statement:

> Activity in recent months has stressed the ideological disagreements between the Bund in Poland and other Bund organizations that are ideologically related to socialist parties in Western Europe ... Accordingly, the Central Committee of the Bund in Poland resolved, in its meeting on 21 March 1948, to secede from the Coordinating Committee of Bund Organizations and from the Socialist International ... The Coordinating Committee of Bund Organizations has no authority to represent the Bund in Poland ...[5]

At the same time the Bund leaders in Poland had informed their colleagues in the United States of their decision.[6]

During those months, the effort to delegitimize the Bund and the Bundist ideology was a central feature in the propaganda activity of the PPR activists on the Central Jewish Committee. It was clear to Zachariasz, Michał Mirski, Hersh Smolar and their colleagues who supported pro-Soviet autarchic rule that the Zionist movements and parties would soon close their headaquarters in Poland and relocate to Palestine. They were not a rival in which time should be invested in undermining its status. By contrast, the idea of Jewish cultural autonomy, the fostering of the national culture in its Bundist version, the social democratic ideology and the heritage of the Bund's anti-Nazi struggle commanded considerable influence among Polish Jewry. The policy that coalesced among the Jewish communists was, on the one hand, to integrate and assimilate the Bund organizations and branches into the PPR in the course of dialogue and coordination, and, on the other hand, to bring down Bundism and its tradition and depict them as reactionary, narrow, conservative and nationalist.[7]

On 3–4 April 1948 major activists in the Bund convened in Wrocław to finalize the resolution disengaging the Bund from the World Coordinating Committee and to plan its gradual integration to activity of the PPR. Summarizing the two-day conference, the Bund released a statement attacking the United States for the Marshall Plan and its policies in Europe, and its support of Franco's fascist regime in Spain. The Bund activists stated that the United States was fomenting a new war in Europe against the socialist regimes, expressed support of the socialist parties in Czechoslovakia and Hungary that had seceded from the Socialist International, and called for the formation of a unified front against the 'forces of reaction in the West'. The Bund leaders urged their comrades and all Polish Jews to cooperate with Jewish members of the PPR in 'building Polish Jewry on independent socialist foundations'.[8]

To accelerate the Bund's integration into PPR activity, the Bund Central Committee and Jewish members of the PPR established a six-person joint committee attended by three PPR members of the Central Jewish Committee (Szymon Zachariasz, Hersh Smolar and Yoel Lazebnik) and three members of the Bund Central Committee. After a series of meetings in May 1948 this committee adopted several resolutions by consensus, calling for the establishment of six-member joint committees – three members from each party – in Polish towns where the Bund was active. These committees were to engage in uniting the Bund and PPR agencies; to organize joint cultural, educational and organizational activities for Jewish members in both parties; and to call two district conferences of Bund members and Jewish members of the PPR – in Wrocław on 30 May 1948, and in Łódź on 6 June 1948 – in order to explain to the members the decisions made by the six-member committee.[9]

Both district conferences adopted two far-reaching resolutions in advance of the Bund's integration into the PPR. One concerned the unification of the Bund's cooperatives with those headed by PPR members; the other spoke of merging the Bundist youth organization SKIF with the general organization of Jewish youth, which was under the influence of the PPR.[10]

The process of liquidating the Bund in Poland as an autonomous political player also had economic significance. The party owned various assets in various parts of Poland – cooperatives, orphanages, chapter houses – of which legal title had to be transferred to the newly established joint agencies. The Bund Central Committee made strenuous efforts in the summer of 1948 to have the Bund cooperatives pay off their accrued debts, since cooperatives with outstanding debts could not merge with those of the PPR.[11]

Concurrently, the Bund leaders took pains to persuade rank-and-file active members of the need to establish the aforementioned Bund–PPR committees that would coordinate actions in advance of the merger. This matter presented no few difficulties. In June 1948, in a letter to PPR activists in the Jewish committee in Ząbkowice (Katowice District), Fiszgrund admitted that he had not managed to persuade the Bundists in this town to establish a joint committee with members of the PPR.[12] Persuasion campaigns on behalf of the merger were also made among Bund activists in Bielawa, Łódź, Wrocław and other towns.[13] A circular from the Central Committee to members in various towns, devoted to the need to reorganize the party, urged party members to rediscuss the Bund ideology in view of the new political situation in Poland.[14]

For all practical purposes, the self-imposed liquidation of the Bund in Poland and its merger with the PZPR was completed in October 1948. At that time, Zachariasz and his colleagues evidently postponed negotiations with the Bund Central Committee concerning coordinated activity between the Bund and PPR representatives on the Jewish committees, in the knowledge that the Bund would be liquidated as an independent party as soon as the PPS and the PPR completed their union. However, the Bund leaders realized that unless they concluded an agreement with the PPR to maintain, somehow, a framework of specific Bund activity, they would totally vanish from the landscape of Jewish life in Poland. In early October 1948 Fiszgrund complained to Zachariasz that PPR activists in the Central Jewish Committee were postponing, on various pretexts, the continuation of talks with the Bund concerning 'continued joint organizing in the Jewish street'.[15] Activists from Tarnów and Bielawa also complained to the Central Committee about PPR procrastination in forming joint agencies for activity.[16] On 23–24 October 1948 the Central Committee sponsored the last conference of the Bund as an independent party in Poland – an assembly of activists in Łódź. Fiszgrund reported that, pursuant to the decision taken at the previous Bund conference in Wrocław in April 1948, to establish a joint action front with the PPR, the Bund leaders and the Jewish members of the PPR Jewish Committee decided to achieve total coordination, both ideological and organizational. The Bund leaders stated that, by joining the PZPR, the Bund had renounced the erroneous, separatist path that it had followed since 1903, when it had seceded from the Russian social democratic movement and headed in its own direction.[17]

By the summer of 1948, rank-and-file Bund members realized that the movement in Poland was doomed and would soon be liquidated as an independent entity. From May 1948 on, dozens of members contacted the American Representation in New York and asked it to arrange emigration visas from Poland as quickly as possible.[18] In Nowogrodzki's estimation, at least 200 Bund members applied to leave Poland during May–June 1948.[19] Szmuel Top, a leading figure in the Bund cooperative in Szczecin, related that he had decided to leave Poland – where a totalitarian Communist regime was consolidating itself – when he received the order from the Jewish Committee to deactivate the party cooperative in that town.[20] The young people in Tsukunft resisted the forced integration into the PPR with special vigour. Various Tsukunft committees resolved to close their branches and terminate their activities for young people on their own, in order to avoid a forced merger with the PPR's youth organizations. The members of these committees were strongly represented among the Bundists who left Poland in the second half of 1948.[21] In the estimation of Bono Winer, a member of the Tsukunft Central Committee and a leading Tsukunft activist in Łódź who also left Poland at this time, about 400 Bund members emigrated from Poland by early 1949.[22]

In March 1948, when the Central Committee in Warsaw adopted its resolution to secede from the Coordinating Committee of Bund Organizations, the Bund leaders in the United States realized that the days of the Bund in Poland were numbered. Nowogrodzki wrote the following to Lucjan Blit in London:

> The recent reports from Poland are the beginning of the end. It is now absolutely clear that the days of an independent socialist movement [in Poland] are numbered. This also pertains to the Bund, of course. I have no concrete plan, but we have a duty to fulfil in getting our members out, and this duty imposes a heavy responsibility on us. Do you have a plan that can contribute something in this matter …?[23]

On 8 April 1948 the Secretariat of the World Coordinating Committee convened in New York to discuss its response to the secession statement from the Bund in Poland. The members in New York were afraid to enter into an open dispute with the party in Poland, lest this exacerbate the rift in the party and risk the emigration of members who wished to leave Poland.[24] With the movement in Poland being liquidated, Bund members in the West were left with one desideratum only: to remove from Poland the many members who had not reconciled themselves to forced integration into the PPR and preferred to emigrate. In June 1948, after efforts by the mission in New York, Nowogrodzki reported to Blit that little could be done for these members. The World Coordinating Committee in New York managed to obtain exit visas for a few members of the Bund Central Committee in Poland and a group of members of Tsukunft. They were unable to do the same for the others who wished to leave and sent them money with which they might attempt to cross the Polish border on their own. Indeed, most rank-and-file Bund members who left Poland in late 1948 did so by slipping across the border, mostly to Germany.[25]

In June 1948 the Secretariat of the World Coordinating Committee convened in Brussels to discuss the Polish Bund's secession from the Bund's worldwide coordinating agency. The statement released by Bund representatives in the West after the meeting officially confirmed, in a manner of speaking, that the Bund had split for good and that the movement in the West and its colleagues in Poland were no longer related.[26]

On 10 January 1949, five members of the 'Liquidation Committee' – an entity that the Bund established in the aftermath of the October 1948 decision in principle to join the PZPR – convened in Wrocław. The members of this committee were Salo Fiszgrund, Szmuel Gurewicz, Ignacy Samsonowicz, Max Brum and Moshe Lederman. The Committee established local committees for various towns in Poland and tasked them with handing the PZPR the property owned by the Bund in Poland. On 16 January 1949 the Bund Central Committee announced the liquidation of party activity and urged members to join the PZPR. The Polish communists refused to allow the Bund to join the united party as a division, as it had allowed the PPS, and required Bund members to join individually.[27] On 24 January the 'Liquidation Committee' resolved to turn over to the PZPR the Bund's resort homes, apartments used by the district committees, several cars and a large warehouse of commodities in Wrocław. The Committee also gave the PZPR Secretariat a list with the names of members of the Bund Central Committee and the branches, along with a detailed list of all party property. It handed the party archives to the PZPR archives. On the basis of an agreement concluded with PZPR members of the local Jewish committees, Bund members were urged not to resign their positions in social and cultural Jewish organizations.[28]

Not all Bund members who remained in Poland joined PZPR. On 28 February the 'Liquidation Committee' convened again and was told that the Bund members' willingness to join the PZPR had run into 'certain difficulties'. The minutes of the meeting indicate that most Bundists in Częstochowa joined the party but that only a minority in Tarnów, Kraków, Łódź, Legnica and various towns in Silesia did so.

On 13 May 1949 the 'Liquidation Committee' decided to complete the liquidation process by the end of that month. A valuation of party property was drawn up, employees of orphanages and schools who were fired because of the deactivation were given severance pay, the cars of the Central Committee in Warsaw and typewriters and other office equipment were given over to the PZPR, and the printers that published the Bund newspapers – which had stopped appearing – merged with the printing facility of the newspaper *Dos naye lebn*. The Bund libraries and the party's book publisher were merged with the Jewish book publisher *Yidish Buch*.[29]

It is difficult to determine exactly how many Bund members joined the PZPR at that time. Among the thousand or so Bund members who remained in Poland after the great migrations of 1946–47, 200–400 left shortly before the party was liquidated in late 1948 and early 1949. The report of the 'Liquidation Committee' for its activities in January–May 1949 spoke of difficulties that had arisen in enlisting Bund members in the PZPR. In various locations, committees of the Communist Party refused to enrol Bundists – evidently those who were known for their anti-communist views in previous years. The report speaks of the admission of some 40 members in Szczecin and a similar number in several other towns.[30] Most Bund members who elected to remain in Poland after the party was liquidated and after the Communist regime solidified did not join. Among members of the post-war Bund Central Committee, only Fiszgrund participated in the final phases of dismantling the Bund. Falk, Finkelstein and Szuldenfrei did not take part in disbanding the Bund, and several of these officials even chose to emigrate. Jaszunski and others resigned from the Bund and joined the PPR before their comrades did so. Among the Bundists who remained in Poland, Marek Edelman and several members of Tsukunft were notable in that they chose to stay in Poland but did not join the PZPR or help to liquidate the Bund.

In the Bund's last year of existence in Poland the process that had begun two years before the party branches were closed for good, its publications stopped appearing and its activists joined the PZPR came to an end. The curtain descended on a movement that for approximately half a century had made a unique contribution in organizing Jewish workers and struggling for their rights as Jews and workers and had been an important player in the singular Jewish culture in Eastern Europe. The demise of the Bund was mainly the consequence of the political reality that evolved throughout Eastern Europe during the late 1940s. A regime that allowed only one party and one ideology no longer had room for a political movement that contained elements of opposition to Communist rule. The liquidation of the Bund in Poland coincided with the liquidation of Polish socialism. The Bund leaders in the West aptly summed up the reasons for the termination of the Bund's half-century of activity in Eastern Europe:

> More than half a century of glorious activities of the Jewish labour movement, under the banner of the Bund, has come to an end in Communist Poland. A movement which withstood successfully severe persecution on part of the Russian tsars, a movement which the reactionary government in pre-war Poland was unable to extinguish, which during the bleak years of Second World War, the Nazi hangmen could not eliminate ... was liquidated by the evil power of the Communist usurpers who, unable to confront an independent socialist movement, exterminate it wherever their power of coercion and terror is established.[31]

Indeed, the liquidation of the Bund in Poland was a consequence of the liquidation of Polish Jewry, on the one hand, and the Communist takeover of Poland, on the other. In Poland, a semblance of Jewish life continued to exist in the 1950s and the 1960s, and the Jews there faced fewer restrictions in Jewish culture, education and historical research than Jews elsewhere in Eastern Europe. However, this milieu left no room whatsoever for the synthesis of an autonomous Jewish culture and a general socialist and democratic movement.

The remnants of the Jewish labour movement were helpless against the powerful and resourceful enemy of unrestricted Jewish life in Eastern Europe – Stalinism and its agents. The demise of the Bund as a movement and way of life in Poland in 1949 marked the continuation of the liquidation process that the Nazis had inflicted on the movement during the war and the occupation. The two great enemies of Eastern European Jewry in the twentieth century – Nazism and Stalinism – left behind nothing but relics and memories of the grand Jewish community that had existed there. One of their victims was the Jewish labour movement – the Bund.

218   *For Our Freedom and Yours*

NOTES

1. Coutouvidis and Reynolds, *Poland 1939-1947*, pp. 297ff; S. Mikołajczyk, *The Rape of Poland* (New York: Whittesey House, 1948), pp. 300–1.
2. Albert, *Najnowsza historia polski*, pp. 566–79; Kersten, *The Establishment of Communist Rule in Poland*, pp. 466–7.
3. Fiszgrund to Wasser, 28 January 1948. AAN, KC PZPR, 30/IV-5, file 1.
4. Circular from to Bund members in Poland concerning conference in Warsaw on 14 March 1948, AAN, KC PZPR, 30/IV-5, file 1.
5. 'Dekleratsye fun Bund in Poyln', *Folkstsaytung*, 8 (36), 1 April 1948; see also *Głos Bundu*, 19 April 1948.
6. Letter from Central Committee of the Bund in Poland to Coordinating Committee of Bund Organizations in New York, 21 March 1948, *The Jewish Labour Bund Bulletin*, 1 (4), April 1948, p. 7.
7. Minutes of meetings of PPR members on the Central Jewish Committee, 5 May and 27 July 1948, AAN, Sz. Zachariasz, 476/19.
8. *Folkstsaytung*, 9(37), 10 April 1948.
9. Circular from Bund Central Committee to party branches in Poland, 22 May 1948, AAN, KC PZPR, 30/IV-5, file 3; Fiszgrund to Bund Central Committee in Wrocław, 21 May 1948, AAN, KC PZPR, 30/IV-5, file 3; *Folkstsaytung*, 12–13 (40–1), 1 June 1948.
10. Report from district conferences in Wrocław on 30 May 1948, and in Łódź on 7 June 1948, *Folkstsaytung*, 14–15 (42–3), 1 July 1948.
11. Falk to the cooperatives in Legnica and Wałbrzych, 28 May 1948, AAN, KC PZPR, 30/IV-5, file 2.
12. Fiszgrund to PPR members of the Jewish committee in Ząbkowice, 20 June 1948, AAN, KC PZPR, 30/IV-7.
13. Circular from Central Committee in Warsaw to various Bund branches in Poland in October 1948, AAN, KC PZPR, 30/IV-5, file 3.
14. Ibid.
15. Fiszgrund to Zachariasz, 9 October 1948, AAN, KC PZPR, 30/IV-5, file 3.
16. Fiszgrund to Bund Committee in Tarnów, 15 June 1948, AAN, KC PZPR, 30/IV-2, file 6, and to Bund Committee in Bielawa, 11 October 1948, AAN, KC PZPR, 30/IV-5, file 3.
17. *Folkstsaytung*, 20 (48) 7 November1948.
18. Emigration applications from Bund members in Poland to American Representation, BA, ME-18/52.
19. Nowogrodzki to Blit, 16 June 1948, BA, ME-18/57.
20. Interview by the author with Szmuel Top, 27 December 1989.
21. Undated statement by seven Tsukunft activists who left Poland, BA, ME-42/59.
22. Interview by the author with Bono Winer, 29–30 June 1988.
23. Nowogrodzki to Blit, 19 March1948, BA, ME-17/71.
24. *The Jewish Labour Bund Bulletin*, 1 (5), May 1948.
25. Nowogrodzki to Blit, 16 June 1948, BA, ME-18/57.
26. *The Jewish Labour Bund Bulletin* 1(8–9), August–September 1948.
27. Sprawozdania z działalności Centralnej Komisji Likwidacyjnej 'Bundu' w Polsce, p. 1, BA, MG-7/11; Nowogrodzki to Rogoff (an editor of the *Forverts*), 7 February 1949, BA, ME-18/68.
28. Sprawozdania z działalności Centralnej Komisji, p. 2.
29. Ibid. In February 1948, the Bund in Poland operated seven public libraries that had 550 volumes. The largest (200 volumes) was in Warsaw. Falk to JLC, 7 February 1948, AAN, KC PZPR, 30/IV-5, file 2.
30. Sprawozdania z działalności Centralnej Komisji, (see note 27).
31. 'The Murder of a Movement', *The Jewish Labour Bund Bulletin*, 2 (15) (March 1949), p. 1.

Conclusion

On the eve of World War II, the Bund in Poland had just crossed a major watershed in its historical development. Never in its history, from its establishment in 1897 in Wilno until 1938–39, had the Bund attained a position of such influence on Eastern European Jewry. After the party's successes in elections to Jewish community organizations and municipal councils in the years preceding the German occupation – triumphs that are impressive in their own right – the spokesmen and leaders of the party felt that, for the first time in Bund history, they indeed represented the Jewish masses in Poland, as they had repeatedly claimed. Even though their initial intention was to represent the Jewish proletariat alone, they believed they had attained in those two years a mandate to represent all of Polish Jewry. Years of efforts to organize Jewish workers, to foster educational and cultural institutions, and to maintain good relations with Jewish labour organizations in the West, and, above all, the internal political realities in Poland, had carried the Bund to the threshold of success in its lengthy struggle with rival ideologies, particularly Zionism. For a brief time it seemed as if Bundism would become the political creed of the majority of Polish Jews.

It was with a sense of self-confidence, inspired by belonging to a large political camp – the socialist movement – that the Bund found itself under German occupation. Like many observers in Poland and elsewhere, no one in the Bund had expected the Polish army to fall in defeat and for Polish independence to vanish within the space of a single month. The response of the party leadership in Warsaw to the collapse of the Polish army and the siege that gradually strangled the Polish capital seems to have been one of confusion and bewilderment. Shortly before the Polish government left the city, the Bund leadership split into two camps: one favouring an exodus from Warsaw together with the government and the heads of the other Jewish parties; the other arguing that the Bund leaders should stay in Warsaw and help defend it gallantly in order to emphasize the shared destiny of the Jewish proletariat and the Polish people and proletariat. By the end of September 1939, a problem that would recur again and again during the occupation appeared for the first time and forced its way onto the Bund's agenda: the need to reconcile the Bund ideology and political doctrine with the new realities of life. By deciding to leave Warsaw and seek shelter outside the German occupation zone, the leaders and prominent activists of the Bund admitted, so to speak, that the danger they faced as leaders of a Jewish party transcended the peril that hovered over the average Polish political activist.

Various centres of Bund activity took shape in late 1939 and early 1940, and it is doubtful that the Bund in those days could be described as a united organizational and ideological framework. In response to the departure of Bundists from Warsaw and the hardships that Bund members encountered in Soviet-occupied eastern Poland, groups of young Bundists, activists in Tsukunft, became increasingly prominent during the first few months of the German occupation. This group assumed the tasks of rehabilitating the movement. It was due to their efforts that the Bund worked out an underground *modus operandi* during the occupation. The Tsukunft leaders understood that they could not leave their rank and file, composed of young adults and teenagers, without any organizational framework while these young Jews' other settings of life – family, education and employment – were disintegrating. Therefore, they created an infrastructure for educational activities, published underground newspapers and organized social groups, thus preserving the Bund as an underground ideological movement that did not collapse even under the conditions of German occupation. The contributions of several veteran party activists such as Maurycy Orzech, Leon Feiner, Bernard Goldstein and others to the Bund's underground activities in 1940–41 placed the Bund on a stronger organizational footing and enhanced its ability to establish relations with the underground outside the ghetto, especially that of the Polish socialists.

The structure and working methods of the Bund in the ghettos of Poland shed light on the nature of the party as it had coalesced in the interwar period. Between the world wars, the Bund in Poland was comprised of a core of dedicated activists surrounded by supporters, whose numbers increased as the Jewish condition in Poland worsened from the mid 1930s onwards. This community of supporters, which adhered to the Bund mainly for pragmatic rather than ideological reasons, terminated nearly all of its Bund activities during the occupation. Except for the Warsaw ghetto, where some 150 Tsukunft members sustained Bund activities in the underground, large-scale movement operations were not perceptible in the ghettos of Poland, some of which were situated in cities where the Bund had been a salient political force until the war. The average Jew was immersed in a desperate struggle for day-to-day survival and had no interest in the dangerous underground actions of a political movement that the Nazi occupation had consigned to irrelevance. The Bundists, like their counterparts in every Jewish party in the underground, were powerless to confront the Jews' problems of day-to-day existence; the only evidence to the contrary came from Tsukunft in its educational and social welfare work. Since the Bund youth organization was part of a larger party framework, unlike the predominantly autonomous Zionist youth movements, its activities were misconstrued as being those of an underground political party.

As long as a response to the Nazis' systematic murder of the Jews was out of the question, the underground Bund was able to avoid a head-on confrontation with the issue of the unique Jewish fate in the war. In several ghettos, conditions permitting, Bund members managed to set up underground activity cells. Their relations with the Polish socialist underground helped them to create a countrywide network of underground activity. The principal importance of relations with the Polish underground was the opportunity it gave Bund activists to report on developments in the ghettos of Poland to the Polish government-in-exile in London and, through it, to the free world. The Bund's special contribution to the Jewish underground in occupied Poland is reflected in Leon Feiner's reports, written in 1942, that informed the world of the tragedy that had overtaken Poland and of the Jews' desperate plight. Relations with the Polish underground also helped Bund member Zygmunt (Zalman) Freidrich to bring to public knowledge the first confirmed reports from Treblinka in July–August 1942.

Once the Nazis' 'final solution to the Jewish problem' became known, the Bund was forced to reconsider two of its principles: belief in the common interests of Jews and Poles in the anti-Nazi struggle; and rejection of political relations with Zionist organizations, which would be tantamount to acknowledgement of a shared Jewish fate. They were disillusioned by the attitude of the Polish underground, especially the socialists among them, who did not regard themselves as sharing the Jews' fate in the war. Although the Polish socialist underground sympathized with the Jews' suffering and protested against the deportations to the death camps (as evinced in the pages of its clandestine press), it considered the extermination of Polish Jewry primarily a *Jewish* tragedy rather than a Polish national one. It was mostly in response to this disillusionment that young Bundists enlisted in the ŻOB (Jewish Fighting Organization) in the Warsaw ghetto during October–November 1942.

The Bund's integration into Jewish combat organizations in Warsaw, Wilno, Białystok and other localities seems to constitute an admission that there was indeed an exclusively Jewish fate. The Tsukunft activists, observing the Jewish tragedy from close quarters and noticing how the Jewish community in which they lived was striving to preserve some kind of cultural, educational and social assistance structure, formed a nucleus around which a new Bund doctrine took shape – a doctrine not shared by Bundists outside Poland during or after the war.

The *modus operandi* of the American Bundists underscored the difference in historical consciousness between the young Tsukunft members in Poland and the veteran leadership outside Poland. The American Representation of the Bund, in which party leaders who had left Poland at the beginning of the occupation joined local activists from American Jewish labour organizations, was an important agency that provided relief and aid for Bund members in occupied Poland and elsewhere. Its extensive relief operations were significant achievements that other political movements, larger than the Bund, failed to match. The American Bundists' devotion to their European counterparts inspired the underground activists to hope that their comrades in the Free World had not forgotten them and were sparing no effort to provide all possible assistance. However, this group of leaders – the pre-war Bund functionaries – did not fully comprehend the significance of the events that were occurring. They continued to assert the importance of relations with Polish politicians in exile – the government-in-exile in London and the Polish socialists – and were reluctant to antagonize them by voicing unconventional views. Moreover, they continued to cross verbal swords with their Jewish political rivals in the pre-war style.

Two Bundists among the dozens who participated in the Bund's wartime political and underground activities stood out for their methods and activities: Abrasha Blum in Warsaw and Szmuel Zygielbojm in London. Among the Bund activists who remained in Warsaw after the veteran leadership had left, Blum was the first to undertake the task of organizing a Bundist underground. He also outperformed all others in enlisting Bund youngsters for the ŻOB and in breaking down the barriers between the Bund and the other constituent youth movements and parties in the ŻOB. How much influence did Blum exert on Bundist ideology during the war? The scanty documentation on Abrasha Blum portrays an organizationally skilled, impressively dynamic man who had a profound influence on young Bundists. Unquestionably charismatic, he was the unchallenged leader of the Tsukunft members. After the Bund joined the ŻOB, Blum became the movement's central figure and a key performer in developing the Bund's fighting cells. Evidently Blum did not concern himself with ideological matters and was not wont to publish ideological articles in the party's underground press. This task was reserved for party leaders, particularly Maurycy Orzech who, by virtue of his status and importance in the pre-war Bund leadership, became a party figurehead in the ghetto. However, Blum was more influential in the Bund's underground development than any other leader in the ghettos of Poland.

Zygielbojm was cut of different cloth. Older than Blum, he retained his pre-war status as a member of the Central Committee. Thus, he was a movement leader in Warsaw in the first months of the occupation, before he left Poland in early 1940, and in 1942 he became the Bund representative on the exiled Polish National Council in London. Although Zygielbojm represented the continuation of the Bund's political activities in exiled Polish institutions and for American Jewish public opinion, he was more acutely aware of the terrible significance of the Holocaust than any other movement leader outside Poland. Zygielbojm held no academic distinction and was not highly regarded among the party's leaders and ideologues. His American colleagues, aware of his intellectual weakness, doubted his ability to fulfil the task that had been assigned to him as a result of the pressure exerted by the Polish government-in-exile (i.e., representing the Bund on the Polish National Council). However, during the year that he held this position – before he took his own life in protest against the world's silence as the Jews were being murdered in Poland – Zygielbojm transformed himself from a drab party official into a Jewish leader who played a historic role in the Holocaust era.

After many years of activity among Jewish workers in Poland, and from his close acquaintance with the life and culture of Polish Jews, Zygielbojm in the autumn of 1942 arrived at the terrible realization that this world was being destroyed before his very eyes. He very quickly dismissed the importance of both political and party interests and did not hesitate to criticize the Polish government harshly. He also clashed with its leaders in order to keep the issue of the devastation of Jewry on the public agenda in Britain. Very few leaders of Polish Jewry in the occupied country, and even fewer outside Poland, were as successful as Zygielbojm in abandoning erstwhile patterns of thought and contemplating the new, tragic realities soberly in the midst of their occurrence.

It is no coincidence that the Bund activists who exerted the greatest influence on the Jewish response during the war did not belong to the party's intellectual cadre. The Bund leaders who shaped the party's pre-war ideological doctrines, Henryk Erlich and Wiktor Alter, were uninvolved in Bund work during the Holocaust period. These two Bund leaders, men of stature in the Jewish leadership of interwar Poland, met their deaths at Soviet hands under political circumstances over which they had no control. It was Zygielbojm and Blum, of all people – men of action rather than ideologues – who were instrumental in shaping the Bund's contours during those terrible years. The ability to fathom the meaning of Jewish life under Nazi occupation, especially with respect to the ongoing slaughter that was being systematically carried out, relied more on intuition than on political, social or ideological analysis. During the occupation, no prominent Bund thinkers were capable of equipping the movement with a new ideology. Although political movements and parties never rush to replace their ideological traditions, even in times of crisis, the few Bund members who understood that the old ideologies no longer met the test of reality made the necessary change – but in their actions, not in their writings.

Of all the Jewish parties that populated Eastern Europe until 1939, only the Bund was liquidated, for all practical purposes, as a result of the destruction of Polish Jewry. The Zionist parties devised alternative settings – similar or identical – in the State of Israel; Orthodoxy rehabilitated itself in the United States, Western Europe and Israel. The Bund, by contrast, virtually disappeared from the map of post-Holocaust Jewish life as a political and ideological movement. The few years of renewed activity in post-war Poland illustrates this most emphatically. The handful of surviving party activists who chose to remain in Poland for various reasons organized a group of members and attempted to resuscitate a movement that was an extension of a bygone culture. Amid the instability of post-war Poland, amid the waves of the departure of Jewish survivors who had returned to or had survived the war there, and amid overt, violent anti-Semitism, these activists managed briefly to infuse their party with a sense of revival. The political changes that swept Poland in the 1940s, however, brought the fleeting efflorescence to an end. Most Bundists who remained in Poland realized this even before 1949, when the last vestiges of autonomous non-Communist political activity were stamped out. Seeing no chance to rehabilitate themselves in Poland, they chose to emigrate.

However, the Bund activists in the West – newly joined by the emigrés – did have an opportunity to set the Bund on a new path that would preserve the movement's heritage as a dynamic player in Jewish life. Therefore, they took a very important step that, in their opinion, would bring this about: the establishment of a world committee of Bund organizations. This marked a watershed in the party's history. The Bund had never envisioned itself as a world Jewish movement, regarding such a configuration as contrary to the essence of the Bundist ideology that espoused the integration of Jews into the surrounding society. The founders of the World Bund Committee intended to follow in the foot-steps of the other Jewish political movements – Zionist and non-Zionist – that had reorganized in the wake of the Holocaust and the establish-ment of the State of Israel. However, the activists and founders of the World Bund Committee, the vast majority of whom had belonged to the party leadership in pre-war Poland, failed to animate an internal ideological rethinking that might have allowed the Bund to sustain its heritage and weave itself into the fabric of post-Holocaust Jewish life. At this juncture, as during the war period, the World Bund Committee members chose to continue in the tradition of rejecting the idea of Jewish statehood. Treating the new Jewish state with suspicion, if not outright hostility, they hoped to transmit their European socialist Jewish heritage, with its Yiddish culture, to Western Jewish communities. The latter, however, had raised a generation that was as far removed from this heritage as east is from west.

The rivalry between the Bund and its opponents, the hostility of Zionist activists and the attitude of some Bund leaders during and after the war concerning relations with Zionist political organizations, place historians who wish to study the Bund's development during those years at a serious disadvantage. Israeli historiography in regard to that period of time has hardly dealt with Bund activities during and after the Holocaust. There are various reasons for this – residues from the past, prevalent ideological influences in Israeli historical research, and the apologetics and factual distortions that pervade the material published by Bund survivors. Those who wish to study the history of the Bund during the Holocaust and to assess its contribution to Jewish survival must disregard the hostility and criticism that Bund opponents expressed with regard to the movement's doctrines; they must also overlook the traditional Bundist apologetics. The Bund, like other political Jewish movements, attempted to chart its course at a time when Jewish life in Poland was disintegrating. However, its members and supporters, like the Jewish community as a whole, faced overwhelming forces. Thus, in order to evaluate properly the wartime activities of the Bund, one has to examine the fullness of Jewish life that continued during the Nazi occupation and at the time of the Jews' struggle for physical and spiritual survival – a struggle to which the Bund contributed to the best of its ability.

Did Bundism fail – as an ideology, a culture and a new Jewish way of life – after 50 years of activity in Eastern Europe? An affirmative reply, in comparison with the success of Zionism, is irrelevant in a historical analysis of Jewish history during the Holocaust. As a general worldview that coalesced in late nineteenth-century Eastern Europe, Bundism was tailored to the Jewish population there; when this community was tragically liquidated during the Holocaust and Jewish life in the Soviet Union became untenable, Bundism lost its relevance. The Bund's defeat at the hands of history is inextricably linked to the downfall of Eastern European Jewry at the hands of the Nazis.

It was not only to history, however, that the Bund lost out. It also forfeited its place in Jewish public consciousness. The Bund has been relegated to the margins of Jewish remembrance of the Holocaust mainly because even its survivors failed to find a way to integrate it into the new chapter in Jewish history. The loss of Bundist ideology to history has also turned out to be its loss in the shaping of memory.

The idea of Diaspora Jewish life that stresses the maintenance of certain cultural indicators – an idea that underlies the Bundist doctrine – has persisted to this day. As a movement, however, the Bund has disappeared. Nothing remains of this magnificent movement, with its hundreds of activists and tens of thousands of supporters – a movement that had published dozens of newspapers, literary and political journals; had maintained a Yiddish-speaking Jewish educational system, a youth movement and numerous Jewish charitable committees; and had struggled against anti-Semitism in Eastern Europe. A handful of members in New York, Australia and South America continue to put out several Yiddish publications, most of which contain translated material from the American and Israeli media or excerpts from the writings of the movement's bygone founders. Yiddish-speaking schools continue to operate in various locations around the world, but they have turned the language into a folklore piece instead of a vernacular in daily use. Where there is no Yiddish culture, no Jewish proletariat, no separate Jewish political activity and no struggle for equal civil rights for Jews, there is no Bund.

Bibliography

ARCHIVES

1. *American Jewish Joint Distribution Committee Archives (AJDC), New York*

   795   Refugees in Wilno
   818   JDC Bureau in Paris
   828   Jewish schools in Poland and Wilno

2. *Archiwum Akt Nowych (AAN), Warsaw*

   KC PZPR Komitet Centralny, Polska Zjednoczona Partia Robotnicza:
   30/III   Bund (1939–45)
   30/IV   Bund (1945–49)
   202   Delegatura
   203   Armia Krajowa
   295   Komitet Centralny PPR
   Cukunft:
   229/1
   229/2
   Sz. Zachariasz:
   476

3. *Archiwum Żydowskiego Instytutu Historycznego, Warsaw*

   Post-war documents

4. *Bund Archives (BA) – YIVO (RG-1400), New York*

   JLC   Jewish labour Committee
   M-7   Bundists in Lithuania
   M-12   Aid to Jewish schools in Poland
             Labour Party, London

ME-16 Sonya Nowogrodzki
M-16/1
MG-2/5
       Szmuel Zygielbojm
ME-17
ME-18
       The American Representation of the Bund
ME-18 PPS in London
ME-42 Emanuel Szerer
MG-1   Aid to Refugees
MG-2   Jewish Labour Committee
       Polish government-in-exile
MG-4   British Foreign Office, the Erlich–Alter affair
MG-7   Documents from Łódź Ghetto
MG-9   Letters from Poland
       Rescue Council for the Jewish Population in Poland
S–2   Interviews

5. *HaShomer haTsa'ir Archives (HHA), Giv'at Haviva*

   1-2   Post-war Poland

6. *Moreshet Archive (MA), Giv'at Haviva*

   A   Testimonies
   D   Documents

7. *Private Collection*

   Winer, Bono, *Dos Togbukh fun Lodzer Geto, 1940, 1943–44*, ed. Na'khum and Henya Raynharts, Perets Zilberberg, Hava Rozenfarb

8. *Public Record Office (PRO), London*

   FO-371   Foreign Office, general correspondence

9. *Yad Vashem Archives, Jerusalem*

   0.25   Michał Zylberberg
   0.3   Collection of testimonies

0.33   Diaries and memoirs
0.55   Alexander Berenfes
M-1/E   Testimonies and diaries
M-2   Ignacy Schwarzbart
M-11   Jewish Historical Committee – Białystok
M-14   Rescue Council for the Jewish Population in Poland
P-5   Wolf-Yasni Collection, Łódź

10. YIVO Institute for Jewish Research, New York

RG-116 Poland 2 (1939–45)
RG-223 Sutzkever-Kaczerginski Collection

ORAL TESTIMONIES

Oral Document Centre of the Institute of Contemporary Jewry, Hebrew University, Jerusalem
17 (93)   Faynzilber Avraham, 3 August 1976
8 (26)   Lau-Lavie, Naphtali, May 1975
8 (20)   Tsanin Mordechai, 9 October 1978

INTERVIEWS

Babitz, Chaim, Tel Aviv, 20 March 1989
Leber, Ya'akov , Kiryat Tiv'on, 27 January 1988
Top, Szmuel, Tel Aviv, 27 December 1989
Winer, Bono, Jerusalem, 29–30 June 1988

NEWSPAPERS AND PERIODICALS

Biuletyn fun 'Bund', Warsaw
Biuletyn fun 'Tsukunft', Brussels
Biuletyn fun Y.B Tsukunft, Warsaw
Dos Naye Lebn, Warsaw
Folkstsaytung, Warsaw
Forverts, New York
The Ghetto Speaks, New York
Głos Bundu, Warsaw

The Jewish Labour Bund Bulletin, New York
Robotnik, London
Unser Shtime, Paris
Yugent Veker, Warsaw

OTHER PRIMARY SOURCES

Ainsztein, R., 'New Light on Szmul Zygielbojm's Suicide', *Yad Vashem Bulletin*, 15 (August 1964), pp. 8–12.
Anders, W., *Bez Ostatniego Rodziału, Wspomnienia z lat 1939–1946* (Newtown, Wales: Montgomeryshire Printing, 1950).
Arad I., Gutman I. and Margaliot A. (eds), *Documents on the Holocaust* (Jerusalem: Yad Vashem, 1981).
Armia Krajowa w Dokumetach [AKWD] 1939–1945, Vols 1–5, (London: Studium Polski Podziemnej, 1970–1989).
Balberyszski, M., *Shtarker fun Ayzn – Iberlebungen in der Hitler Tekufe* (Tel Aviv: Farlag Hamenora,1967).
Bartoszewski, W., *1859 Dni Warszawy* (Kraków: Znak, 1984).
— *Dni walczącej stolicy* (Warsaw: Wydawnictwo ALFA, 1989).
Ben-Menahem, A and Rab, Y. (eds), *Chronika Shel Geto Lodź*, Vols 1–4 (Jerusalem: Yad Vashem, 1986–89).
Berman, A. A., *BaMakom asher Ya'ad li haGoral* (Tel Aviv: HaKibuts haMe'uhad, 1978).
Bernstein, M., 'Bundistn in Ratnfarband bes der Tsveyter Velt-Milkhome', *Unser Tsayt*, 11/12 (1957), pp. 88–91.
Blayvays, A., 'Geto Epizodn …', *Unser Tsayt*, 4/5 (1967), p. 28.
Blumental, N. (ed.), *Te'udot meGeto Lublin – Udenrat lelo Derech* (Jerusalem: Yad Vashem, 1967).
'Bona', 'Jak Bund święcił 1 maja 1941r. w getcie łódzkim?', *Biuletyn Żydowskiego Instytutu Historycznego* 54 (1965), pp.113–15.
Brener, L., *Vidershtand un Umkum in Tsenstachower Geto* (Warsaw: Yidisher Historische Institut in Poyln, 1950).
Documents on Polish–Soviet Relations 1939–1945 (DSPR), Vol. 1 (London: Heinemann, 1961).
Dray – Andenkbuch (Tel Aviv: Ringelblum-institut, 1966).
Dworzecki, M., *Yerushalaym de-Lita in Kamf un Umkum* (Paris: Union Populaire Juive, 1948).
Edelman, M., *Getto walczy* (Warsaw: C.K. Bund, 1946).
Eth Ezkera, Sefer Kehilat Tzoyzmir (Sandomierz) (Tel Aviv: Association of Tzoyzmir Jews and Moreshet, 1993).

Fogel, G., 'O działalności Bundu w getcie łódzkim w 1940r', *Biuletyn Żydowskiego Instytutu Historycznego*, 54 (1965), pp. 103–12.

Gliksman, J., *Tell the West* (New York: Greshman Press, 1948).

Goldstein, B., *Finf Yor in Varshever Geto* (New York: Unser Tsayt, 1947).

Grossman, C., *An'shei haMahteret* (Merhavia: Sifriat Poalim, 1965).

Gutman, I., *Mered haNetsurim* (Tel Aviv: Sifriat Poalim, 1963).

Hartglas, A., *Na pograniczu dwóch światów* (Warsaw: Oficyna Wydawnicza, 1996).

Henryk Erlich und Wiktor Alter (New York: Unser Tsayt, 1951).

Hertz, Y.S. (ed.), *Zygielbojm Bukh* (New York: Unser Tsayt, 1947).

— (ed.), *In di Yorn fun Yidishn Khurbn* (New York: Unser Tsayt, 1948).

Hilberg, R. Staron, S. and Kermisz, J. (eds), *The Warsaw Diary of Adam Czerniaków: Prelude to Doom* (New York: Stein & Day, 1979).

Hirszowicz, L., 'NKVD Documents Shed New Light on Fate of Erlich and Alter', *East European Jewish Affairs*, 22–2 (1992), pp. 65–85.

Historishe Zamelbukh, Materyalen un Dokumenten tsu der Geshikhte fun Algemaynem Yidishn Arbeter-Bund (Warsaw: Ringen, 1947).

Kaplan, C.A., *Scroll of Agony: The Warsaw Diary of Chaim A. Kaplan* (London: Hamish Hamilton, 1966).

Karski, J. *The Story of a Secret State* (Boston, MA: Houghton Mifflin, 1944).

Kermish, J., Bialostocki, Y. and Shaham, I. (eds), *Itonut haMahteret haYehudit beVarsha*, Vols 1–6 (Jerusalem: Yad Vashem, 1979–97).

Klayn, D., *Mitn Malakh Hamaves untern Orem – Mayne Iberlebungen in Poyln bes der Nazi Okupatsie* (Tel Aviv: Peretz Farlag, 1968).

Korczak, R., *Lehavot baEfer* (Tel Aviv: Sifriyat Poalim, 1965).

Korzec, P., 'The Riddle of the Murder of Henryk Erlich and Wiktor Alter by the Soviets', *Gal-Ed*, 10 (1987), pp. 281–310.

Krall, H., *Shielding the Flame* (New York: Henry Holt, 1986).

Kruk, H., *Togbukh fun Vilner Geto* (New York: YIVO, 1961).

Kupersztayn, H., 'Di Bundishe *Folkstsaytung* bes der Nazi-Daytshe Balagerung fun Varshe', *Unser Tsayt*, 10, (1984), pp. 10–12.

Kurts, Y., *Sefer Edut* (Tel Aviv: Am Oved, 1944).

Lewinski, L., 'Działalność Bundu w Łodźi w latach 1939–1944', *Biuletyn Żydowskiego Instytutu Historycznego*, 54 (1965), pp. 112–13.

Mayus, 'Historishe Tog in Lublin', *Unser Tsayt*, 8 (1941), pp. 25–8.

Meltz, Y. and Levi-Landau N. (eds), *Piótrków-Tribunalski vehaSeviva* (Tel Aviv: Piótrków Tryb. Landsmanschaften, n.d.).

Mikołajczyk, S., *The Rape of Poland* (New York: Whittesey House, 1948).

M.K., 'Yosef Aronovitz in Sovietishe Tefisa', *Unser Tsayt*, 7/8 (1951), pp. 37–40.

Musnik, Y., 'Der Lebn un Likvidatsie fun Vilner Geto', in Y.S. Hertz, *In di Yorn fun Yidishn Khurbn* (New York, Unser Tsayt, 1948).

Neustadt, M. (ed.), *Hurban vaMered shel Yehudei Varsha* (Tel Aviv: The General Federation of Labour, 1947).

Nirenberg, Y., 'Die Geshikhe fun Lodzer Geto', in Y.S. Hertz (ed.), *In die Yorn fun Yidishn Khurbn* (New York, Unser Tsayt, 1948).

Nunberg, A., 'Mit a Kav durkh der "Griner Grenets"', *Unser Tsayt*, 4 (1953), pp. 26–8.

Olkusz, Sefer Zikaron leKehilat Olkusz (Tel Aviv: Olkusz Association in Israel 1972).

Pat, J., *Ash un Fayer* (New York: Cyco Bicher-Farlag, 1946).

— 'Bundistn und Bund in Poyln', *Unser Tsayt*, 5 (1946), pp. 14–17.

— 'A bisl Apikorses Vegn Velt-Tsuzamenfar fun "Bund"', *Unser Tsayt*, 12 (1946), pp. 15–18.

Pinsk, Sefer Zikaron leKehilat Pinsk-Karolyn (Tel Aviv: Irgun Yotsei Pinsk biMedinat Israel, 1966).

Polewski, S., 'Bundishe Tetikayt in Vilner Geto', *Unser Tsayt*, 9 (1958), pp. 24–6.

Portnoy, S. A. (ed.), *Henryk Erlich and Victor Alter: Two Heroes and Martyrs for Jewish Socialism* (New York: Ktav, 1990).

Pużak, K., 'Wspomnienia, 1939–1945', *Zeszyty Historyczne*, 41 (1977), pp. 3–196.

Reysha (Rzeszów) Sefer Zikaron (Tel Aviv: Rzeszów societies in Israel and United States, 1967).

Ringelblum E., *Ksovim fun Geto* (Tel Aviv: Peretz Farlag, 1985).

— *Stosunki polsko-żydowskie w czasie drugiej wojny światowej* (Warsaw: Czytelnik, 1988).

Rotenberg, Y., *Fun Varshe biz Shankhay* (Mexico City: Shlomo Mendelsohn fund, 1948).

Sarid, L. A. 'Teshuvat Abba Kovner leMastinav', *Yalkut Moreshet*, 47 (1989), pp. 7–96.

Schwartz, P., 'Vegn Ayner a Rede', *Unser Tsayt* , 7 (1941), pp. 18–20.

— *Dos is Geven der Anhayb* (New York: Arbeter Ring, 1943).

Shashkes, C., *Bletter fun a Geto Togbukh* (New York: C.H. Glants, 1943).

Stein, A.S., *Haver Artur, Demuyot uFerakim miHayei haBund* (Tel Aviv: M. Newman, 1963).

Szerer, E., *Jewish Future* (London, 1947).

Tenenbaum-Tamaroff, M., *Dapim min haDeleka* (Tel Aviv: Hakibuts HaMe'uhad, 1947).

Tetikayts-Barikht fun Tsentral-Komitet fun de Yidn in Poyln fun 1 Yanuar 1946 biz dem 30 Yuni 1946 (Warsaw, 1947).

Trunk, I., 'Kultur Arbet in Shatn fun Toyt', *Yugent Veker*, 3 (4), April 1947, p. 19.

Tsanin, M. *Grenetsn biz zum Himl* (Tel Aviv: HaMenora, 1970).

Tselemenski, Y., *Mitn Farshnitenem Folk* (New York: Unser Tsayt, 1963).

Vladka, *Mishnei Evrei haHomah* (HaKibuts HaMe'uhad, n.d.).

Warhaftig, Z., *Palit veSarid Bimey haShoah* (Jerusalem: Yad Vashem, 1984).

Waychert, M., *Yidishe Aleynhilf 1939–1945* (Tel Aviv: Menora Farlag, 1962).

Y.A., 'Mit 35 Yor Tsorik …', *Unser Tsayt*, 2 (1975), pp. 27–9.

Yarnushkewits, T., 'Mit H. Erlichn in Sovietisher Tefise', *Unser Tsayt*, 1 (1957), pp. 20–21.

Zagórski, W., *Wolność w niewoli* (London: Nakładem autora, 1971).

Zaltzman, M., *Bella Szapiro – di Populere Froyn-Geshtalt* (Paris, 1983).

Zaremba, Z., *Wojna i konspiracja* (Kraków: Wydawnictwo Literackie, 1991).

Zuckerman, Y., *BaGeto uvaMered* (Tel Aviv: Beit Lohamei haGeta'ot and HaKibuts haMeh'uhad, 1985).

— *A Surplus of Memory: Chronical of the Warsaw Ghetto Uprising* (Berkeley, Oxford: University of California Press, 1993).

Zygielbojm, F., *Der Koyakh tsu Shtorbn* (Tel Aviv: Peretz Farlag, 1976).

SECONDARY SOURCES

Adelson, J., 'W Polsce zwanej ludową,' in J. Tomaszewski (ed.), *Najnowsze dzieje Żydów w Polsce* (Warsaw: Wydawnictwo Naukowe PWN, 1993).

Albert, A., *Najnowsza historia Polski 1918–1980* (London: Puls, 1991).

Aly, G., *Final Solution: Nazi Population Policy and the Murder of the European Jews*, (London and New York: Arnold, 1999).

Arad, I., 'Concentration of Refugees in Wilno on the Eve of the Holocaust', *Yad Vashem Studies*, 9 (1973), pp. 201–14.

— *Ghetto in Flames, the Struggle and Destruction of the Jews in Wilno in the Holocaust* (New York: Holocaust Library, 1982).

Bauer, Y., *Flight and Rescue: Berichah* (New York: Random House, 1970).

— 'Rescue Operations through Wilno', *Yad Vashem Studies*, 9 (1973), pp. 215–23.

— *American Jewry and the Holocaust* (Detroit: Wayne University Press, 1981).

— *Out of the Ashes: The Impact of American Jews on Post-Holocaust European Jewry* (Oxford: Pergamon Press, 1989).

Blatman, D., 'On a Mission against All Odds: Szmuel Zygielbojm in London (April 1942–May 1943), *Yad Vashem Studies*, 20 (1990), pp. 237–71.

— 'No'ar Tsiyoni veBunda'i veHitgabshut Ra'ayon haMered', *Dapim leHeker Tekufat haShoa*, 12 (1995), pp. 139–57.

— 'The Bund in Poland 1935–1939', *Polin*, 9 (1996), pp. 58–82.

Breitman, R., *The Architect of Genocide* (New York: Alfred A. Knopf, 1991).

Ciechanowski, J.M., *Powstanie warszawskie* (Warsaw: Państwowy Instytut Wydawniczy, 1989).

Coutouvidis, J. and Reynolds, J., *Poland, 1939–1947* (Leicester: Leicester University Press, 1986).

Cygański, M., *Z dziejów okupacji hitlerowskiej w Łodzi 1939–1945* (Łódź: Wydawnictwo Łódzkie, 1965).

Dambrowska, D. and Wein, A. (eds), *Pinkas haKehillot –Polin*, Vol. 1, (Jerusalem: Yad Vashem, 1976).

Dieckmann, C., 'Der Krieg und die Ermordung der litauischen Juden', in U. Herbert (ed.), *Nationalsozialistische Vernichtungspolitik 1939–1945* (Frankfurt a.m.: Fisher Taschenbuch Verlag, 1998).

Dobroszycki, L., *Survivors of the Holocaust in Poland: A Portrait Based on Jewish Community Records 1944–1947* (Armonk, NY, and London: M. E. Sharpe, 1994).

Duraczyński, E., *Rząd Polski na uchodźstwie 1939–1945* (Warsaw: Książka i Wiedza, 1993).

Engel, D., 'The Polish Government-in-Exile and the Deportations of Polish Jews From France in 1942', *Yad Vashem Studies*, 15 (1983), pp. 91–123.

— *In the Shadow of Auschwitz, The Polish Government-in-Exile and the Jews 1939–1942* (Chapel Hill and London: University of North Carolina Press, 1987).

— *Facing a Holocaust, The Polish Government-in-Exile and the Jews 1943–1945* (Chapel Hill, NC, and London: University of North Carolina Press, 1993).

— *Beyn Shihrur liBerichah* (Tel Aviv: Am Oved, 1996).

— 'Patterns of Anti-Jewish Violence in Poland 1944–1946', *Yad Vashem Studies*, 26 (1998), pp. 43–85.

Enziklopedia Shel Galuyot – Grodno (Jerusalem: Enziklopedia Shel Galuyot, 1973).

Frankel, J., *Socialism, Nationalism, and the Russian Jews 1862–1917* (New York: Cambridge University Press, 1981).

Gutman, I., 'The Jews in Anders' Army in the Soviet Union', *Yad Vashem Studies* 12 (1977), pp. 231–96.

— *The Jews of Warsaw,1939–1943: Ghetto, Underground, Revolt* (Bloomington, IN: Indiana University Press, 1982).

— *HaYehudim beFolin Aharei Milhemet ha'Olam haSheniyah*, (Jerusalem: Zalman Shazar, 1985).

Gutman, I. and Blatman, D., 'Youth and Resistance Movements in Historical Perspective', *Yad Vashem Studies*, 23 (1993), pp. 1–71.

Gutman, I. and Krakowski, S., *Unequal Victims: Poles and Jews During World War II* (New York: Holocaust Library, 1986).

Hertz, Y. S. (ed.), *Doyres Bundistn*, Vols 1–3 (New York: Unser Tsayt, 1956–68).

— *Di Geshikhte fun Bund in Lodź* (New York: Unser Tsayt, 1958).

Hilberg, R., *The Destruction of the European* Jews, Vols 1–3 (New York: Holmes & Meier, 1985).

The Historical Encyclopedia of World War II (New York: Facts on File, 1980).

Holzer, J., *PPS szkic dziejów* (Warsaw: Wiedza Powszechna, 1977).

Johnpoll, K. B., *The Politics of Futility: The General Jewish Workers Bund of Poland 1917–1943* (Ithaca, NY: Cornell University Press, 1967).

Kacewicz, G. U., *Great Britain, the Soviet Union, and the Polish Government in Exile (1939–1945)* (The Hague: M. Nijhoff, 1979).

Kersten, K., *The Establishment of Communist Rule in Poland 1943–1948* (Berkeley, CA/Oxford: University of California Press, 1991).

— *Polacy-Żydzi-Komunizm. Anatomia półprawd 1939–68* (Warsaw: Niezależna Oficyna Wydawnicza, 1992).

Kranzler, D. H., *Japanese, Nazis and Jews: The Jewish Refugee Community in Shanghai, 1938–1945* (New York: Yeshiva University Press, 1976).

Levin, D., *The Lesser of Two Evils: Eastern European Jewry Under Soviet Rule, 1939–1941* (Philadelphia, PN: The Jewish Publication Society, 1995).

Litvak, Y., *Pelitim Yehudim miPolin biVerit-haMo'atsot, 1939–1946* (Tel Aviv: HaKibuts haMe'uhad, 1988).

Madajczyk, C., *Polityka III Rzeszy w okupowanej Polsce*, 2 vols (Warsaw: Państwowe Wydawnictwo Naukowe, 1970).

Perlis, R., *Tenu'ot haNo'ar haHalutsiyot beFolin haKevushah* (Tel Aviv: HaKibuts haMe'uhad, 1987).

Pickhan, G., 'Das NKVD-Dossier über Henryk Erlich und Wiktor Alter', *Berliner Jahrbuch für osteuropäische Geschichte*, 2 (1994), pp. 155–86.

Piechota, Z., 'Eksterminacja inteligencji oraz grup przywódczych w

Łodźi i okręgu Łódźkim w latach 1939–1940', *Biuletyn Okręgowej Komisji Badania Zbrodni Hitlerowskich w Łodźi*, I (1989), pp. 12–23.

Pinczuk, B. Z., *Yehudei Berit-haMo'atsot mul Penei haShoa, Mehkar beVe'ayot haHaglaya veHapinuy* (Tel Aviv: haAguda leHeker Toldot haYehudim, 1979).

Prekerowa, T., *Konspiracyjna Rada Pomocy Żydom w Warszawie 1942–1945* (Warsaw: Państwowy Instytut Wydawniczy, 1982).

Redlich, S., *War, Holocaust and Stalinism* (Luxemburg: Harwood, 1995).

Sakowska, R., *Ludzie z dzielnicy zamkniętej* (Warsaw: Wydawnictwo Naukowe PWN, 1993).

Shlomi, H., 'Reshit Hit'argenut Yehudei Polin beShil'ei Milhemet ha'Olam haSheniyah', *Gal-Ed*, 2 (1975), pp. 287–331.

— 'Pe'ilut Yehudei Polin lema'an Hidush Hayei ha Yehudim baMedina, Yanuar 1945–Yuni 1945', *Gal-Ed*, 10 (1987), pp. 207–25.

Sierocki, T., 'Polski ruch socjalistyczny w latach wojny i okupacja' in W. Góra (ed.), *Wojna i okpuacja na ziemiach polskich 1939–1945* (Warsaw: Książka i Wiedza, 1984).

Stola, D., *Nadzieja i zagłada* (Warsaw: Oficyna Naukowa, 1995).

Suleja, W., *Polska Partia Socjalistyczna 1892–1948, Zarys dziejów* (Warsaw: Wydawnictwo Szkolne i Pedagogiczne, 1988).

Szarota, T., *Okupowanej Warszawy dzień powszedni* (Warsaw: Czytelik, 1988).

Szaynok, B., *Pogrom Żydów w Kielcach 4 lipca 1946* (Wrocław: Wydawnictwo Bellona, 1992).

— 'Ludność Żydowska na Dolnym Śląsku 1945–1950', PhD dissertation (University of Wrocław, 1993).

Tombs, I. 'Erlich and Alter, "The Sacco and Vanzetti of the USSR": An Episode in the Wartime History of International Socialism', *Journal of Contemporary History*, 23–4 (1988), pp. 531–49.

Trunk, I., *Lodzer Geto* (New York: YIVO, 1962).

— *Judenrat: The Jewish Councils in Eastern Europe Under Nazi Occupation* (New York: Macmillan, 1972).

Yapou, E., 'Lama Hutsu Erlich ve-Alter LaHoreg?', *Gesher*, 111/12 (1985), pp. 101–7.

Weinberg, G. L., *A World at War: A Global History of World War II* (New York: Cambridge University Press, 1994).

Wolf-Yasni, A., *Di Geshikhte fun Yidn in Lodź in di Yorn fun der Daytsher Yidn-Oysratung*, Vol. I (Tel Aviv: Peretz Farlag, 1960).

Index